Antiracist Professional Development for In-Service Teachers:

Emerging Research and Opportunities

Jenice L. View
George Mason University, USA

Elizabeth K. DeMulder
George Mason University, USA

Stacia M. Stribling
George Mason University, USA

Laura L. Dallman
George Mason University, USA

A volume in the Advances in
Higher Education and Professional
Development (AHEPD) Book Series

Published in the United States of America by
    IGI Global
    Information Science Reference (an imprint of IGI Global)
    701 E. Chocolate Avenue
    Hershey PA, USA 17033
    Tel: 717-533-8845
    Fax: 717-533-8661
    E-mail: cust@igi-global.com
    Web site: http://www.igi-global.com

Library of Congress Cataloging-in-Publication Data

Names: View, Jenice L., 1958- author. | DeMulder, Elizabeth K., 1959- author. |
  Stribling, Stacia M., 1973- author. | Dallman, Laura L., 1960- author.
Title: Anti-racist professional development for in-service teachers :
  emerging research and opportunities / by Jenice L. View, Elizabeth K.
  DeMulder, Stacia M. Stribling, Laura L. Dallman.
Description: Hershey, PA : Information Science Reference, 2021. | Includes
  bibliographical references and index. | Summary: "This book addresses
  the vital need to support P-12 classroom teachers in all disciplines to
  provide well-rounded and anti-racist education to all students"--
  Provided by publisher.
Identifiers: LCCN 2020011730 (print) | LCCN 2020011731 (ebook) | ISBN
  9781799856498 (hardcover) | ISBN 9781799856504 (paperback) | ISBN
  9781799856511 (ebook)
Subjects: LCSH: Multicultural education--United States. | Culturally
  relevant pedagogy--United States. | Teachers--In-service
  training--United States. | Anti-racism--Study and teaching--United
  States.
Classification: LCC LC1099.3 .V54 2021 (print) | LCC LC1099.3 (ebook) |
  DDC 370.1170973--dc23
LC record available at https://lccn.loc.gov/2020011730
LC ebook record available at https://lccn.loc.gov/2020011731

This book is published in the IGI Global book series Advances in Higher Education and Professional Development (AHEPD) (ISSN: 2327-6983; eISSN: 2327-6991)

British Cataloguing in Publication Data
A Cataloguing in Publication record for this book is available from the British Library.

All work contributed to this book is new, previously-unpublished material.
The views expressed in this book are those of the authors, but not necessarily of the publisher.

For electronic access to this publication, please contact: eresources@igi-global.com.

Advances in Higher Education and Professional Development (AHEPD) Book Series

ISSN:2327-6983
EISSN:2327-6991

Editor-in-Chief: Jared Keengwe, University of North Dakota, USA

MISSION

As world economies continue to shift and change in response to global financial situations, job markets have begun to demand a more highly-skilled workforce. In many industries a college degree is the minimum requirement and further educational development is expected to advance. With these current trends in mind, the **Advances in Higher Education & Professional Development (AHEPD) Book Series** provides an outlet for researchers and academics to publish their research in these areas and to distribute these works to practitioners and other researchers.

AHEPD encompasses all research dealing with higher education pedagogy, development, and curriculum design, as well as all areas of professional development, regardless of focus.

COVERAGE

- Adult Education
- Assessment in Higher Education
- Career Training
- Coaching and Mentoring
- Continuing Professional Development
- Governance in Higher Education
- Higher Education Policy
- Pedagogy of Teaching Higher Education
- Vocational Education

IGI Global is currently accepting manuscripts for publication within this series. To submit a proposal for a volume in this series, please contact our Acquisition Editors at Acquisitions@igi-global.com or visit: http://www.igi-global.com/publish/.

The Advances in Higher Education and Professional Development (AHEPD) Book Series (ISSN 2327-6983) is published by IGI Global, 701 E. Chocolate Avenue, Hershey, PA 17033-1240, USA, www.igi-global.com. This series is composed of titles available for purchase individually; each title is edited to be contextually exclusive from any other title within the series. For pricing and ordering information please visit http://www.igi-global.com/book-series/advances-higher-education-professional-development/73681. Postmaster: Send all address changes to above address. Copyright © 2020 IGI Global. All rights, including translation in other languages reserved by the publisher. No part of this series may be reproduced or used in any form or by any means – graphics, electronic, or mechanical, including photocopying, recording, taping, or information and retrieval systems – without written permission from the publisher, except for non commercial, educational use, including classroom teaching purposes. The views expressed in this series are those of the authors, but not necessarily of IGI Global.

Titles in this Series

For a list of additional titles in this series, please visit:
http://www.igi-global.com/book-series/advances-higher-education-professional-development/73681

Handbook of Research on Diversity and Social Justice in Higher Education
Jared Keengwe (University of North Dakota, USA)
Information Science Reference • © 2020 • 380pp • H/C (ISBN: 9781799852681) • US $255.00

Accessibility and Diversity in the 21st Century University
Gary A. Berg (California State University Channel Islands (Retired), USA) and Linda Venis (UCLA (Retired), USA)
Information Science Reference • © 2020 • 331pp • H/C (ISBN: 9781799827832) • US $195.00

Higher Education Accessibility Behind and Beyond Prison Walls
Dani V. McMay (State University of New York at Fredonia, USA) and Rebekah D. Kimble (Via Evaluation, USA)
Information Science Reference • © 2020 • 400pp • H/C (ISBN: 9781799830566) • US $255.00

Practice-Based Professional Development in Education
Crystal Loose (West Chester University, USA)
Information Science Reference • © 2020 • 202pp • H/C (ISBN: 9781799846222) • US $165.00

Handbook of Research on Ethical Challenges in Higher Education Leadership and Administration
Victor Wang (Liberty University, USA)
Information Science Reference • © 2020 • 466pp • H/C (ISBN: 9781799841418) • US $255.00

For an entire list of titles in this series, please visit:
http://www.igi-global.com/book-series/advances-higher-education-professional-development/73681

701 East Chocolate Avenue, Hershey, PA 17033, USA
Tel: 717-533-8845 x100 • Fax: 717-533-8661
E-Mail: cust@igi-global.com • www.igi-global.com

Table of Contents

Preface

The six chapters of the book—1. "When Asked, Teachers 'Said...: Contemplating a New Teacher Professional Development Manifesto," 2. "Identity Work," 3. "Critical Reflective Practice, Critical Pedagogy, and Culturally Relevant Pedagogy," 4. "Teaching/Learning Relational Dynamics," 5. "Teacher Leadership and Collegial Relationships," and 6. "A Policy Manifesto for Antiracist Teacher Professional Development"—are rooted in several theoretical frameworks, and in the authors' work as teacher educators for over 20 years in a master's degree professional development program for practicing educators at all grade levels and in all subjects/disciplines (including some instructional coaches and museum educators). In each chapter, the authors define the central idea of the chapter; the importance of the central idea to promoting antiracist teacher professional development; how the authors worked with P-12 teachers, using critical reflection, critical dialogue, and their teacher-learner relationships, to explore the central ideas; the outcomes of these explorations, both those that were hoped for and the actual outcomes; and the tensions and dilemmas that were revealed in the course of these explorations, particularly as related to adult development school/culture/context, university culture, and societal trends and policies.

The elements of the master's degree program and the operating theoretical frameworks that have informed the program evolution are described below.

MASTER'S DEGREE TEACHER PROFESSIONAL PROGRAM

The authors are faculty in a 30-credit master's degree teacher professional development program at a public university in the mid-Atlantic United States. Their teaching philosophies are strongly rooted in social change, humanistic and progressive approaches, including an antiracist stance. They have worked to shift the dispositions and stance of more than 2,000 practicing P-12 teachers since 1996, first in a face-to-face and then in a hybrid online program. The program was designed to develop in-service teachers' capacities to engage in critical pedagogy and critical literacy, school-based and community-based inquiry, collaboration, transformative leadership and continuous improvement in an effort to encourage them to remain in the classroom as educational leaders and change agents. In the course of that time the authors have seen the transformation of individual teachers and their teaching, but we continue to struggle with the challenges of making systemic change. Figure 1 is a graphic that portrays program goals over the course of the two years.

Figure 1. Teacher professional development program goals

Reconceptualize teaching and learning as critical educators using a social justice framework

Recognize the need for and power of collective action to bring about positive change

Identify individual goals for personal, professional, and leadership development

Seek out multiple perspectives and engage in multiple perspective-taking

Build capacities, skills, and commitment to engage in critical dialogue

Consider how cultural identity impacts teaching and learning

Construct a powerful and supportive learning community

Develop "critical" attitudes toward received knowledge

Build a foundation for constructivist meaning-making

Cultivate supportive professional relationships

Seek out complexities and personal challenge

Explore our roles as activists and advocates

Seek to understand our multiple identities

Develop our capacity for deep reflection

Create a learner-centered environment

Grow our tolerance for ambiguity

Broaden our ideas of leadership

Cultivate an attitude of inquiry

Develop teacher voice

Foster creativity

Build trust

In its face-to-face incarnation, the program required that the teachers, who joined in school-based teams, attend eight-hour class days for two 2-week summer sessions, a third summer session of one week, and four 8-hour class days per academic semester during the intervening years. In the hybrid version of the program, teachers attended a five-day face-to-face orientation, online instruction for the first and second academic years, and a second summer five-day face to face session in between the academic years.

Throughout the program, teachers were required to keep reflective journals about their experiences and evolving ideas about education specifically related to teacher agency, school/societal structures related to race, class and gender, moral professionalism, social justice, and language and culture both implicitly and explicitly embedded in their classrooms. They were also expected to engage in their own action research projects in which they deeply explored areas of their teaching practice in order to better understand and hopefully improve the interactions and learning within their classrooms. Consistent with a learner-centered approach, after each class day, teachers shared reflective written feedback on the ways in which they experienced the graduate school curriculum.

The teacher professional development challenge was twofold. To create meaningful, positive identity forming educational experiences for P-12 youth, it is important to create teacher professional development that does the same. Therefore, the authors attempted to model learner-centered instruction, educator collaboration, self-reflection and self-correction by engaging in rigorous critical dialogue. All of the courses, in the face-to-face and hybrid versions of the program, were team taught by all of the faculty, with small group and individual mentoring for each teacher in the program.

The success of a program such as this is manifest in the changes in classroom teacher practice that occur outside of the professional development milieu and the authors have attempted to track those outcomes through the coursework of P-12 teachers enrolled in the program, their data and reporting of their students' outcomes, anonymous alumni surveys and one-on-one alumni interviews.

OPERATING THEORETICAL FRAMEWORKS

The program design was originally based on research on teacher professional development that focused on the "ideal" duration, schedule, and composition of content and participants. In addition, several frameworks have shaped the authors' work: adult development; moral professionalism; critical pedagogies and theories; culturally relevant pedagogy; women's ways of knowing; and more recently, critical race theory; and antiracist practice and policy development and the related theorists mentioned below.

A word about our language choices: Race is a social construct that artificially separates humans into "races." Yet, racism is also a social construct that creates "whiteness" and intentionally (sometimes violently) reserves the assets of society to lighter-skinned people. We refer collectively to Indigenous/Native, Black, Latinx, and Asian Pacific Islanders as People of Color, a flat and inadequate way to define darker-skinned people in the U.S. who share elements of specific cultures and are negatively impacted by structural racism. We intentionally use Black as an inclusive term to refer to anyone with ancestry in the African diaspora, including the continent of Africa, the Caribbean, South America, Europe, Asia, and the Americas. We only use African American and black when citing authors and teachers who explicitly use this terminology, or when referring only to African-descended people from the United States. Brown and Latinx are gender-neutral ways to refer to the widely diverse people from the Caribbean, Central and South America; similarly, we only use Hispanic when citing authors or teachers.

While copy-editing the book, we were struck by how the word "white" dominated the narrative. The American Psychological Association 7th edition style guide requires that we capitalize the "w" when we refer to U.S. people who are racially white. We choose, instead, to stand in solidarity with Dumas (2016) who argues that "white is nothing but a social construct, and does not describe a group with a sense of common experiences or kinship" (p. 13), in the way that "European" or "French" is an accurate cultural or political descriptor. If antiracism encourages the decentering of whiteness, it starts with the language we use to describe human beings.

WHY THIS BOOK

Several chapters in the *Handbook of Professional Development in Education* (Martin, Kragler, Quatroche, & Bauserman, 2014) acknowledge the evolving landscape of public schools, including the deepening inequalities and the changing racial demographics of the student population. However, the *Handbook* on the whole, accepts neo-liberal schooling as "the new normal" and offers teacher professional development methods for working within existing structures. The five characteristics of successful professional development that the *Handbook* documents – professional development that is instructive, reflective, active, collaborative, and substantive – assumes the existing accountability regime, the continuation of global comparisons, measures of teacher quality that are tied to student scores on standardized tests, standards-driven instruction (however poorly supported), technology solutions to the high cost of high-quality teacher professional development, and the growth of data-driven decision- making (Martin et al, 2014, p. xi – xviii). It is a pragmatic book that offers a vision of teacher professional development that continues to hold Eurocentric curriculum and accountability pedagogies as normative. The *Handbook* treats teachers as professionals and intellectuals, yet not necessarily as artists, citizens or antiracist pedagogues.

Many of the scholars used in the graduate program and who inform the authors' individual research and scholarship include: Wayne Au, Stephen Brookfield, Marilyn Cochran-Smith, Linda Darling-Hammond, Jeffrey Duncan-Andrade, Michael Dumas, Paulo Friere, Geneva Gay, Paul Gorski, Patricia Hinchey, Ibram Kendi, LaGarrett King, Alfie Kohn, Kevin Kumashiro, Sonya Douglass Horsford, Gloria Ladson-Billings, Sonia Nieto, Hugh Sockett, Mariana Souto-Manning, David Stovall, Katy Swalwell, Joan Wink, Kenneth Zeichner, and many other critical scholars and texts that critique neo-liberal educational policies. The authors' respect for their work is immeasurable, yet there remains the need to continuously construct new curricula based on the theories and frameworks of these scholars to meet the daily and changing needs of P-12 classroom teachers. There is nothing the authors can (or should) "plug and play" from the work of these researchers.

Zeichner's 2018 publication, *The Struggle for the Soul of Teacher Education*, offers an important theoretical framing useful to the authors as teacher educators and scholars. Most important is the reassertion of social justice and respect for the knowledge of P-12 practitioners and non-professional educators in communities in teacher educator programs (p. 175). Zeichner also explicates the three types of professionalism – organizational (state control), occupational (collegial authority), and democratic professionalism – that can govern teacher professional development, arguing strongly for the "collaborative and cooperative action between teachers and other education stakeholders…[as a] needed response to growing forms of occupational professionalism and excessive bureaucratic controls in teaching and teacher education" (p. 44). As bracing as is this text, it focuses attention on pre-service teacher education with little attention to the needs and concerns of in-service, veteran P-12 teachers.

No More Culturally Irrelevant Teaching by Souto-Manning, Llerena, Martell, Maguire, and Arce-Boardman (2018) is also a balm for teachers and teacher educators. It is aimed at a practitioner audience already poised to embrace and practice culturally relevant teaching strategies. The book offers specific practices and stances that emerge both from critical theoretical frameworks and an analysis of the current policy environment. Yet, it only hints at the type of structured antiracist teacher professional development that P-12 teachers can practice and reflect on in a collegial environment, particularly in settings where there are few teachers with a critical stance.

The work of Sonya Douglass Horsford and colleagues on educational leadership offers insights for teacher educators and policy makers for changing the conditions of teacher professional development toward antiracist policies; these ideas are explored further in the final chapter of this book.

Content-specific scholars such as LaGarrett King, Prentice Chandler, Anthony Brown, Keffrelyn Brown, and Cinthia Salinas (social studies), and Danny Martin, Nicole Joseph, and Toya Jones Frank (mathematics) offer important theories that may be transferable to other disciplines. All of these scholars bring a lens of antiracist theory and practice to their disciplinary research. Nevertheless, few address practice or praxis, or are directed particularly at the practice of veteran in-service teachers across disciplines and grade levels, and in multiracial settings.

For all of the ways that the authors respect, if not revere, these intellectuals and practitioners, they believe this book offers additional insight to how to design teacher professional development experiences for in-service P-12 teachers that help to dismantle educational racism and inequity, starting in the classroom.

REFERENCES

Dumas, M. J. (2016). Against the dark: Antiblackness in education policy and discourse. *Theory into Practice*, *55*(1), 11–19. doi:10.1080/00405841.2016.1116852

Martin, L. E., Kragler, S., Quatroche, D. J., & Bauserman, K. L. (Eds.). (2014). *Handbook of professional development in education: Successful models and practices, PreK-12*. The Guilford Press.

Souto-Manning, M., Llerena, C. L., Martell, J., Maguire, A. S., & Arce-Boardman, A. (2018). *No more culturally irrelevant teaching*. Heinemann.

Zeichner, K. (2018). *The struggle for the soul of teacher education: Critical social thought*. Routledge.

Acknowledgment

Many of these chapters began life as scholarly presentations at international and national conferences, including the American Education Research Association, the National Association of Multicultural Education, the Critical Questions in Education Conference, the Central and Eastern European Schools Association conference, the Conference on Higher Education Pedagogy, and the Peace and Justice Studies Association conference.

We are grateful to:

Our colleagues over the 20+ years of the teacher professional development master's degree program who have provided creativity, skills, hard questions, and inspiration.

Laura Dallman served multiple roles in the creation of this book: thought leader, chapter author, a doctoral graduate assistant, and the person who interviewed alumni to allow the other authors to analyze the data anonymously.

The P-12 classroom teachers who have been our teachers, in addition to being learners in the master's degree programs in both the fully face-to-face and the hybrid incarnation of the program. Many of these teachers also participated in the anonymous alumni surveys and interviews.

Elizabeth (Lissa) Soergel, who graciously copy edited the entire manuscript.

Our beloved friends and families who have supported us through this long journey of living (and documenting) our work.

Chapter 1

When Asked, Teachers Said... :
Contemplating a New
Teacher Professional

ABSTRACT

The authors perceive that institutionalized racial hierarchies are the greatest barrier to educational equity in the United States. While P-12 teachers may express the desire to make their classrooms spaces of joy, creativity, and intellectual brilliance, it is primarily through intentional skills development that teachers succeed. The authors assert the need for greater investments by school districts and teacher education programs in professional development for in-service P-12 teachers that further empower them and, in turn, their students, to contribute to the dismantling of racism in the U.S. Teacher educators, administrators and policy makers need to position themselves as cultivators and supporters of P-12 teachers in ways that encourage and sustain their antiracist advocacy and equity work in their teaching.

Teaching is a profession that requires lifelong training --response from an alumni survey

DOI: 10.4018/978-1-7998-5649-8.ch001

INTRODUCTION

Public school teachers are the first line of defense to change the classroom experiences of children and youth, all of whom are negatively impacted by educational inequities. We perceive that institutionalized racial hierarchies are the greatest barrier to educational equity in the United States. While talented teachers may express the desire to make their individual classrooms spaces of joy, creativity, and intellectual brilliance, it is primarily through intentional and collaborative skills development that teachers succeed. Guided by the results from a national survey of teachers, a local survey, our experiences from more than 20 years of providing teacher professional development, and the theoretical frameworks offered by scholars of race, teacher professional development, and adult development, we assert the need for greater investments by school districts and teacher education programs in professional development for in-service teachers that further empower them and, in turn, their students to contribute to the dismantling of racism in the U.S.

The data are well-known that document how the structural inequities of employment, housing, health, and wealth accumulation negatively and disproportionately impact the educational attainment and achievement of Children and Youth of Color (Kendi, 2016; Race the Power of an Illusion, n.d.). We know that the efforts of teachers as "street level bureaucrats" to act as "equity warriors" too often fail, because Teachers of Color experience racial battle fatigue (Acuff, 2018), and many white teachers, even those who self-report as equity minded, resist or are unaware of strategies to make structural change (Rochmes, Penner & Loeb, 2017). To rely on classroom teachers to bear the full burden of transforming educational inequities is unconscionable. To offer sustained support through ongoing and antiracist teacher professional development, as offered by this book, we stand a chance of breaking the overwhelming "whiteness" of U.S. schooling in order to capture and elevate the intellectual brilliance of all students in U.S. schools and communities.

In the following five chapters of the book, we offer a sequence of explorations that can lead to antiracist teacher professional development experiences: engaging in deep racial identity work; methods for unpacking assumptions; examining teaching-learning relational dynamics; nurturing teacher leadership and collegial relations; and policy proposals based on a "manifesto" for how to broaden the practice of antiracist teacher professional development across U.S. school districts. Each section includes examples of how P-12 teachers in a graduate teacher professional development program engaged with these explorations and the outcomes, tensions and dilemmas that emerged. Although our work identifies multiple areas of inequity/oppression in schools, such as gender, language, class, and abilities, in this book we are focused on race/ethnicity as the most challenging area of educational inequity.

Brief History of Educational Inequities

Access to U.S. public educational opportunity has always been unequal. Not only has access been unequal, but the cultural attitudes we struggle with today have been codified since the early years of our country's history. In the late 18th century, Thomas Jefferson drafted "A Bill for the More General Diffusion of Knowledge" and his "Notes on the State of Virginia." His educational plan called for a two-track system for "the laboring and the learned" that would allow a very few of the laboring class to advance, such that "twenty of the best geniuses will be raked from the rubbish annually, and be instructed, at the public expense" (Jefferson, 1784). One hundred years later, jurisdictions attempted to implement many of Horace Mann's ideas for universal, secular public education with well-trained professional teachers (e.g., Cremin, n.d.), with a caveat that perpetuated Jefferson's systemic inequities. In most public school systems, the white laboring class, and those populations that became part of the ascending American Empire (e.g. Collier, 1993) – Indigenous people, the formerly enslaved Africans, the immigrants from Europe and Asia, the displaced Mexicans, Cubans, Puerto Ricans, native Hawaiians, Guamanians, American Samoans, Filipinos, and Mariana Islanders – did not merit equal expenditures on public education or access to a high-quality common curriculum (e.g., Singer, 2016).

By 1896, the legal codification of educational inequities took the form of the U.S. Supreme Court decision upholding the constitutionality of racial segregation in public accommodations (*Plessy v. Ferguson* 1896a and 1896b). Rossi and Montgomery (1994) detail the history of separate and unequal schooling for Children of Color as encoded in law, justified by pseudo-science and reinforced by social mores. The curriculum offered to the children in segregated, underfunded schools was explicitly Eurocentric and celebrated the victories of elite Europeans in the Americas. Social experiments in education – such as the early years of Hampton Institute, U.S. government funded Indian boarding schools, and Americanization programs – were designed to "kill the [Indian, African, Mexican, Asian, immigrant], save the child," or otherwise prepare children for manual and industrial labor and second-class citizenship (e.g., Anderson 1988; Buffalohead & Molin 1996; Hoffman & Hoffman, 1976; Rossi & Montgomery 1994; Singer, 2016). The structural and cultural violence (Galtung 1969; Galtung 1990) promoted through schooling during the period of legal racial segregation and forced cultural assimilation would now be considered bad pedagogy, if not an outright violation of human rights (Ho 2007).

The More Things Change, The More They Stay the Same

Schooling in the early 21st century perpetuates the structural inequities of the last 200-plus years. Simultaneously, a "perfect storm" of four important trends is brewing that threatens to fortify these structures rather than dismantle them. First, the common belief in the value of public schools is under attack. Rooks (2017) describes a toxic alliance of venture capitalists, hedge fund investors, corporations and philanthropists that profit from "segrenomics," or the persistent and intentional racial and economic segregation of public schooling (p. 2). In 2012 fewer than a third (29%) of Americans polled indicated "a great deal" or "quite a lot" of confidence in public schools, compared with 33% in 2007, or 58% in 1973 (Jones, 2012). White parents in some localities around the country strategize to "secede" from school districts where they are likely to encounter African American and Latinx families (e.g., Felton, 2017). The family of U.S. Secretary of Education Betsy DeVos has contributed millions of dollars since the late 1990s to the cause of school choice and unregulated charter expansion in her home state. Her policy preferences include vouchers that transfer taxpayer dollars to private and parochial schools, private investment in charter schools, and opposition to teachers' unions (Strauss, 2016; Wallace, Vazquez, & Marsh, 2017). There is a great deal of concern that disinvestments in public education will be led by federal government policy over the next decade (Partelow, Shapiro, McDaniels, & Brown, 2018).

Secondly, the student population (and future workforce) reflects the "Browning" of the United States (e.g., Caldwell, 2015; Frey, 2014; Uriarte, 1991). By 2022 projections are that Children of Color will constitute nearly 55% of the public school student population (NCES, 2014). Most classroom teachers (82%) are white, middle-class women (NCES, 2012). The racialized identities of these school inhabitants were first formed centuries ago. We are living with the legacy of the Virginia Slave Codes of 1705 when "whiteness" was first invented to prevent poor, "white" indentured servants from forming alliances with Indigenous people and indentured and enslaved Africans to gain economic and political power over wealthy colonists (Coates, 2014; Foner, 2009; Kendi, 2017; Smedley, 1997). These racialized identities have evolved and have persisted into the 21st century, as subsequent waves of immigrants arrived and populations were subsumed by an expanding nation (e.g., Chaudhary, 2015). Efforts to ignore or downplay the impact of race in the student-teacher relationship treat teachers as technicians or "educational clerks... who implement scripted teaching strategies and curriculum" (Zeichner, 2018, p. 29; see also View & Gorski, 2014). These efforts also disregard the work of scholars such as Pollock, Deckman, Mira and Shalaby (2010) who describe the feeling among (white) teachers that tackling race in the classroom requires superhuman effort at every level of engagement. Their research into the dyadic, teacher-student relationship, examines the classroom level, the school level and outside the classroom at the level of public policy. In particular, Pollock and her colleagues describe three core tensions that especially plague teachers: 1. the desire for "concrete" applications of "theoretical" ideas about race, 2. persistent questions about the potential for "everyday" activity to dismantle inequitable "structures," and 3. a wrestling with the need for both professional and personal development on racial issues. Critical race theory (CRT) scholars also acknowledge the need to infuse a CRT lens into teacher education, teacher professional development, and school culture (e.g., Brown-Jeffy & Cooper, 2011; Hayes & Juarez, 2012; Kohli, 2016, Ladson-Billings, 2013a, 2013b; Milner & Laughter, 2015; Milner, 2017; Stovall, 2016), but also the need for more examples of how to address the core tensions and practical needs of teachers and children.

Thirdly, the U.S. faces greater economic competition from global economies, even as it continues to rank among the strongest global economies (e.g. The Global Competitiveness Index, 2015). The ability to leverage talent is at the heart of an economy's competitiveness, and talent-driven economies are the ones that are in the best position to adapt to and benefit from technology-driven changes. Teachers are the linchpin to America's ability to remain globally competitive. In most of the highest-performing global economies, teachers are drawn from the top one-third of all students completing college degrees (Barber & Mourshed 2007). This cannot be said of the United States. Rockoff (2004) suggests that teacher effectiveness is the most important school-based determinant of student achievement and likely plays a decisive role in their success. Lacking coordinated strategies to recruit, retain, and develop more capable teachers, the U.S. is ignoring "a vital national priority" (West, 2004).

We know there is a cultural mismatch of classroom teachers with the growing population of Students of Color. There are lessons that *should* be learned from Teachers of Color on how to improve educational outcomes for all children (e.g., Battey, Levya, Williams, Belizario, Greco & Shah, 2018; Cherng & Halpin, 2016; Eddy & Easton-Brooks, 2011; Easton-Brooks, Lewis & Zhang, 2009). Yet, the efforts to recruit and retain more Black, Latinx, Indigenous, and Asian teachers are sorely lacking.

Finally, schools face a shortage of teachers of all races and ethnicities, with too few teachers entering the profession to begin with and too many leaving prematurely. The inadequate supply of teachers, particularly skilled veteran teachers is due to factors that discourage teachers from making long-term commitments to teaching, including underfunded schools and the deprofessionalization of the teaching profession (e.g., Carver-Thomas & Darling-Hammond, 2017; Horsford, Scott, & Anderson, 2019; Sutcher, Darling-Hammond & Carver-Thomas, 2016; Zeichner & Ndimande, 2008). It is estimated by the Economic Policy Institute that the actual teacher shortage far exceeds that of the 112,000 per year predicted in 2017 and that those numbers will increase annually (Garcia & Weiss, 2019).

The rising public expressions of racism, class hostilities, and anti-immigration fervor pose for teachers and their students a binary dilemma: do they stick with the pacing guide and standardized test preparations that dominate curricula because these efforts will serve to support and sustain the systems and outcomes they know, or do they ask questions of the world and of one another to learn deeply and to develop the critical skills needed to create a new world? While addressing the question of what is the purpose of education, James Harvey of the Center on Reinventing Public Education states that, "The most significant skill [young people] can develop in the 21st century is the same skill that served them well in prior centuries: a mind equipped to think, the most important work skill of them all" (Harvey, quoted in Sloan, 2012).

The too few teachers who remain to advocate for all students and to work to make Americans schools great, lack support. Always an instrument of advancing the nation's political and economic policies (Martin, Kragler, Quatroche & Bauserman, 2014), rather than serving the expressed needs of children, teacher professional development efforts in the early 21st century tend to be chaotic, idiosyncratic, and regarded by most classroom teachers in our recent national survey as only "somewhat useful" or "poor," lacking immediate applicability to classroom practice, and failing to be engaging for teachers (*How does teacher professional development matter survey*, 2018).

If Harvey (2012) is correct regarding the purpose of education, what specific resources and strategies do teachers need to help develop critical thinking skills for themselves and in their students? How can teacher professional development be a tool for transforming an inequitable and hostile social order starting in the classroom? And, why should teacher educators, administrators, and policy makers invest in this kind of teacher professional development? These questions are addressed in the following sections.

Why Antiracist Teacher Professional Development?

We will address the last question first, regarding why such an investment is important. Kendi (2019) argues that policies serve the self-interest of people and communities. We perceive that all children in the U.S. face psychic injury given the history of institutional racism in the United States, the role of formal public education as an instrument of institutional racism, the systemic deprofessionalization of the teaching profession as it has become whiter and more female, and the role that U.S. society expects adults to play in shaping the lives of children. We argue that one purpose of teacher professional development is to treat teachers with the same regard as medical professionals, lawyers, and engineers – practitioners who are responsible for life-and- death decisions of safety and care for others, and also who are afforded a degree of autonomy and judgment consistent with their training and experience. Increasingly, these professions are insisting that an excellent doctor, lawyer, or engineer must demonstrate familiarity and comfort with cultural difference, if not advocacy toward dismantling systemic inequities (Clear Communication, 2017; Jesiek, Shen & Haller, 2012; Madaan, 2017; Trent, Dooley, & Dougé, 2019). Therefore, we perceive an emergency – a life and death decision – regarding the desperate need for critical, race-conscious teacher professional development as an antidote to the psychic racial injuries our children experience.

Antiracist teacher professional development addresses the type of "interest convergence," first defined by Derrick Bell (Bell, 1980). In an essay on the meaning of the 1954 U.S. Supreme Court *Brown v. Board of Education* decision, Bell wondered why 100 years of organizing and activism by African Americans finally resulted in a constitutional change regarding racially segregated public schooling. Without discrediting the legal genius and the decades long struggle of the NAACP Legal Defense team, Bell stated that "the interest of blacks[sic] in achieving racial equality will be accommodated only when it converges with the interests of whites" (p.523). In the case of the *Brown* decision, Bell outlined four interests held by American whites of the post-World War II era. Many perceived the immorality of domestic racial inequality fresh from fighting a four-year war against Nazism in Europe. Whites were aware (if not fearful) of the growing anger and radicalization of Black WWII veterans who returned to racialized violence and legal discrimination in their own nation. These whites understood the Cold War contradiction of winning the "hearts and minds" of emerging nations if all Americans were not being treated in accordance with rhetoric stating that "all men are created equal." Finally, Bell perceived that an economic interest by wealthy, largely northern, corporations to industrialize the rural South was stymied by ongoing state-sponsored segregation.

As was attempted with the legal desegregation of public schools, antiracist teacher professional development can serve a moral interest in that it promotes conditions for all children – white, People of Color, affluent, low-income, English fluent, English language learners, citizens, undocumented, and so on – to receive a high-quality education that nurtures the whole child. The cofounder of the National School Climate Center states that, "it is essential that all children, particularly the disadvantaged and the poor, have the opportunity to develop the social-emotional competencies and ethical dispositions that provide the foundation for the tests of life, health, relationships, and adult work" (Cohen, 2006, pp. 226-227). Even more than "disadvantaged and poor children," classroom teachers, particularly those who are white middle-class women, need social-emotional competencies and ethical dispositions to create these opportunities for all children, including for white affluent children. Cain (2016) created the *Multicultural Teacher Capacity Scale* to help teachers engage in a self-assessment regarding their dispositions, knowledge and skills to promote educational equity in their classrooms, schools and beyond. (See Table 1)

Although our interest in antiracist teacher professional development is to advance issues of educational equity, it has the additional advantage of helping to create a strong and highly skilled teaching force by supporting teachers to attain content expertise, to develop deeper pedagogical talent, and to practice agency as a rapid response to the current events of schooling. Among the characteristics of expert teachers identified in Table 2, we would expand Characteristic #11 (Have high respect for students) to include "being an equity advocate" as a practical tool for improving school climate and reducing the distractions that interrupt learning. The Cain rubric offers guidance for how to be such advocates.

Table 1. The Multicultural Teacher Capacity Scale (Cain Rubric)

Background: Although multicultural is a common term used in education, it is often used in inconsistent and superficial ways. In this study, multicultural education refers to a school-based reform movement and a multicultural teacher is one who has the knowledge, skills, and dispositions to promote educational equity in their classrooms, schools, and ultimately society. Acknowledging that teachers are not simply multicultural or not, multicultural teacher capacity describes the extent to which teachers feel that they are multicultural.

Description: The Multicultural Teacher Capacity Scale (MTCS) is a self-assessment tool designed to capture the extent to which teachers feel that they are multicultural as outlined by the included characteristics. Teachers reflect on the 11 multicultural characteristics as they are described along a continuum of levels teachers identify their location. The MTCS is designed for formative use to better understand where teachers fall on the continuum and to then seek ways to promote growth. As depicted in the model below, multicultural teacher capacity is organized into three domains: dispositions, knowledge, and skills. Dispositions are the values, attitudes, and beliefs that shape how teachers interpret knowledge and apply skills. The next layer is knowledge, which is the information that is used to inform the skills. Skills describe teaching practices that impact the classroom and beyond. Domains are the organizing categories and within each is a set of characteristics. Each characteristic is described along a continuum of five levels: nascent, emerging, progressing, advancing, and transformational. The goal is for everyone to find a place on the continuum. At the nascent level, teachers have not yet acquired the disposition, knowledge, or skill. At the emerging level, the teachers are developing an awareness, which then becomes acknowledgement at the progressing level. Social action begins at the advancing level and is intentional and sustained at the transformational level. The ultimate goal is for teachers to be intentionally engaged in social action that leads to long-lasting changes in their classrooms and beyond. By reflecting on their multicultural characteristics, teachers develop an awareness of their current level and the subsequent level present areas to work toward. This tool has implications for teacher education programs, teacher educators, teachers, and administrators who are committed to educational equity.

Instructions: To identify their respective levels, teachers review each characteristic and reflect on the descriptors beginning with nascent and continuing to the subsequent level until they reach a point where they do not meet the criteria listed. Levels are cumulative. As such, each descriptor under the levels must be met in order to progress to the subsequent level. It can be overwhelming to focus on 11 characteristics, therefore after reflecting on each characteristic, emphasis should be placed on 1-3 at a time.

We perceive that included with the children who experience interrupted learning are affluent, largely white, suburban children caught in the 'race to nowhere,' attending high-pressure schools and engaging in stress-related behaviors (cheating, depression, self-harming, and suicide), as adults push to distinguish these children from others (Abeles, 2010; Kain, 2011; Martin, 2011; Mathews, 2011). In fact, most (75%) whites support efforts to racially integrate schools and say they would be comfortable sending their children to schools that were up to 50% Black, making a lie of the rhetoric regarding parental preferences (Frankenberg & Jacobsen, 2011). We perceive that the more that children and youth learn to be critical thinkers, problem-solvers, and ethically-minded, empathic and active citizens, the greater their readiness for solving the social, economic, political, scientific, cultural, and moral problems of the 21st century. Squandering the talents and creativities of children, especially Children of Color and poor whites in order to preserve the socially constructed privilege of a diminishing percentage of affluent white children, seems to be self-defeating public policy. Professional teachers, who have the perspective of working with hundreds of children over the course of their careers and who are supported by intentional and ongoing teacher

Table 2. Skills and attributes of expert teachers

1. Organize and use content knowledge with more depth, integration, interdisciplinarity and insight
2. Adopt a problem-solving stance to their work
3. Anticipate, plan, and improvise as required by the situation
4. Are better decision-makers and can identify what decisions are important and which are less important decisions
5. Are proficient at creating an optimal classroom climate for learning.
6. Have a multidimensionally complex perception of classroom situations
7. Are more context-dependent and have high situation cognition
8. Are more adept at monitoring student problems and assessing their level of understanding and progress, and they provide much more relevant, useful feedback
9. Are more adept at developing and testing hypotheses about learning difficulties or instructional strategies
10. Are more automatic
11. Have high respect for students
12. Are passionate about teaching and learning.
13. Engage students in learning and develop in their students' self-regulation, involvement in mastery learning, enhanced self-efficacy, and self-esteem as learners
14. Provide appropriate challenging tasks and goals for students
15. Have positive influences on students' achievement
16. Enhance surface and deep learning

Adapted from: Distinguishing Expert Teachers from Novice and Experienced Teachers, Hattie, J.A C. (2002). What are the attributes of excellent teachers? In *Teachers make a difference: What is the research evidence?* (pp. 3-26). Wellington: New Zealand Council for Educational Research.

professional development, are in an excellent position to be anti-oppression advocates in partnership with parents.

Finally, public education's structural inequities and cultural attitudes make it difficult to achieve our vital economic goals. It is in the interest of U.S. policymakers to retain and uplift the professional teachers that devote their lives to educating the nation's 36 million public elementary and middle school children and the 15 million public high school children (National Center for Education Statistics, 2017). With turnover rates ranging from 11-17% nationwide per year (and as much as 80% for teachers who are certified outside of traditional teacher certification processes) at a cost of more than $20,000 to replace each departing teacher, we are wasting tens of millions of dollars and squandering the talents and creativities of adults charged with educating the next generation of changemakers (Ashoka, n.d.).

Antiracist Teacher Professional Development as a Tool for Transformation

Several factors make antiracist teacher professional development transformational: it encourages teachers to reflect deeply on their own identities as actors with agency in their classrooms; it encourages deep reflection on their practice, and within the context of systems of schooling (P-12, pre-service, and in-service education) and educational policies that shape their classroom practice; it offers teachers tools for gathering and analyzing data to support their claims concerning educational inequities; and it offers classroom teachers tools for working with others to correct those inequities.

In examining how teacher professional development can be a tool for transforming an inequitable and hostile social order starting in the classroom, we turned to teachers for clues. Using snowball sampling through networks of practicing teachers, we circulated a 27-question anonymous Survey Monkey to teachers. Receiving 144 responses from teachers in 11 states (AZ, DC, FL, IL, IN, IA, MD, NV, NY, OR, and VA), we analyzed their responses to queries about their teaching experiences and the type and quality of professional development they have received. One of the limitations of the survey was that we cannot ignore the social desirability factor when considering teacher responses, nor can we know exactly how teachers defined terms such as "awareness of student difference/differentiation" and "culturally relevant lessons." Follow-up research included interviews with teachers who were alumni of our program to gain more insight regarding these limitations.

However, when asked, "Does teacher professional development matter?" nearly all (96.6%) said that it does. This teacher's response captures many of the reasons respondents gave for why teacher professional development matters: "So we can fix the broken system."

As teacher educators in a teacher professional development master's degree program, it is reassuring that teachers see value in the idea of teacher professional development. Yet, we and they know that teacher professional development, in and of itself, does not transform teaching practice immediately or permanently. At best, we maintain critical hope (Duncan-Andrade, 2009) that antiracist teacher professional development can support teachers to radically transform their practice, believing that it is essential to help teachers take on the task of "provid[ing] the materials that students need to name and deal with the myriad issues that impact their lives" (Shear in Chandler, p. xi)." We believe that teachers and students together need to share in the process of unpacking the byproducts of an oppressive society and that teachers should take "audacious steps to seek to understand and feel students' pains and dreams as their own" and, in the process, model acceptance and care (Duncan-Andrade, 2009, p. 11). Alone, professional development cannot change the larger contexts in which teachers must work, but it can support teachers to change the lives of their students, their classroom communities, and practices at their schools. In addition, antiracist teacher professional development can support teachers to have a stronger voice in the policy arena beyond their schools, where the crucial voice of teachers is largely absent.

When asked, "Why do you teach?" the majority of teachers in the national survey described teaching, essentially, as a calling. Less inspired by the academic schedule (32%), a family legacy of teaching (23%), the portability of the work (17%), love of subject matter (46%), money (9%), or status (1%), most respondents indicated that their motivation for teaching was to nurture the development and learning of children (75%), because teaching is a passion (73%), because they derive a sense of purpose from the profession (69%), and because they love children and adolescents (68%).

As can be seen in Table 3, survey respondents were similar to the demographic profile of contemporary U.S. teachers in that most were female (86%), white (79%), licensed (80%), and had experience teaching in public schools (90%) (NCES data does not indicate whether private school teachers have any public school experience). Other characteristics of the survey

Table 3. Demographic profile of teacher professional development survey respondents

	Teacher Professional Development Survey	U.S. 2015-2016
Gender: Female (assumes gender binary statistics)[a]	86%	77%
Race: white [b]	79%	80%
Licensure [c]	80%	90%
Public school teaching experience [d]	90%	86%
More than 5 years' experience [e]	71%	88.1%*
Intends to stay in the profession "until retirement" [f]	63%	<28-75%

*indicates four or more years teaching experience
Note:
[a, b, d, e]National Center for Education Statistics:https://nces.ed.gov/surveys/ntps/tables/ntps1516_111617_t1n.asp;
[c]National Center for Education Statisticshttps://nces.ed.gov/surveys/ntps/tables/ntps1516_111617_t1n.asp;
[f]National Center for Education Statistics
https://nces.ed.gov/fastfacts/display.asp?id=28; and Goldring, Taie, & Riddles 2014; Ingersoll, Merrill, & Stuckey, 2014; McGee & Winters 2013, Morrissey 2015, 2017; Raue & Gray 2015; Rhee & Fornia, 2016.

respondents were that most were veteran teachers with more than five years of experience in the education profession (NCES data queries 4 or more years of experience) and most intended to stay in the profession "until retirement" (national and state data sets on teacher attrition and retention explore the receipt of full pensions as a proxy for retention or explore persons "leaving" the profession).

Beyond the Individual Classroom

A greater challenge is equipping teachers to participate in dismantling systems of oppression, particularly the intractable systems of racism and white supremacy that shape public schooling. This is not to say that the largely "white" teaching force is inherently and hopelessly racist; it is to say that teachers operate with decreasing autonomy within a system that reinforces a status quo designed centuries ago to deny high-quality schooling to poor whites and to all people who are American Indian/Native Alaskan, Black/African American, Hispanic/Latinx, and Asian Pacific Islander, particularly if their first language is other than English.

In our survey teachers indicated that high-quality teacher professional development would be the sort that offered the tools for addressing issues of race within their classrooms and schools. Nearly all respondents indicated that they agree or strongly agree that high-quality teacher professional development includes immediately applicable information and techniques that can enhance student learning (98%), collaboration with professional colleagues (97%), critical dialogue with peers (96%), awareness of student difference/differentiation (94%), the opportunity to learn about learner-centered instruction (93%), the opportunity for self-reflection (93%), and the opportunity to create culturally relevant lessons (92%).

When offered teacher professional development, teachers indicated that most of it is only "somewhat useful" (59%) or "poor" (15%). Typical descriptions of their teacher professional development experiences include irrelevant information, boring lectures and PowerPoints, and arrogant and ill-informed presenters. Teachers were especially resentful of the "wasted time" when the teacher professional development was mandatory, was run by the school district or administrators, and/or was essentially a sales pitch for new products. Many teachers referred to feelings of being demeaned and "treated as idiots" by teacher professional development presenters. Example critiques include:

- The worst professional development presentations are the mandatory ones held by the school division given by people who are in leadership roles and have been out of the classroom for a very long time and have no idea what is really going on in the classrooms from day to day.
- The current model of professional development is subject area weekly meetings. Teachers spend more time trying to figure out how to bullshit the administration into thinking we are doing what they want instead of spending time figuring out what the kids need and the best ways to get them that.
- Anything given to me by [my school district is poor quality]. They assume we are idiots, insinuate and/or say insulting things, assume we do not have the best intentions of our students and don't want to do what we are told, are top-down – try to "model" for the classroom as if we are children and force us to pay attention in inauthentic ways, give poor discussion questions, and you name it.
- [The worst PD is] ESL [English as a Second Language] PD that exclusively focuse[s] on higher proficiency ELLs [English Language Learners] (students who can be fully integrated into general education without targeted language support). The presenter told me I would "never have a student in [my] class who speaks no English at all, so don't worry about it," [but] I teach the newcomers class!

Frustrations included teacher professional development experiences that teachers perceived were downright silly, including a "graduate course where early childhood teachers had to do crafts with paper bags, crayons, glue. Demeaning." Or a session on "how to use fragrance in your classroom to enhance learning. Not kidding. A total waste of time." Or "learning how to use coloring books to teach AP Social Studies."

These same teachers were much more effusive when describing their best teacher professional development experiences. They characterized high-quality teacher professional development as being hands-on, practical, research-based, intensive, participatory, collaborative, interdisciplinary, and self-selected. teacher professional development that focuses on rote standards rather than on the impediments to addressing educational inequities fail to serve the express desires of teachers. We believe that antiracist teacher professional development, with a race-conscious lens, is a step in the right direction for delivering high-quality support to teachers.

The Specifics of Antiracist Teacher Professional Development

Figuring out how to deliver antiracist teacher professional development requires revisiting the three core tensions regarding race with which teachers struggle: the desire for "concrete" applications of "theoretical" ideas about race, the persistent questions about the potential for "everyday" activity to dismantle inequitable "structures," and a wrestling with the need for both professional and personal development on racial issues. Pollock and her colleagues assert that the most successful teachers serving Children of Color were those who "pledged to continue ongoing inquiry to both sides of each tension" (2010, p. 221), and that with explicit attention to issues of race in teacher professional development, teacher educators can encourage teachers to keep all three tensions in play for the duration of their careers.

Yet, the teachers who responded to our survey indicate challenges that are consistent with what happens when complexity theory (describing complex systems such as public schools as being bigger than the sum of their component parts) encounters critical realism (Cochran-Smith, Ell, Grudnoff, Ludlow, Haigh & Hill, 2014). Researchers are tasked with investigating the multiple interacting and mutually dependent parts and players to understand how the system works. They are then expected to unearth causal explanations for the system's functioning that include what the various players believe about the processes and contexts in which they are located and their own agency in making change. Finally, researchers and teacher educators using this framework must analyze how pre-service and in-service teachers can learn to navigate these complex systems to address social inequality, power, and access to opportunity (Cochran-Smith et al, 2014, p. 111). Opfer and Pedder (2011) suggest that teacher professional development often fails because of a shallow understanding of this interplay between complexity theory and critical realism and the fact that teacher learning is "deeply embedded in their professional lives and in the complex working conditions of their schools" (p. 379). Where teacher professional development is successful in helping teachers develop "patterns of practice for equity," that success is a result of sustained interaction among three specific elements: the teachers' personal beliefs and values, mentor teachers, and children in classrooms (Walby, 2007, p. 116-117).

The survey respondents may believe that teacher professional development matters because of a belief that changing micro level variables will have systemic effects throughout education. Out of their affection for children and adolescents and their dedication to the profession, they might say that the path toward racial equity and justice is frustratingly slow and incremental and that staying the course is essential if change is to occur. They might agree that teacher professional development matters through the ripple effects of critically engaging teachers – one at a time.

A macro-level view, however, sharpens the focus on the broader, deeper, and entrenched systemic inequities highlighted by Critical Race Theory literature and shines a bright light on the urgency of pain that all children and youth are experiencing as a result of these inequities. For adults there is value in both developing a critical stance and working with children and youth to provide the scaffolding for children to develop their own critical stance (i.e., all children should/could be "groomed" to help dismantle systems of oppression and inequity). First, in order for that to happen, teachers themselves need the support in antiracist teacher professional development to develop their own critical stance.

What do we need to do differently in teacher professional development to support the development of the changemakers we so urgently need? We seek to respond positively to the call from Aileen Kennedy (2014) who noted:

"[There is] a plethora of articles exploring particular models or approaches [to teacher professional development], [but] very little that synthesised these models and even less that sought to theorise such syntheses in relation to broader concerns such as policy, power and professionalism, taking the contribution beyond simply creating typologies of [professional development] models." (p. 2-3)

To do so, for over 20 years we have engaged in our own reflective practice as teacher educators, studying and experimenting with strategies, tools, experiences, assignments, theories and practices along with the P-12 classroom teachers enrolled in a two-year master's degree professional development program. We have invited our colleagues to reflect with us, formally and informally, through dialogue, collaborative practice, and policy actions.

Despite our laser focus on P-12 classroom teachers, most conversations about education begin with at least a token reference to the children we hope to educate. And we all do so blindly: We do not know whether the rapid expansion of the gig economy or the globalized economy is the result of, or the prompt for, a changing consensus about public education in the United States. We do not know if heightened racial tensions and anti-immigrant hatred are the dying gasps of an old socio-political structure or the beginning of a century-long retrenchment that requires us to gather our children close to their tribes. But we believe that the millennia of human existence created the consensus that we want our individual children, if not our collective children, to have the abilities to meet their basic human needs, to have meaningful relationships, to find and follow their passions, and to make meaningful contributions to their communities. Formal and informal educators help children to achieve these goals. As we contemplated the impact of our program, we looked for data from classrooms that offer evidence of teachers' efforts to uplift student voice, of student academic impact, and of the extent to which teachers are meeting the academic and socio-emotional needs of their students.

In examining the data from the national survey and the teacher professional development literature, we attempted to state more clearly what classroom teachers needed and wanted from their professional development experiences. These aspirations are framed from the perspective of moral professionalism (e.g., Sockett, 1993) and considering the ethical dilemmas (e.g., Levinson & Fay, 2016) teachers experience. We have been guided by a notion that teachers are, and should be treated as, artists, intellectuals and citizens (e.g., View & DeMulder, 2009). That is to say that professional educators who are prepared for a future that promotes educational equity for all children will be those who maintain a critical stance, who are creative and flexible, who use their adult voices in the public square, and who teach children to have a critical stance, to uplift their youthful voices and to engage in youth civic action.

We perceive that school superintendents and principals are not the only school leaders and that they and teachers together should behave as *democratic professionals* (e.g., Horsford, Scott, & Anderson, 2019, pp. 155-158). Rather than encouraging teachers to be merely compliant (or obedient), we have coached teachers toward deeper inquiry. With guided practice in classrooms, we want teachers to see how inquiry and race-conscious pedagogies work for all children. Beyond caring and holding good intentions, we have sought conversations with classroom teachers and teacher educators about how to redefine the role of teachers as change agents against institutional racism. We believe that practice moves us all closer to "perfect."

In reflecting on our practice as teacher educators, we place our work in the context of the teacher professional development typologies (e.g. Kennedy, 2014), and consider many of the experiments and outcomes for meaning-making among in-service classroom teachers and their P-12 students. These experiments include the afore-mentioned racial identity work, methods for unpacking assumptions, examinations of teaching-learning relational dynamics, the promotion of teacher leadership and collegial relations and the development of school-based and public policy proposals. We continuously discuss the good, the bad and the ugly that result from our efforts to more intentionally infuse race-consciousness in teacher professional development.

Finally, we are interested in making antiracist teacher professional development a vibrant reality. We looked to Fairfax, Virginia, among the top-ranked school districts in the nation (Newsweek, August 2016), to gauge the possibilities. Fairfax County, Virginia, expands on the state vision of a "portrait of a graduate," and suggests where teacher professional development should lead. The Fairfax County Portrait of a Graduate describes children and youth who are communicators, collaborators, ethical global citizens, creators, critical thinkers, and goal-directed and resilient individuals. In order for students to graduate with these attributes, they will need teachers who receive high-quality and ongoing professional development.

We perceive that the nation is at an important threshold for discerning how to implement race-conscious teacher professional development with the white, middle- class, women who represent the majority of U.S. public school teachers, at the same time as recruiting and retaining Teachers of Color who enter the profession and rewarding all teachers who demonstrate an ability to sustain educational equity. Accordingly, we perceive that parallel "portraits" teachers and teacher educators would match and embolden similar characteristics in pre-service and in-service teachers. These "portraits" would regard teachers as antiracist leaders who pave the way for the future of education and for the next generation of informed citizens. Appropriate antiracist teacher professional development is essential to cultivate that leadership by supporting teachers to have an amplified voice, not only in their schools but also in shaping education policy.

Toward achieving this goal, we have encouraged teachers and teacher educators to actively seek out growth opportunities to transform society from the grassroots up. Growth requires discomfort (e.g., Csikszentmihalyi, 1992). Fear and discomfort prevent people from doing the hard work of change (e.g., Baily, & Katradis, 2016). Educators must lean into the discomfort for the sake of their own growth and on behalf of all children and to engage in the pedagogies of courage (Emdin, 2016a) and vulnerability (Brantmeier, 2011). We need to address and work to eliminate the public ignorance and hatred we have seen around the nation. High school graduates, younger children and their teachers must be educated and empowered to seek justice. Interest convergence says, "That thing that you are calling justice is also profitable for us." Fear and hatred create a sense of scarcity and narrow self-interest; in contrast, we believe that by working together, innovation can create intellectual and spiritual abundance toward justice.

Antiracist teacher professional development may offer the tools that penetrate the equity resistance described by Gorski (2019) and documented by Rochmes, Penner and Loeb (2017). By learning from scholars and Teachers of Color such as Ndemanu (2014), and Lapayese, Aldana and Lara (2014) about how existing teacher education for pre-service teachers continues to reify "whiteness" and predicts the attrition of Teachers of Color, we can redesign in-service teacher professional development that serves all teachers. LaCroix and Kuehl (2019) suggest a Diversity in Teacher Education Framework for pre-service teachers that can be adapted for in-service teachers, since all teachers beyond white preservice teachers need this knowledge (p. 40). The framework includes awareness of racial positioning, knowledge of history of racial inequities, open attitudes regarding learning about experiences of "race," and collaborative learning experiences and experience with practicing culturally responsive pedagogies. Antiracist teacher professional development would prepare teachers for formal evaluations of their knowledge of racialized experiences and racism, it would embed a meaningful critical study of whiteness and privilege in order to alleviate the invisibility of this social location (Lapayese et al, 2014), it would incorporate Yosso's concept of community cultural wealth (2005), and it would offer incentives to teachers who demonstrate growth toward narrowing the opportunity gap/education debt (Ladson-Billings, 2006). It would offer instruction and practice in Emdin's Seven C's (co-generative dialogue, co-teaching, cosmopolitanism, context, content, competition and curation) for effective teaching that promote deep relationships between teachers and students – discussed in more detail in chapter 3 (Emdin, 2016b).

Teachers are uniquely positioned to "be the change we wish to see." Teacher educators, administrators and policy makers need to position themselves as cultivators and supporters of teachers in ways that encourage and sustain their antiracist advocacy and equity work in their teaching. We trust that teachers, with thoughtfully developed knowledge, dispositions and the right set of tools (e.g., Cain, 2016), can lead the way toward a more equitable and "profitable" educational enterprise and a more just world. We believe that our nation needs to do this work. We acknowledge that it is hard and imperfect. And we believe it can, and should, be taught.

REFERENCES

Abeles, V., & Congdon, J. (Directors), (2010). *The race to nowhere: Transforming education from the ground up* [Film]. Reel Link Films. http://www.racetonowhere.com/about-film

Acuff, J. (2018). Confronting racial battle fatigue and comforting my Blackness as an educator. *Multicultural Perspectives, 20*(3), 174–181. doi:10.1080/15 210960.2018.1467767

Anderson, J. (1988). *The education of blacks in the south, 1865 – 1930*. The University of North Carolina Press.

Baily, S., & Katradis, M. (2016). "Pretty much fear!!" Rationalizing teacher (dis)engagement in social justice education. *Equity & Excellence in Education, 49*(2), 215–227.

Baker, B. D., Farrie, D., & Sciarra, D. (2018). *Is school funding fair? A national report card* (7th ed.). Education Law Center. https://edlawcenter.org/ assets/files/pdfs/ publications/National_Report_Card_2017.pdf

Barber, M., & Mourshed, M. (2007). *How the World's Best-Performing School Systems Come Out on Top*. McKinsey and Company. https://www.mckinsey.com/ industries/social-sector/our-insights/how-the-worlds-best-performing-school-systems-come-out-on-top

Battey, D., Leyva, L. A., Williams, I., Belizario, V. A., Greco, R., & Shah, R. (2018). Racial (mis)match in middle school mathematics classrooms: Relational interactions as a racialized mechanism. *Harvard Educational Review, 88*(4), 455-484. https://searchproquest.com.mutex.gmu.edu/docvie w/2237547502?accountid=14541

Bell, D. A. (1980). Brown v. Board of Education and the interest-convergence dilemma. *Harvard Law Review, 93*(3), 518–533. http://www.jstor.org/stable/1340546

Brantmeier, E. J. (2013). Pedagogy of vulnerability: Definitions, assumptions, and applications. In J. Lin, R. Oxford, & E. J. Brantmeier (Eds.), RE-envisioning higher education: Embodied pathways to wisdom and transformation (pp. 95–106). Information Age Publishing.

Brown-Jeffy, S., & Cooper, J. E. (2011). Toward a conceptual framework of culturally relevant pedagogy: An overview of the conceptual and theoretical literature. *Teacher Education Quarterly*, *38*(1), 65–84.

Buffalohead, W. R., & Molin, P. F. (1996). A nucleus of civilization: American Indian families at Hampton Institute in the late nineteenth century. *Journal of American Indian Education*, *35*(3), 59–94. https://www.jstor.org/stable/24398297

Cain, J. M. (2015). *Clarifying Multicultural: The Development and Initial Validation of the Multicultural Teacher Capacity Scale* [Unpublished doctoral dissertation]. University of North Carolina at Chapel Hill.

Caldwell, C. (2014-15, Winter). The Browning of America [Review of the book *Diversity Explosion: How New Racial Demographics Are Remaking America*, by W. H. Frey]. *Claremont Review of Books, 15*(1). https://claremontreviewofbooks.com/the-browning-of-america/

Carver-Thomas, D., & Darling-Hammond, L. (2017). *Teacher turnover: Why it matters and what we can do about it*. Learning Policy Institute.

Chaudhary, A. R. (2015). Racialized incorporation: The effects of race and generational status on self-employment and industry-sector prestige in the United States. *The International Migration Review*, *49*(2), 318–354. doi:10.1111/imre.12087

Cherng, H. S., & Halpin, P. F. (2016). The importance of minority teachers: Student perceptions of minority versus white teachers. *Educational Researcher*, *45*(7), 407–420. doi:10.3102/0013189X16671718

Clear Communication. (n.d.). *Cultural Respect*. National Institutes of Health, U.S. Department of Health and Human Services. https://www.nih.gov/institutes nih/nih-office-director/office-communications-public-liaison/clear communication/cultural-respect

Coates, T. (2014, June 23). How racism invented race in America and the case for reparations: a narrative bibliography. *The Atlantic Monthly*. https://www.theatlantic.com/politics/archive/2014/06/the-case-for-reparations-a-narrative-bibliography/372000/

Cochran-Smith, M., Ell, F., Grudnoff, L., Ludlow, L., Haigh, M., & Hill, M. (2014). When complexity theory meets critical realism: A platform for research on initial teacher education. *Teacher Education Quarterly*, *41*(1), 105. https://www.jstor.org/stable/teaceducquar.41.1.105

Cohen, J. (2006). Social, emotional, ethical and academic education: Creating a climate for learning, participation in democracy and well-being. *Harvard Educational Review*, *76*(2), 201–237. doi:10.17763/haer.76.2.j44854x1524644vn

Coles-Ritchie, M., & Smith, R. R. (2017). Taking the risk to engage in race talk: Professional development in elementary schools. *International Journal of Inclusive Education*, *21*(2), 172–186. doi:10.1080/13603116.2016.1193562

Collier, E. C. (1993). *Instances of use of United States forces abroad, 1798-1993*. Congressional Research Service. http://www.ambriente.com/nexum/documents/usaforces.pdf

Cremin, L. A. (n.d.). Horace Mann: American educator. In *Encyclopedia Britannica*. https://www.britannica.com/biography/Horace-Mann

Csikszentmihalyi, M. (1992). *Flow: The psychology of happiness*. Rider Press.

Dodman, S. L., DeMulder, E. K., View, J. L., Swalwell, K., Stribling, S. M., Ra, S. S., & Dallman, L. (2018). Equity audits as a tool of critical data-driven decision making: Preparing teachers to see beyond achievement gaps and bubbles. *Action in Teacher Education*, *41*(1), 4–22. doi:10.1080/01626620.2018.1536900

Dumas, M. J. (2016). Against the dark: Antiblackness in education policy and discourse. *Theory into Practice*, *55*, 11–19. doi:10.1080/00405841.2016.1116852

Duncan-Andrade, J., & Morrell, E. (2005). Turn up that radio, teacher: Popular cultural pedagogy in new century urban schools. *Journal of School Leadership*, *15*(3), 284–308. doi:10.1177/105268460501500304

Duncan-Andrade, J., & Morrell, E. (2008). *The Art of Critical Pedagogy: The Promises of Moving from Theory to Practice in Urban Schools*. Peter Lang.

Easton-Brooks, D., Lewis, C. W., & Zhang, Y. (2009). Ethnic matching: The influence of African American teachers on the reading scores of African American students. *The National Journal of Urban Education & Practice*, *3*(1), 230–243.

Eddy, C. M., & Easton-Brooks, D. (2011). Ethnic-matching, school placement, and mathematics achievement of African American students from kindergarten through fifth grade. *Urban Education*, *46*(6), 1280–1299. doi:10.1177/0042085911413149

Emdin, C. (2011). Moving beyond the boat without a paddle: Reality pedagogy, Black youth and urban science education. *The Journal of Negro Education*, *80*(3), 284–295. https://www.jstor.org/stable/41341134

Emdin, C. (2016a). *For White folks who teach in the hood ... and the rest of y'all too: Reality pedagogy and Urban education*. Beacon Press.

Emdin, C. (2016b). Seven C's for effective teaching. *Educational Leadership*, *74*(1). http://www.ascd.org/publications/educational-leadership/sept16/vol74/num01/Seven-Cs-for-Effective-Teaching.aspx

Felton, E. (2017, September 6). The Department of Justice Is overseeing the resegregation of American schools. *The Nation*. https://www.thenation.com/article/the-department-of-justice-is-overseeing-the-resegregation-of-american-schools/

Foner, E. (2009). *Give Me Liberty!: An American History*. W.W. Norton & Company.

Frankenberg, E., & Jacobsen, R. (2011). Trends school integration polls. *Public Opinion Quarterly*, *75*(4), 788–811. doi:10.1093/poq/nfr016

Freire, P. (1970). Pedagogy of the oppressed. *Continuum*.

Frey, W. H. (2018). *Diversity explosion: How new racial demographics are remaking America*. Brookings Institution Press.

Galtung, J. (1969). Violence, peace, and peace research. *Journal of Peace Research*, *6*(3), 167–191.

Galtung, J. (1990). Cultural violence. *Journal of Peace Research*, *27*(3), 291–305.

Garcia, E., & Weiss, E. (2019, March 26). *The teacher shortage is real, large and growing, and worse than we thought*. The first report in The Perfect Storm in the Teacher Labor Market Series Report. Economic Policy Institute.

Goldring, R., Taie, S., & Riddles, M. (2014). *Teacher Attrition and Mobility: Results from the 2012–13 Teacher Follow-up Survey*. *U.S. Department of Education*. National Center for Education Statistics.

Gorski, P. (2019, April). Avoiding racial equity detours. *Educational Leadership*, 56–61.

Hayes, C., & Juarez, B. (2012). There is no culturally responsive teaching spoken here: A critical race perspective. *Democracy & Education*, *20*(1), 1–14. https://democracyeducationjournal.org/cgi/viewcontent.cgi?article=1023&context=home

Herbes-Sommers, C., Strain, T. H., & Smith, L. (Directors). (2003). *Race: The Power of an Illusion*. California Newsreel. http://www.racepowerofanillusion.org

Historical Timeline of Public Education in the US. (2017). Race Forward. https://www.raceforward.org/research/reports/historical-timeline-public-education-us

Ho, K. (2007). Structural violence as a human rights violation. *Essex Human Rights*, *4*(2), 1–17.

Hoffman, A. M., & Hoffman, D. B. (1976). A History of Vocational Education. ERIC. *RE:view*, *4*(2), 1–17. https://eric.ed.gov/?id=ED132283

Horsford, S. D., Alemán, E. A., & Smith, P. A. (2019). Our separate struggles are really one: Building political race coalitions for educational justice. *Leadership and Policy in Schools*, *18*(2), 226–236. doi:10.1080/15700763.2019.1611868

Horsford, S. D., Scott, J. T., & Anderson, G. L. (2019). *The politics of education policy in an era of inequality: Possibilities for democratic schooling*. Routledge.

Horsford, S. D., Stovall, D., Hopson, R., & D'Amico, D. (2019). School leadership in the New Jim Crow: Reclaiming justice, resisting reform. *Leadership and Policy in Schools*, *18*(2), 177–179. doi:10.1080/15700763.2019.161r872

Ingersoll, R., Merrill, L., & Stuckey, D. (2014). *Seven trends: the transformation of the teaching force, updated April 2014*. CPRE Report (#RR-80). Consortium for Policy Research in Education. https://files.eric.ed.gov/fulltext/ED566879.pdf

Jefferson, T. (1784). *Notes on the State of Virginia*. University of North Carolina Press for the Institute of Early American History and Culture. The Founders' Constitution, Volume 1, Chapter 18, Document 16. http://press-pubs.uchicago.edu/founders/documents/v1ch18s16.html

Jesiek, B. K., Shen, Y., & Haller, Y. (2012). Cross-Cultural Competence: A Comparative Assessment of Engineering Students. *International Journal of Engineering Education, 28*(1), 144–155.

Jones, J. M. (2012). *Confidence in U.S. Public schools at new low*. Retrieved from News.Gallup.com. https://news.gallup.com/poll/155258/Confidence-Public-Schools-New-Low.aspx

Kain, E. (2011, May 19). Watching "Race to Nowhere" and "The Lottery". *Forbes.* https://www.forbes.com/sites/erikkain/2011/05/19/watching-race-to-nowhere-and-the-lottery/#580ce19e4c40

Kendi, I. X. (2016). *Stamped from the beginning, The definitive history of racist ideas in America*. Nation Books/Bold Type Books.

Kennedy, A. (2014). Understanding continuing professional development: The need for theory to impact on policy and practice. *Professional Development in Education, 40*(5), 688–697. doi:10.1080/19415257.2014.955122

Kincheloe, J. (2008). *Critical pedagogy*. Peter Lang Publishing.

Kohli, R. (2016). Behind school doors: The Impact of hostile racial climates on urban teachers of color. *Urban Education,* 1–27. Doi:10.1177/0042085916636653

LaCroix, T. J., & Kuehl, R. (2019, Spring). Working toward equity: A framework for exploring racial and ethnic diversity in teacher education programs. *The Teacher Educators' Journal, 12*(1), 25–49.

Ladson-Billings, G. (2006). From the achievement gap to the education debt: Understanding achievement in US schools. *Educational Researcher, 35*(7), 3–12. https://www.jstor.org/stable/3876731

Ladson-Billings, G. (2013a). "Stakes is high:" Educating new century students. *The Journal of Negro Education, 82*(2), 105–110. doi:10.7709/jnegroeducation.82.2.0105

Ladson-Billings, G. (2013b). Critical Race Theory—What it is Not! In *Handbook of Critical Race Theory in Education*. Routledge. Accessed on: 06 Oct 2017 https://www.routledgehandbooks.com/doi/10.4324/9780203155721.ch3

Lapayese, Y. V., Aldana, U. S., & Lara, E. (2014). A Racio–economic Analysis of Teach for America: Counterstories of TFA Teachers of Color. *Perspectives on Urban Education*, *11*(1), 11–25.

Levinson, M., & Fay, J. (Eds.). (2016). *Dilemmas of educational ethics: Cases and commentaries.* Harvard Education Press.

Madaan, A. (2016). Cultural competency and the practice of law in the 21st century. *Probate & Property Magazine 30*(2). https://heinonline.org/HOL/LandingPage?handle=hein.journals/probpro30&div=23&id=&page=

Martin, J. (2011, March 7). Race to Nowhere: One Principal's Response. *Connected Principals blog.* http://connectedprincipals.com/archives/2925

Martin, L. E., Kragler, S., Quatroche, D. J., & Bauserman, K. L. (Eds.). (2014). *Handbook of professional development in education: Successful models and practices, PreK-12.* The Guilford Press.

Mathews, J. (2011, May 3). Why Race to Nowhere documentary is wrong. *Washington Post.* https://www.washingtonpost.com/blogs/class-struggle/post/why-race-to-nowhere-documentary-is wrong/2011/04/03/AFBt27VC_blog.html?utm_term=.6ec433039379

McGee, J., & Winters, M. (2013, September). *Better pay, fairer pensions: Reforming teacher compensation.* Civic Report No. 79. Center for State and Local Leadership at the Manhattan Institute.

Milner, H. R. (2017). Opening commentary: The permanence of racism, critical race theory, and expanding analytic sites. *Peabody Journal of Education*, *92*(3), 294–301. doi:10.1080/0161956X.2017.1324656

Milner, H. R., & Laughter, J. C. (2015). But good intentions are not enough: Preparing teachers to center race and poverty. *The Urban Review*, *47*, 341–363. doi:10.100711256-014-0295-4

Morrissey, M. (2015, March 5). *Will switching government workers to account-type plans save taxpayers money?* Economic Policy Institute. https://www.epi.org/publication/will-switching-government-workers-to-account-type-plans-save-taxpayers-money/

Morrissey, M. (2017, October 17). *Teachers and schools are well served by teacher pensions.* Economic Policy Institute. https://files.eric.ed.gov/fulltext/ED587804.pdf

National Center for Education Statistics. (2017). *Fast Facts*. https://nces.ed.gov/fastfacts/display.asp?id=372

Ndemanu, M. T. (2014). Multicultural teacher education courses are not designed for all pre–service teachers: An African American student teacher's perspective. *Journal of Instructional Psychology*, *41*(3), 64–78.

Partelow, L., Shapiro, S., McDaniels, A., & Brown, C. (2018, September 20). *Fixing chronic disinvestment in K-12 Schools*. Center for American Progress. http://nmcel.org/uploads/PDFs/employment/2.K12_Disinvestment_Brief.pdf

Pollock, M., Deckman, S., Mira, M., & Shalaby, C. (2010). "But what can I do?": Three necessary tensions in teaching teachers about race. *Journal of Teacher Education*, *61*(3), 211–224. doi:10.1177/0022487109354089

Raue, K., & Gray, L. (2015). *Career paths of beginning public school teachers results from the first through fifth waves of the 2007—08 Beginning Teacher Longitudinal Study*. Stats in Brief. NCES 2015-196. National Center for Education Statistics. https://files.eric.ed.gov/fulltext/ED560730.pdf

Rhee, N., & Fornia, W. B. (2016). *Are California teachers better off with a pension or 401(k)?* University of California, Berkeley Center for Labor Research and Education. http://laborcenter.berkeley.edu/pdf/2016/California_Teachers_Pension_401k.pdf

Rochmes, J., Penner, E. K., & Loeb, S. (2017). *Educators As "Equity Warriors"* (CEPA Working Paper No.17-11). Stanford Center for Education Policy Analysis. https://cepa.stanford.edu/wp17-11

Rockoff, J. E. (2004). The impact of teachers on student achievement: Evidence from panel data. *The American Economic Review*, *94*(2), 247–252. https://www.jstor.org/stable/3592891

Rooks, N. (2017). *Cutting school: Privatization, segregation, and the end of public education*. The New Press.

Rossi, R., & Montgomery, A. (Eds.). (1994). Education reform and students at risk: historical overview – separate and unequal. In *A Review of the Current State of the Art*. U.S. Department of Education. Retrieved from https://www.ed.gov/pubs/EdReformStudies/EdReforms/chap1b.html

Singer, A. (2016, September 16). A brief history of education in the United States, Part 2. *HuffPost*. https://www.huffingtonpost.com/alan-singer/a-brief-history-of-educat_b_8144756.html

Sloan, W. J. (2012, July). What Is the purpose of education? *Educator's Update*, *54*(7). http://www.ascd.org/publications/newsletters/education-update/jul12/vol54/num07/What-Is-the-Purpose-of-Education%C2%A2.aspx

Smedley, A. (1997, November). The origin of the idea of race. *Anthropology Newsletter*. http://www.pbs.org/race/000_About/002_04-background-02-09.htm

Sockett, H. (1993). *The moral base for teacher professionalism.* Teachers College.

Stovall, D. (2016). Out of adolescence and into adulthood: Critical race theory, retrenchment, and the imperative of praxis. *Urban Education*, *51*(3), 274–286. doi:10.1177/0042085915618718

Strauss, V. (2016, December 8). A sobering look at what Betsy DeVos did to education in Michigan — and what she might do as secretary of education. *The Washington Post.* https://www.washingtonpost.com/news/answer-sheet/wp/2016/12/08/a-sobering-look-at-what-betsy-devos-did-to-education-in-michigan-and-what-she-might-do-as-secretary-of-education/

Strauss, V. (2018, February 9). This is what inadequate funding at a public school looks and feels like- as told by an entire faculty. *The Washington Post.* https://www.washingtonpost.com/news/answer-sheet/wp/2018/02/09/this-is-what-inadequate-funding-at-a-public-school-looks-and-feels-like-as-told-by-an-entire-faculty/

Sutcher, L., Darling-Hammond, L., & Carver-Thomas, D. (2016). *A coming crisis in teaching? Teacher supply, demand, and shortages in the U.S.* Learning Policy Institute. https://learningpolicyinstitute.org/product/coming-crisis-teaching

The Global Competitiveness Index. (2015–2016). *Rankings Report.* World Economic Forum. http://reports.weforum.org/global-competitiveness-report-2015-2016/report-highlights/

The New Leam. (2017, September 18). *Excerpt from Critical pedagogy: teachers as transformative intellectuals* https://thenewleam.com/2017/09/critical-pedagogy-teachers-transformative-intellectuals-henry-giroux/)

Trent, M., Dooley, D.G., & Dougé J., (2019). The impact of racism on child and adolescent health. *Pediatrics, 144*(2). Doi:10.1542/peds.2019-1765

Uriarte, M. (1991). *The meaning of the browning of America.* Gastón Institute Publications. https://scholarworks.umb.edu/gaston_pubs/1

View, J. L., & DeMulder, E. K. (2009). Teacher as artist, intellectual and citizen: Using a critical framework in teacher professional development that empowers voice and transforms practice. *Democracy & Education, 18*(2), 33–39.

View, J. L., & Gorski, P. (2014, May/June). *Whites and* Brown. In *Urban Education: Issues and Solutions, Season Five.* George Mason University Television. https://vimeo.com/channels/urbaneducation/115079655

Wallace, G., Vazquez, M., & Marsh, R. (2017, October 29). What Betsy DeVos' schedule tells us about her agenda. *CNN.com.* https://www.cnn.com/2017/10/28/politics/devos-schedules-education/index.html

West, M. R. (2012). Education and Global Competitiveness. In K. Hassett (Ed.), *Rethinking Competitiveness.* American Enterprise Institute Press. http://nrs.harvard.edu/urn-3:HUL.InstRepos:9544459

Yosso, T. J. (2005). Whose culture has capital? A critical race theory discussion of community cultural wealth. *Race, Ethnicity and Education, 8*(1), 69–91. doi:10.1080/1361332052000341006

Zeichner, K. (2018). *The struggle for the soul of teacher education: Critical social thought.* Routledge.

Zeichner, K., & Ndimande, B. (2008). Contradictions and tensions in the place of teachers in educational reform: Reflections on teacher preparation in the US and Namibia. *Teachers and Teaching, 14*(4), 331–343. doi:10.1080/13540600802037751

Chapter 2
Identity Work

ABSTRACT

The authors describe the first crucial step in antiracist teacher professional development – developing a deep understanding of one's identity. After providing the theoretical framework behind this approach and sharing their own stories of their identity development as antiracist educators, the authors describe the curricular approaches they used to engage teachers in exploring the self. They also share the outcomes of these efforts and the tensions and dilemmas that arise when supporting teachers to examine their identities in the process of becoming antiracist educators.

As Kendi (2019) reminds us, "…racist and antiracist are not fixed identities. We can be racist one minute and an antiracist the next" (p. 10). In other words, the work is on-going and requires constant reflection on the self. We need to be aware of the identities we claim related to race, gender, ethnicity, language, etc. and how these complex interconnected identities drive our worldviews, dispositions, behaviors, attitudes, and actions (see example identity web in Figure 1). Furthermore, it is imperative that we deepen our understanding of the role our experiences play in shaping these identities and ultimately how these identities we bring to our classroom then impact students' learning. Through deep reflection, we can become more aware of the ways in which our actions in the classroom are (or are not) "supporting an antiracist policy... or expressing an antiracist idea" (Kendi, 2019, p. 13).

Scholars (e.g., Brookfield, 2012; Eryaman, 2007; Mezirow, 1990; Schön, 1983; Wink, 2011) have become ready references for practicing classroom

DOI: 10.4018/978-1-7998-5649-8.ch002

Figure 1. Example Identity Web

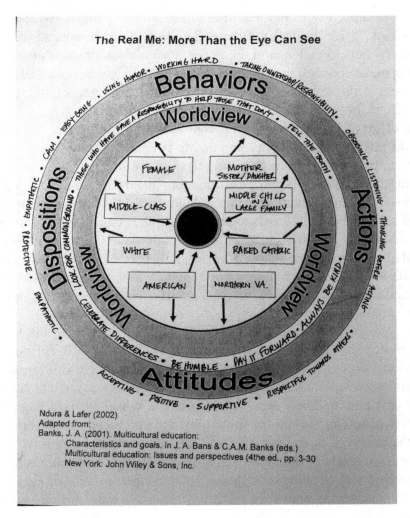

The Real Me: More Than the Eye Can See

Ndura & Lafer (2002)
Adapted from:
Banks, J. A. (2001). Multicultural education:
    Characteristics and goals. In J. A. Bans & C.A.M. Banks (eds.)
    Multicultural education: Issues and perspectives (4the ed., pp. 3-30
    New York: John Wiley & Sons, Inc.

teachers (both P-12 and higher education teachers) seeking to develop their reflective practice. Teacher professional development programs that expand the spaces for teachers to engage in critical reflection, including on issues of identity (their own and that of their students), support teachers in discovering the power of their own voices and in re-envisioning their roles as critical educators who empower their own students (Howard, 2003; Milner, 2003; View, DeMulder, Stribling & Kayler, 2009). There is substantial evidence that interpersonal relationships provide support for individual development and learning. In particular, the adults in a child's life influence the extent to which that child thrives in a learning environment (Briggs, 2012; Mendes, 2003; Heick, 2015; Rimm-Kaufman & Sandilos, 2016; Townsend, 2012). We wanted teachers to understand the importance of relationships in their lives and then make connections with their own students. We also wanted teachers to recognize through their own practice the importance of interpersonal connections for supporting students' development and learning.

Our efforts fall into what Carter Andrews, Brown, Castillo, Jackson, and Vallenki (2019) identify as a humanizing pedagogy. They maintain that a humanizing pedagogy is rooted in efforts to develop critical consciousness for both teacher educators and their students – in our case, in-service teachers. The three core tenets underlying this pedagogy are: "1) engaging in sustained critical self-reflection, 2) resisting binaries, and 3) enacting ontological and epistemological plurality" (Carter Andrews et al., 2019, p. 12). Our work around identity and positionality is an on-going part of our two-year program, a foundational piece of each one of our courses, as we strive to problematize race (and other identity markers) particularly related to issues of teaching and learning.

Recognizing positionality necessarily challenged our teachers to notice their privilege and to understand the ways in which racism still permeates our institutional structures and policies. Because all teachers were at different places in their own development, we had to be prepared for a myriad of responses to our curriculum. There were white teachers who had been engaging in this level of self-reflection for some time and embraced the opportunity to continue the work in a supportive and intentional space. There were white teachers who had been operating under the assumption that being color-blind was the best way to address (or rather NOT address) issues of race in their classrooms; over the course of the 2-year program most of them grew into budding antiracist teachers. We also worked with Teachers of Color, though commensurate with national statistics, any given cohort was made up of anywhere from 0 to 10% of this population. While some of these Teachers of Color contributed life experiences that reflected a deep understanding of their positionality and of the broader racist system in which they lived and worked, there were some who internalized their oppression (e.g., David, 2015) and clung tightly to the assumptions and practices embedded in hegemonic structures. Regardless of where teachers were in their development when they began their professional development journey with us, our goal was to grow their capacity as antiracist teachers who actively resist and challenge white supremacy culture and its structures and practices, which afford un-equitable opportunities for the students they teach. Focusing on themselves allowed teachers to examine their own implicit bias that impacts who they are and how they operate within their classroom and school settings. A recent study by Zimmerman and Kao (2020) used national data of first-grade teachers' ratings of students to show how teachers' assessment of student abilities was greatly influenced by their interpretation of students' noncognitive skills. When comparing students with identical non-cognitive skills and test scores, teachers were more likely to rate Black students as less capable in math and Asian students more capable in literacy. This study also looked at implicit bias related to gender and the intersectionality of race and gender. Not surprisingly, though still disappointingly, girls and Girls of Color were continually rated less capable by teachers. Naming, reflecting on, and acting to combat these implicit biases begins with identity work and an examination of one's positionality, experiences, beliefs, and assumptions.

One of the greatest benefits of the identity work we incorporated into our curricular experiences was the groundwork it laid for developing a community of learners who trusted each other with their stories, their successes, and their struggles. We contend that it is not possible to become an antiracist educator and to do the work of antiracist teaching in isolation (more on this in Chapter 4). The greatest hope for doing this work well lay in the communities we built that allowed space for respectful sharing, agreeing, disagreeing, challenging, and growing. It is by knowing who we are, stepping outside of ourselves, and seeing the world through each other's experiences that we can begin to develop our critical consciousness.

As part of this learning community and the developers of a humanizing pedagogy (Carter Andrews et al., 2019), our own efforts to be antiracist were an important part of this story; how could we understand and support our teachers if we did not first understand ourselves? Similarly, our goal for teachers was to use their own self-reflection as a means to better understand and to better support their students. Therefore, we modeled "radical honesty" (Williams, 2016) in our own truth telling as we shared personal experiences and efforts to act in ways that created more equitable and socially just learning experiences for all. And so, we begin with our stories…

JENICE

I am a third-generation native of Washington, DC, grandchild of the Great Migration of Black people from South Carolina, Virginia, and eastern

Tennessee, and enslaved people from Gabon. In 2012 after an uncomfortable exchange with white P-12 classroom teachers in our master's degree program, I wrote the following poem:

The reason we are not post-racial

(in response to "The Help" and all of its apologists)

human relations being what they are

it is possible that my grandmother loved you

as much as you think she did

she was always described

by family

and church members

as loving and kind

she would have felt warmly toward you

if your mother were kind and respectful

and if you imitated your mother's example.

if you were a snot and cute

and under the age of six

she would have forgiven your bratty ways

but be clear:

the only reason

she labored

in your mother's house

is because

she loved us more

My parents taught me that Black is beautiful; that natural hair is "better;" that white people are not superior partly because – globally – People of Color outnumber whites; and that sometimes, in an employment setting, it can be easier to work with whites than with People of Color.

For first through third grades my family lived in Pittsburgh, PA. In first grade we attended the Black school in the neighborhood. Second and third grades included adventures in school busing to the white school, where I had my first exposure to educational inequities. In Pennsylvania at the time teachers were allowed to practice corporal punishment; I was aware that the 3rd grade teacher was always unfairly hitting the Black boys from our neighborhood with rulers. We moved back to Washington and lived in an affluent white neighborhood in Ward 3 that was experimenting with housing desegregation, making us one of the few Black families living within the school's boundaries. The school was responding to a desegregation lawsuit by busing Black kids from crowded all-Black schools in Southeast to under-enrolled white schools in Ward 3. As a result, my fourth grade teacher was under my Dad's surveillance because she was openly racist. He would often show up in the window of her classroom door to let her know he was watching.

That same year, my "friend" referred to my mother as a Black bitch; Mom told me the next time to hit her with a brick. I was shocked since we had heard non-violent messages all of our lives. Later that same school year, Dr. King was assassinated on Thursday, April 4. On Friday April 5, as the city was aflame with riots continuing from the night before, our fourth grade teacher tried to be overly solicitous of the Black students in class until one of the girls bused in from Southeast said, "My mother told me not to talk to white people today." My Mom also first taught me about apartheid in South Africa and said she wished all of the white South Africans were driven into the ocean to their deaths – another shocking sentiment. I learned later that we were targeted with vandalism by white teen boys in the neighborhood, prompting Mom and Dad to move the following year to an intentionally racially integrated neighborhood.

By middle school and high school, DC was thoroughly Chocolate City, so the racialized tensions were more muted, even though I continued to live, attend school, and worship in racially integrated settings. My tensions around race tended to have more to do with identity formation in adolescence and making decisions about which white friends could be trusted. Meanwhile, I loved it when Howard University students and other older Black people would call me "Little Sister" in passing, and when I got affirmation about being a dark-skinned, very skinny, nappy-headed female because despite the rhetoric, many of my peers and many elders did not truly believe that Black was beautiful. It was in a cosmopolitan setting such as DC that I got a lot more "love" than other Black girls of that era.

My parents, my husband, and I believed in public schools, especially the community schools with historically strong Black educators. Some of the best teachers I ever had (including Ivy League graduate school professors) were Black DC public school teachers. By the time our daughters were school age, middle-class Black families were migrating to the suburbs, and those who lived in the city were disinclined to send their children to DC public schools, even if they were themselves DCPS educators. My husband and I were pleased with the education that our two daughters received at their predominantly Black public schools. Yet most public statements about DC public schools were negative, supported by examples of corruption among the teachers union leadership, inefficiencies in the downtown bureaucracy, and horrendous facilities in the all-Black, low-income schools.

After changing careers to teach in middle school and then at the university level, I became offended by the rhetoric that young white teachers were better for Black public school kids than veteran Black master teachers, despite my personal experience and the growing research about the excellence and "superpowers" of mission-driven Black teachers with all students. Faced with the statistic that 80% of public school teachers nationally are white and with some of those young white teachers in our master's degree program who were eager to make a difference in schools, my unspoken metric became, "Would I place one of my own children in this teacher's class?" Was it possible for P-12 white teachers to be as effective at antiracist education as for non-assimilated, mission-driven Teachers of Color? Was it possible for any teacher to be empowered to challenge central bureaucracies and corrupt policy makers and racist curriculum and class biases to teach all children to their highest potential? Could a master's degree teacher professional development program nurture P-12 classroom teachers to step into such an identity with confidence and with a "posse" of like-minded teachers and administrators?

ELIZABETH (BETSY)

My ancestors were white Anglo-Saxon Protestants who immigrated to the US from the British Isles and Germany many generations ago. Like for most young children, my heritage was a given and "fairness" was an ongoing concern. Early on, gender equity was of particular significance. I grew up with four brothers. As the only girl I was aware of some privilege. For example, I had my own room while all but my youngest brother shared a bedroom. I didn't object to that. However, there were also differential, stereotypical expectations about how girls and boys behave that partially framed my understanding of who I was and what role I should play in the family. I was groomed to be the inside (Mama's) helper and peacekeeper. Gender expectations irked me and I did feel a sense of righteous indignation when those expectations limited my freedom. For example, even though I was very athletic, physically strong and competitive, my father forbade me to play football with the neighborhood kids because he thought girls were too fragile for such games, which didn't make sense to me since I was stronger, a faster runner and better catcher than most of the other kids. So I resisted and played anyway. I pushed back in many ways on gender stereotypes that were still quite prevalent as I was growing up. In the 60's when I was in elementary school, girls were required to wear dresses to school and, for too long, I endured the snickering of little boys looking up my dress when I played on the monkey bars and participated in (and won) the Presidential Physical Fitness competitions. I resisted by asking my mother to make a case for changing the school policy so that girls could wear pants and she successfully advocated for me. Looking back, while gender inequity seemed like a constant needling concern, sometimes my indignation was a bit misguided. I thought I wanted to be a ballet dancer (fitting right in to the gender stereotype but I did love to dance) and was allowed to start taking lessons when I was seven years old. After a couple of years of lessons, my mother took me to audition for the National Ballet's annual production of The Nutcracker. My older brother came along for the ride. Many girls and very few boys auditioned. You can imagine my outrage when my brother was "chosen" and I was not.

On the whole, I would say I was woefully unaware of racial tensions when I was young, even though I lived in the Washington D.C. suburbs during the latter part of the civil rights era when race riots were occurring in many major cities. I was aware of racial and income disparities, however. Although my white family was not wealthy (my father was a music teacher and my mother was a stay-at-home mom) we had the privilege of owning a home (passed down from my grandmother) that was literally on a hill overlooking a large government housing project. Many African American families lived there and I went to school with the children in the neighborhood. I saw early on a distinction between the "haves" and "have nots," but I didn't understand the history and the sources of the disparities and so I felt sad and compassionate toward my classmates but don't remember feeling a strong sense of injustice. I certainly didn't recognize my white privilege. I once made a birthday cake and delivered it to a classmate in the "projects" believing that her family wouldn't be able to afford to give her one. I'm sure that I felt pity for her and that I congratulated myself for being thoughtful and kind. I cringe now at my naïveté.

I have always been attuned to others' feelings and suffering (an empath for sure), but over the years I have moved beyond pity — learning to recognize and examine underlying racist assumptions and beliefs (including my own) and to identify and work to address the structures, policies, practices and attitudes that create and perpetuate racism and other inequities.

As I got older, education and other life experiences broadened my understanding and deepened my concern about inequities in general and racial inequities in particular. As an undergraduate and graduate student, I studied developmental psychology and gained a deeper understanding of how life experiences impact social, emotional, and intellectual development. I also came to have a more critical perspective on how the academic and school communities use the terms "at risk" and "achievement gap" without acknowledging and acting on the historical and current racist structures that create these "conditions."

The opportunities I had to live in England for four years and to travel around the US and to other parts of the world as a young adult allowed me to experience a diversity of cultures, languages and perspectives. I also learned a little about what it felt like to be the "other" and to see more clearly how "othering" and the myth of a hierarchy of human value has grossly limited opportunities for many people, both historically and currently.

My concerns for equity had a strong influence on my career path. At one of my first academic conferences, a prominent male researcher made a statement in his presentation that angers me still. He said that the science of psychology suffers from the inclusion of women researchers since they "just want to help people." It was an outrageous misogynistic statement that I suspect discouraged many up-and-coming women scientists. I was outraged and not deterred. (Another prominent male researcher who heard this said in his later presentation that he made psychology his life's work because he wanted to help people.)

As a developmental research psychologist, I sought out an academic home that would allow me to have a strong applied orientation in the education field so that I could not only advance the science but also help people. My research concerns the influences of interpersonal relationships and learning environments on child and adult development. A passion and focus of my work has been to study young children's development in environments where there are many challenging conditions (e.g., poverty, racism, poor-quality child care) but also many potential protective conditions (e.g., social supports, strong parent-child relationships, educational opportunities) that can be supported through community action initiatives. I've conducted some of this research in the context of preschools and communities that are making efforts to support low-income and immigrant children and families. I've also studied the ways teaching and learning relationships and experiences can affect teachers' professional and personal development that may impact their ability to change classroom practices to support their own and their students' meaning-making capacities. The intention is that this work will support teachers' and children's development as individuals and as citizens who are committed to equity, justice, and peace and who are motivated to speak and act for the common good.

Our unique teacher professional development programs have allowed me, for the past 25 years, to collaboratively create, implement and study equity-oriented curricula to advance our understanding of antiracist, culturally relevant work with teachers and to make a difference on the ground in schools and classrooms. The long-term relationships and learning experiences with colleagues and students of different races, genders, ages and backgrounds have been invaluable in my own ongoing process of learning, unlearning, and relearning in pursuit of becoming an antiracist.

STACIA

I am white. I did not always understand the significance of this identity since race was not something I ever had to consider as I moved through a world where people who looked like me had substantial power and privilege. If pressed to contemplate what it feels like to be marginalized, I likely would have relayed stories related to my identity as a female or to my ethnicity. I am a third generation American whose great grandparents all immigrated from Poland in the early 1900's. They settled in ethnic enclaves outside of New York City, surrounding themselves with other Polish-Americans where they continued to speak their native language, enjoy their native food, and maintain their traditions. Their ability to retain their language and culture was a privilege afforded them partly because it was their choice to travel across the ocean. My family believed in the American Dream and while they held tight to their heritage, they also willingly assimilated to the new land, a feat that was easier for them than for many because their skin color allowed them to blend when needed. Growing up, it was drilled into me that if I worked hard enough, I could accomplish anything. I learned to roll my eyes at Polish jokes and to use myself and my family members as evidence that our people were in fact intelligent. Only now can I recognize how ethnic racism drove my sense of self in relation to others (Kendi, 2019). Among white immigrants I rejected the racist ideas about my own ethnic group while embracing racist ideas about other ethnic groups. Stereotypes about the Italians or the Irish were peppered into my family's discourse in an effort to place our own ethnic group on a higher rung of the social ladder. In fact, each generation of my family became more educated and wealthier – in essence, "proving" to my family that meritocracy was alive and well. Anyone who didn't succeed was just not trying hard enough and was likely flawed due to their less-desirable heritage.

My parents' successes provided us a comfortable home in an upper-middle class neighborhood on Long Island, New York. This area was also predominantly white. In addition, it was an area where many people were deeply connected to their ethnic heritage. I remember, as a third grader, completing a Heritage Day project where all of the students wrote reports on the countries of their ancestors. It culminated in a celebration that included dressing up in traditional clothes and cooking traditional food to share with the class. It was not until I was an adult teaching in a rural farming community that I realized how unique it was to be part of a class where everyone had a recent immigration story and had intimate knowledge of and connections to their ancestry. This ancestry, however, included mostly European countries (e.g. Poland, Italy, Ireland, England) and was not at all racially diverse. I can count on one hand the number of Black students who attended my high school; in fact, there was only one Black male in my graduating class of 220. Furthermore, there was only one Black female in the entire school throughout my four-year high school career. She was two years behind me and was my younger brother's prom date. I remember my family joking about how we should not let Grandma know, while at the same time thinking that my parents were so "cool" and "aware" because they were not bothered by the relationship. In retrospect, I was that white person who had one Black friend...so I certainly could not be racist.

I left Long Island in 1991 to attend college in the south. While the campus where I lived and learned was much more diverse than my childhood hometown, I was still able to exist in my bubble of whiteness. I could easily find people, room with people, date people, etc. who looked like me and who shared similar life experiences. It was in my education courses that my reality was challenged and my professors began the process of planting the seeds of diversity and critical literacy. I recall my children's literature course where I was tasked with critiquing the subtle messages conveyed by character choices, language choices, perspective, etc. Looking at who was represented in text and who was not and the "truths" that were portrayed in historical texts began to open my eyes to the larger world beyond my own personal experiences. While racial inequities were part of this dialogue, it was the conversations around gender that stuck out most to me, probably because these were the inequities to which I could personally relate. At this point I began to reflect back on the messages I received and internalized around being female. My parents had always told me I could do and be anything I wanted. But at the same time, I was never tapped by my father to go on the roof to clean the gutters or to fix electrical issues or to go to the local hardware store to get supplies for the next house project – those tasks were often given to my brother. I remembered complaining about this at the time – especially about not getting to go on the roof! – and now had a way to frame these experiences and an action plan for addressing these issues in my own elementary school classroom; I became intentional about choosing literature that depicted people in gender diverse roles. Some of my favorites became books about kick-ass princesses who either save the prince and/or do not marry him in the end. I became adept at seeing sexism and speaking out against it.

I believe that these undergraduate experiences primed me for recognizing other injustices in the world. Upon graduating I moved to a rural farming town to teach first grade. I remember being surprised when my principal referred to the students in the school as middle-class as they did not look like the middle-class I thought I knew. For the first time I recognized the privilege I had been afforded growing up in a rather sheltered upper middle-class family in the suburbs of a major city and began to see how this had shaped my assumptions about the world. After a very difficult first year of teaching, I decided to pursue a Master's degree in Education; I felt that there was so much more left to learn if I were to teach these children well, and for me lectures and books by more knowledgeable others held the answers. My degree program turned out to be the pivotal experience I needed to begin my growth as an antiracist educator. While there were books and theories that helped me make better sense of my charge as a teacher, it was the self-reflection and the relationships built with both my peers in the program and my students who became my partners in education that transformed my thinking and therefore my practice. There was one conversation in particular during a class on moral professionalism where an African American teacher became extremely emotional in her response to a white peer who said that racism was a thing of the past. I remember being taken aback by the exchange, but there was something – my previous examination of sexism? my recent insights into socio-economic status and privilege? –that told me to suspend my judgment and conclusions and to listen. I "listened" for days as I mulled over that conversation and considered how my whiteness shaped my experiences and therefore the ways in which I viewed the world. Had I denied the unique identities and experiences of the Black students who attended my high school? If I could ask them now, what might they say about their educational and social experiences? I would have assumed that their stories would be similar to mine, but how could they have been? It was a turning point for me. I began to critically question and to "see" racism where I had previously had the privilege to "not see." This was not an overnight transformation, but rather has been a gradual growth journey –that continues still. . And it is not a journey I can take alone. My colleagues have become a vital part of my quest, presenting me with new examples, listening to me talk through my questions and understandings, offering me grace when I miss the mark or get tripped up in my own whiteness, and challenging me to always dig deeper.

I am now a mother, which has added another layer of urgency to the work that I feel compelled to do. My two children were adopted through the foster care system. They are white, and while they do not have first-hand experiences of racial injustice in school systems, they have been marginalized for not fitting the mold of the "successful" student due to their myriad special needs associated with drug and alcohol exposure in utero and developmental trauma. Assumptions are made about their behavior and therefore about my parenting that do not take into account the impacts of all they have experienced in their young lives. Parenting them has allowed me to see even more clearly the ways in which public schools are not designed (and teachers are not adequately trained) to meet the unique needs of all students. We cannot afford to let this continue. Furthermore, I have a responsibility to make sure that my children do not find themselves sitting in a graduate course one day and finally coming to the realization that they are white. My purpose for engaging in antiracist work has always been the children, and I will always be a work in progress.

LAURA

It was a muddy trip along busy traffic filled streets, the day I so proudly walked to Grants department store in suburban Chicago. The source of my pride was my independence in walking two miles, despite the rain and cars that splashed urban puddles onto the greater source of my pride – my new-to-me cool clothes. It was 1969 and the "hippie" look was in. Sure, my clothes were too big and worn through, but that was cool, right?

I was nine years old on a quest to return an ill-fitting dog collar. Taught to respect authority and do the right thing, I waited my turn in the check-out line, then pulled the chain collar from my "new" coat pocket and asked for an exchange. The cashier said "no way" as I didn't have a receipt or tag – just a chain.

Since it was December and I had already made the long walk, I re-entered the store to find some Christmas presents. As I shopped, I noticed a store employee on the other side of a display point at me and say to the man next to her, "That's the girl I was talking about." They continued to watch and follow me until I embarrassedly chose a sweatshirt for my brother, paid for it, and left the store.

I broke down crying at dinner that night when my parents asked me about my day. What disturbed me was the store employees' blindness to whom I believed myself to be and their summary categorization of me as a potential thief – a characterization diametrically opposite to the person I strove to be.

Now all of these years later, I can still feel the shock and disturbance of that experience, but with reflection beyond my own ego, I also realize the privilege I had and have. Unlike People of Color, as a white, middle class girl, I could shed the self-impression that others had judged unfairly. I could discard the (apparently not so cool) clothes and could wash the mud from my shoes, hands, and hair. As the daughter of a Lutheran Pastor and stay-at-home mom in an exclusively Caucasian community, I could easily return to "normal" without any need to be self-conscious or self-questioning – or fear of being misperceived.

About the same time, educational missionaries from our church shared slides of their experience in New Guinea. It sparked an enduring curiosity about people who are different from me – people of differing colors, people with differing religions, people from differing cultures, and people with unique life paths. Well fed, well loved, and a member of the hegemonic culture, I had the privilege of finding my own background boring and yearned to explore something new.

Pursuing greater understanding of others but still adhering to the authority of my parents, I studied economics and business as an undergraduate for my dad and psychology for me. Never meant to be a businesswoman, I then went on to receive a Masters of Divinity degree. While in divinity school I read Karl Barth's *Church Dogmatics*. Barth's conception of the *imago dei* is based on humanity's capacity for relatedness – first to God and then to others.

Taking it from divine speculation to simple observation: our mammalian nature requires people to be in relationship. Mulling this over, I concluded that relationships provide for three essential existential needs. First, through simple acknowledgment, others confirm that we are. Listening to another's story makes their story real – makes *them* real. Second, our relationships help ground us in this world. The connections among people tether them to society. Third, in relationship, people have a role in society: parent, employee, helper, leader, etc. As Carol Gilligan highlights in, "In A Different Voice", connection is my moral goal.

As the spouse of a diplomat, I have also been privileged to nurture my curiosity for and connection to others. With our four now- grown children we lived in some of the poorest countries of the world, as well as in some of the most affluent circumstances in wealthy countries. We lived in countries that are predominately Black and Brown and countries that are predominately Muslim. We lived in countries experiencing economic transitions and political, sometimes violent, turmoil. These were all cultures that are very different from my own.

Of course, living in these places doesn't make one "woke." I was still a white, American woman, wife of an American diplomat, who happened to live a life of even greater privilege in places where many wanted for even the most basic necessities. I was stymied by the disparity. My peaceful homogeneous upbringing did not prepare me to enact the "love your neighbor" precept in a diverse, disparate, and, at times, desperate world. Received scripts were inadequate. As relatively rich and privileged as I was (am), and as well-meaning as I was (hope I am), the orphaned child was going to die before I returned. And she would be replaced by another in a never-ending stream of children whose parents could not care for them.

I was naïve. In the recesses of my heart and mind I had thought I could save the world – or at least parts of it. Love and kindness would triumph. But confronted with starving orphans, intractable conflict, and rife corruption, I was humbled to see the world more fully to include Hobbesian characters intent on their exclusive survival and thriving. Not everyone "loves their neighbor."

As an author of this book, I am embarrassed to admit that the manifestation of my diversity curiosity and experience has remained at the personal and interpersonal levels. I have not been a crusader against unjust social structures and barriers. Instead my experience with diversity and global injustice has led me to carefully and deliberatively connect to others – to seek the other, hear their story, affirm their existence, and to help them know that at least one social tether values their unique presence.

This has been my focus as an educator: the building, nurturing, and sustaining of young people. After short stints on Capitol Hill and as a lobbyist in DC, I became an elementary school teacher when my own children reached preschool age. The decision to become a teacher was, again, a matter of privilege. The host country schools at the time lacked electricity, so being the well-resourced American mother that I was, I started a school for my kids and other English-speaking children. Local children attended unheated schools.

Eventually, I received my teaching license and subsequently taught kindergarten and second grade in International Schools in Haiti, Belgium, and Russia and in public schools in Northern Virginia. Again, I was fortunate to teach in schools that utilized the Primary Years Program, an elementary curriculum of the International Baccalaureate, which values and highlights cultural diversity.

Because there are many cultures represented in international schools, there are also varying educational and pedagogical expectations. In meeting the needs of all of our students, a former principal advised that our job as educators was to take each child the next step in their learning – whatever that was. Not a graduate or instructor of the program here discussed, I would have benefited from the tutelage of my co-authors. My sensitively finding and understanding that next level would have been enhanced with the work they have their students do. Working with them has opened my eyes to my own privilege and to a deeper appreciation of others' experience. I hope that in recognizing some of my own advantage, I am less inclined to misjudge the character and learning ability of my students whose background differs from my own and appreciate the unique gifts each child brings.

Currently, I am collecting data for my doctoral dissertation. I am exploring the roles of teacher emotional intelligence and cultural intelligence in the creation of supportive teacher relationships with diverse groups of students. It is my goal to help teachers develop the capacities to form these all-important relationships with their students.

ENGAGING TEACHERS IN IDENTITY WORK

It was important for us to develop a teacher professional development program with space for this kind of identity exploration through self-reflection as a force for moving from knowledge transmission toward cultural transformation (Warford, 2011, p. 257). Of particular concern in our teacher education program is the extent to which this self-reflective process: 1) can address cultural disconnects between the majority of teachers who are white middle-class women and the growing percentage of P-12 students who are Children of Color; and 2) can challenge the perpetuation of dominant Eurocentric narratives in schooling (e.g., Hayes & Juarez, 2012).

While self-reflection was embedded throughout the two-year program, we created several specific learning experiences for the initial face-to-face summer course that would get teachers started on this work. We were intentional in naming the scaffolding we put in place, explaining the importance of knowing and understanding oneself before being able to know, understand, and teach others. Most teacher professional development opportunities dive right into teaching strategies – how to use coupons to teach money skills, how to use running records to guide reading instruction, how to teach science concepts through fun and engaging experiments, etc. Unfortunately, these strategies too often focus on *what* needs to be taught without consideration for *who* is being taught, *who* is doing the teaching, or the larger context in which the knowledge we are tasked to teach is constructed. Needless to say, our approach to teacher professional development was unlike anything most of our teachers had experienced prior to our graduate program and, it turns out, was a most welcome change for them.

Identity Web

One of the first activities we undertook with our teachers during the initial face-to-face week-long summer session, was to have them create an identity web (see the example at the start of this chapter). Teachers began by identifying aspects of their individual culture. We provided some examples of what this might include such as gender, race, age, ethnicity, exceptionalities, language, religion, etc. Teachers were then tasked with brainstorming how these identity pieces shaped their worldview and were asked to capture that worldview using phrases and/or rich description. Finally, they identified how that worldview was manifested in their behaviors, actions, attitudes, and dispositions. This was not easy work for the teachers as many of them had never considered themselves as having "culture" – particularly those teachers who were white and middle-class. Furthermore, they were challenged to think about how their identity shaped how they lived and interacted in the world. When they did see connections, they were mostly related to aspects of their identity that had been marginalized in some way, and teachers were challenged to recognize the role that privilege played in shaping their worldviews. This identity web became a living document to which we referred throughout the two-year program and laid the foundation for the identity work that undergirds antiracist teacher professional development.

Personal Photo Narrative

One important aspect of a teacher's identity is her/his own personal history of schooling and of being a student. These early schooling experiences impact the work that teachers do, from the assumptions they make about the teaching and learning process, to the experiences they create for their own students, to the connections they make or do not make with children who both share similar identities and also claim identities that are vastly different from theirs. Naming this history has the power to help teachers better understand and empathize with their students, particularly around justice issues related to gender, culture, and race. There have been projects that ask students to define their own experience of schooling including the Through Students' Eyes project (2013) and What Kids Can Do (Cook-Sather, 2006). Less common, however, are studies that examine the formation of teacher identity and practice as rooted in teacher memories or experiences of schooling as students. While scholars such as Robin (2008), and Skouge and Rao (2009) have explored the use of digital storytelling as a teacher education tool for revealing the stories of P-12 students or pre-service teachers, we were interested in using it as a tool for teacher identity development, particularly for in-service teachers.

In the first face-to-face week of our program, we asked educators to reflect on their own P-12 schooling. Guiding questions were adapted from the Through Students' Eyes project (2013):

- What was the purpose of school for you?
- What helped you succeed as a student?
- What got in the way?

Teachers were instructed to take or retrieve no more than ten photos of things/ people/images that helped them answer these questions. They were then asked to use the photos to create a narrative (story) about their P-12 schooling using as few words as possible (at most, captions to describe the images). They were asked to share the photo narrative at the end of the week-long course with the large group. Our purpose for having them share broadly was to help build community among the cohort, but also to allow them to learn from each other's childhood experiences and schooling, identifying themes and making connections to their own students' experiences.

Racial Identity Development Work

Over the years of working with classroom teachers, we have become more intentional about infusing readings, conversations, reflections, and theories related to race. Our purpose has been to deepen teachers' examination of self and identity and to plant the seed for how they might begin to understand the experiences and identities of others. On the first day of class during our first face-to-face summer session and after completing their identity webs, we tasked the teachers with reading several rubrics on racial identity development for both white people and People of Color (e.g., RacialEquityTools.org). They did a pair/share with a peer, took some notes on their thoughts and conversations, and took part in a whole-class debrief. Then they were to write a 300-word essay describing their understanding of where they were in their own identity development to be handed in by the end of the week. This is unconventional for a graduate program in Curriculum and Instruction, but, from the beginning, we wanted to emphasize what matters most to us and to the future of education –`` there was no time to waste. Starting the program with the sharing of personal identity work was beneficial. We often received feedback later in the program about how this initial work around racial identity development eventually had a major impact on teachers' thinking about themselves and their students. The seeds of critical thinking and individual positionality had the time to germinate.

Building a trusting learning community was an additional benefit of starting the program with the sharing of personal identity work. Because teachers were often reticent to resist in that first week of class (at least out loud), sharing with their colleagues allowed them time to build trust with their learning cohort and to reflect on what all of this means. In fact, we often received feedback later in the program about how this initial work around racial identity development eventually had a major impact on their thinking about themselves and their students.

We returned to these racial identity rubrics a year later in our second face-to-face summer session. Although we may not have directly referred to the rubrics in the intervening year, we did ask teachers to consider race as an aspect of all the work we did; work with teacher research, technology, democratic practices, and critical theories. During that second summer session, teachers engaged in a marginalizing/mattering activity in which they considered a time they were treated as if they were not valued and one in which they felt they really mattered using the lenses of gender, language, class, and race. Although all "lenses" were discussed, we continuously emphasized the centrality of racial identity on all social experience. This emphasis was especially important as we examined questions of teacher leadership and policy.

We returned to these racial identity rubrics a year later in our second face-to-face summer session. Teachers reflected on the extent to which they recognized themselves in the stages of racial identity development; whether or not they saw themselves in the same stage they identified the prior summer, if they had moved and why, and what might hinder them from moving from one stage to another. To further hone their understanding of racial identity in that second summer, we also shared video clips of elementary students sharing their identity stories. Teachers were tasked with identifying where each student was in his/her racial identity development and explaining why they thought so. Teachers were also asked to consider the lenses they used to understand this child and to further consider what they might learn from the student that could challenge their own assumptions and teaching practices.

Websites and Films

In their framing of a humanizing pedagogy, Carter Andrews et al. (2019) highlight the importance of multiple learning modalities. Privileging printed text as the only way to access knowledge and experiences denies the multiple ways in which we actually engage in the world. So, in addition to narratives and research studies, we used films, websites, video clips, and social media platforms to engage teachers in observation of and self-reflection on identity and positionality. These mediums proved to be powerful entries into examining both racist and antiracist practices and policies.

OUTCOMES

The development of a safe and caring community was an important outcome of our identity work. Teachers indicated that our exploration of identity through multimodal opportunities over time contributed to the development of this safe community. We do not mean "safe" here in the sense that all teachers felt comfortable and affirmed, but rather safe in that all teachers recognized that their contributions would be respected as avenues toward growth as antiracist practitioners. They felt able to participate because they knew we would not shun them for their comments, but would rather use their missteps as entry points into further explorations and learning. As one teacher reflected:

When it came time for me to record the part [of my photo narrative] about my middle school experience with bullying, I had to rewrite the portion of the script several times. I was unsure how personal to get in describing the barriers I faced during those years. I wanted to be authentic in my responses to the guiding questions, but I did not want to overshare either. When I thought back to how supportive everyone in the class had been towards each other, I knew that I had to, as my students say, 'keep it real' when describing my experience. I am proud of my efforts in this photo narrative and I am proud of myself for taking the opportunity to be vulnerable in this experience.

Another teacher reflected on what it meant to share her story with others. As a child, she was not afforded many of the privileges that others had, so she worried about the pity the class might bestow on her. Courageously, he stayed true to her story, and in so doing recognized the value of being honest, not only with her graduate learning community, but with her own students as well:

Once I completed my photo narrative, I watched it and remember thinking... 'my gosh, what a sad story!' I wanted to delete it and start over. I didn't want my classmates to feel sorry for me, because I assumed their education would have been better than mine. While watching everyone's narrative, it made me feel part of the group. We all face unique challenges and that makes us who we are. For this reason, I didn't go back and start over. I wouldn't want to portray someone I'm not to my students.

Another teacher noted the importance of building this community for supporting the learning that was yet to come:

The photo narrative turned out to be one of my favorite experiences from the week. Not only did it give me a better sense of who I am and the opportunity to share that, but it gave me the chance to get to know my peers on a deeper level. This experience helped to bond us even further, and from that bond we will be able to learn from each other exponentially.

Another outcome was teachers' increased awareness. In implementing the curricular practices outlined above, one main goal was for teachers to become more aware of their own identities and how these identities position them in the world and specifically in their classrooms. We have ample evidence that this work had a positive impact on teachers' awareness and understanding of who they are in relation to others. For example, in a final program reflection, one teacher stated:

The activity we did at the beginning of our program two summers ago was such a powerful step in the beginning process of my own understanding of who I am. At the time, I didn't see why doing an identity web was so important, but I have come to know that one can't change if they don't really see themselves as others may see them, nor can one even begin to understand the role one's identity plays in every aspect of their lives. Because I was raised in a lower-middle-class home in a rural Southern community, I had never considered the power and privilege I was afforded just for being white. It was only after moving to such a diverse area of [the state] that I began to think about my race, and only after beginning the [program] that I truly began to understand.

Teacher awareness was expanded through the creation of their photo narrative in the first summer of the program. Many insights into identity emerged from that project.. Themes that teachers expressed as having shaped their identity as a learner and as a teacher included family influence (positive and negative); the impact of non-academic subjects (sports and the arts) and extracurricular activities; positive socializing; a particular teacher who changed the course of their lives; learning disabilities and chronic medical conditions; the importance of the social aspect of school; and status as first-generation college-bound students.

When asked to reflect on the purpose of school and their successes and obstacles, teachers were less concerned with specific academic content than they were on the emotional and contextual impact of their schooling experience, including the positive or negative effects of relationships with their teachers. Evidence suggests that this insight provided by the photo narrative assignment provoked teachers' empathy and compassion for their current students. They recognized similarities between their own stories and those of their students and also became aware of how their own childhood experiences molded their current teaching practices. Barb, a secondary teacher, reflected:

The reflection really reinforced for me just how important influences 'outside' the classroom are on the success of my students. It is not reasonable to expect students to leave their personal lives at the door. Adults can't do that half the time – K-12 students are rarely (if ever) emotionally ready to operate in that way.

While this teacher did not specifically reference experiences around race as an aspect of students' personal lives that they cannot leave "at the door," we had extensive conversations after these reflections about how racial identity is part of what we need to acknowledge as teachers. What this teacher did explicitly address, however, is the connection between her own emotional struggles and those of her students. How can we ask students to master something that is a struggle for most adults? Other teachers made similar connections between their own experiences and those of their students. For example, one Latinx teacher said:

I know most of my students have similar struggles as I had growing up. I should put myself in their shoes and remember how I felt with the workload and the struggles at home. I shouldn't take it personal[ly] when they aren't engaged or show effort in class. Instead, I should develop and foster relationships with

them and remind myself why I became an ELL teacher. I should be opening
doors to those who need assistance navigating their way in a new country.

Having been an English Language Learner (ELL) herself and then working
with the ELL population, this teacher had fallen into the hegemonic trap of
blaming the students for their struggles rather than the system that sets them
up for failure. Through an exploration of her own identity, she was able to
recognize the need to come back to an antiracist teaching approach that
honored and supported these students' realities.

Similarly, the work we did around racial identity development challenged
teachers – particularly our white teachers – to acknowledge how race has
impacted who they are as teachers. Shelley, a secondary math teacher, started
to unearth biases and assumptions of which she was not previously aware.
She reflected on the implication for her students if she continued to leave
these assumptions unexamined:

Where am I with my own racial identity development? I think I am somewhere
between "Disintegration" and "Integration". It's quite a wide range but I am
still learning and growing about my own biases, particularly the ones that
I am not conscious of. I grew up in a middle-class community with Blacks
and whites and Asians. My two favorite elementary school teachers were
Black, my softball coach was Black, and my first crush in middle school
was Black. I was raised in a family that lived by the golden rule, "Do unto
others as you would have them do unto you", in fact, that is still displayed
above the fireplace in my childhood home today. So, I am not a racist right?
Or am I? So why after watching the videos and discussing articles in our
class, are my subconscious biases surfacing, ones that I didn't even know I
had? Are they stereotypes or true racist thoughts? What is the difference? I
cannot be complicit in letting these subconscious thoughts carry over into
the classroom (or elsewhere) if I am going to try to make the culture in my
classroom a positive and safe one for all. I must start with trying to understand
my own identity before I can accomplish this in the classroom. I need more
experiences, to have more conversations, and to learn more about different
perspectives to even begin to understand how to subdue and, dare I say,
admonish, my subconscious biases. Will that be possible? My identity is not
set and will grow and change as I become more aware of these biases, engage
in meaningful relationships with non-whites, and acquire new information.
I may never feel what it is like to be a minority, but I will continue to engage

in learning about antiracism, learn to recognize when my own biases surface (and nip them in the bud), and embrace all cultures and races.

More deeply exploring their identities not only helped teachers look inward to better understand how their experiences shaped their worldviews, but it helped them to recognize how structures and institutions can either oppress or support people based on those identities. This was sometimes a difficult realization, but it provided a powerful impetus for considering the role they might play in perpetuating those structures. They realized the importance of staying aware – remaining open to learn from others and their experiences. For example, Kelsey, a white high school Physical Education teacher reflected that people are still afforded different opportunities based on race:

It upset me as I began reading the Wink text, specifically her examples of things going on in schools. My initial reaction was denial – 'This isn't true,' 'People don't think like that anymore,' 'I don't hear things like that happening today' ...Through this [first summer session] experience, I have gained insight into how to evaluate life from the non-dominant race point of view. In doing so, I know I am even more prepared to proceed in life, to do more in teaching, and show more compassion to others. The presentations, videos, and discussions made things so clear that I can't just look at things from my point of view or take the stance that there are plenty of opportunities for minorities so race can't be an issue anymore.

Teachers' awareness was not confined to our classroom or to theirs. A white elementary school music teacher, Linda, was so affected by our summer session identity exercises that she found the courage to discuss race with an African American friend. This conversation offered further evidence that racism is not just about individual acts of hatred, but is about larger systems that privilege some over others:

I had a very powerful experience yesterday in relation to everything I have learned in this class. I was running with an acquaintance. She is a middle-aged African American woman. We had many miles ahead of us, so I asked her if I could talk to her about what may be an uncomfortable topic for her. She agreed. I asked her what it was like growing up as an African American woman in today's world. This is a question I never would have dreamed to ask a week ago. She was very surprised and eager to talk to me. The story she told shocked me. She spoke of being marginalized by her friends' parents growing up, and she spoke of the racism she experiences now as an adult. She told me that she and her husband felt they could not buy a house in a certain neighborhood because they did not think the neighbors would accept them because they were African American. Hearing the world from her lens was completely different from how I grew up. Again, it is amazing how one world can be experienced in so many different ways.

While reflections that indicate awareness and new knowledge were important, they are not enough to show that teachers were being antiracist in their practice; we needed to see evidence of action or plans for action. For some teachers the photo narrative assignment and reflection on their own schooling histories made them more mindful of how their own practice hinders their students or facilitates success, and they identified specific changes in their practice, such as offering students more "wait time" and creating space for more student voice. One teacher reflected:

Talking about my negative experiences in school made me realize that many of my students have probably had similar experiences with lack of confidence in a subject. It's important for me to not foster these fears and to make sure my students don't get "lost" or feel undermined in ways that I sometimes did in school. I also thought about how important it is for me to make sure I don't do the things teachers did to make school negative for me; this way I can attempt to make school a more positive environment for my students.

Another teacher said:

It also made me aware of what I am saying in the room. I still have memories of my teachers yelling at me for picking up my pencil during cursive word or volunteering the wrong answer. I never want students to shut down and be afraid to answer questions and participate like I was, so this was a great eye-opener for the upcoming school year.

Both of these teachers were white, and it is not clear that they connected their struggles with the struggles that Students of Color might encounter in their classes. Luckily, this assignment/learning experience was only the start of our work with teachers, and we used their reflections to guide our own next steps with them to continue our support on their journey toward antiracist teaching.

The following is an example of a teacher who did use the identity work in the first summer session as an opportunity to reflect on what it meant to be a white teacher in a Black community and her plans for continued growth as an antiracist teacher:

After the first initial panic attack upon seeing the identity web, I found myself naming feelings and thoughts I had not said out loud before. For example, my feelings about being a white teacher in a predominantly African American community. I know this is a conversation my school has not yet addressed but should start to. This could be a non-example of conscientization, knowing what I know but not acting on it, or possibly an example of problem posing. I am looking forward to talking about these situations throughout the semester and hopefully finding my voice to address them.

Angelo, a white elementary ELL teacher, reflected on the need to continue challenging his assumptions about what students need and want from their schooling experience in order to meet their needs:

This process has been cause for me to begin redefining my role as a teacher and what a teacher does. I am realizing that students come to school with any number of ideals as to what the purpose is for them and that they need me to continue to challenge my assumptions, so that I am serving their best interests instead of someone else's, or my own.

The following reflection from an elementary school teacher shows her commitment to examine her curriculum and to be the antiracist teacher she never had as a student herself:

As I try to answer these questions, I keep coming back to social studies. In fourth grade students learn [state] history, content rife with examples of hegemony. And if I am teaching that history in the same way it was presented to me in elementary school, using the traditional banking model, to a classroom where the majority of students come from countries and cultures historically oppressed and marginalized by the white European power structures of American society, then I am perpetuating those racist ideas. This year I need to make sure that I reexamine each lesson, pull out the big ideas and themes around power and think about how to give students the tools and space to think about, question and learn [state] history different from how I was taught history in elementary school.

TENSIONS AND DILEMMAS

Examining racial identity and positionality and how these constructs impact teaching and learning is not always an easy, painless task. Teachers were challenged to name long-held assumptions about how they viewed others and about their intentions in their classrooms, both of which caused cognitive dissonance for some (Gorski, 2009; McDermott, 2017). While resistance and outright anger were reactions that we faced in the earliest years of the program, these reactions became less prevalent as we became more intentional in our recruiting information and class sizes became smaller for our online iteration of the program.

We also wondered though, whether the "muted" reactions to the curriculum may have been influenced by the larger social and political movements in the U.S.. The Black Lives Matter movement, use of social media to document treatment in public spaces, and heated debates about the polarizing stances on national policy made it more difficult to deny that people were living different realities based on the color of their skin. Even so, it was clear that some teachers were uncomfortable with what we were asking them to consider and do. Sometimes their discomfort was something we sensed, and other times they felt comfortable enough to reflect on it. Linda, one of our white elementary school music teachers, articulated her feelings in her final portfolio at the completion of the two-year program. She named the identity web as one of her most powerful learning experiences but admitted that it took her a while to get to that point:

At first, I did not understand what this [identity web] was or how it related to this graduate program (I thought I was here to learn how to be a better teacher!). However, I soon realized that this web was such a powerful tool in understanding how I view the world through my own lens.

She went on to say,

Once I realized that I view the world a certain way because of my own experiences and identity, I could realize and understand that my students see the world completely differently than I do. This allowed me to make my teaching more student-centered and democratic. I started asking my students their opinions instead of putting my opinions on them. I started asking myself, 'Why do they not understand this concept? What can I do to help them?'

instead of asking, 'They should understand this, what is wrong with them?'
This has allowed me to become much more compassionate and understanding.

It is interesting that learning how to be a better teacher was not initially connected to who she was or how she viewed her students. When we minimize teaching to strategies and "cute, engaging" lessons, we miss the whole point of what an antiracist democratic education is meant to be.

DiAngelo's (2018) work around white fragility, offers a useful framework for understanding how some of our teachers experienced our curriculum and the tensions that arose when engaging in antiracist teacher professional development. For example, Becky, a white elementary school teacher, took every opportunity to express her love for and admiration of her diverse class of students. Embedded within these comments, however, were examples of "aversive racism," particularly through her use of "racially coded terms" (DiAngelo, 2018, p. 43). Becky wrote:

I have always assumed that I grew up in a fairly diverse environment. I say 'fairly diverse' as I know my upbringing and education was not in the type of environment I teach in now, which is 'all diverse' if you will.

At the time, she taught in a school that was majority Latinx with some African American students. She conflates "diverse" with "People of Color," rather than recognizing that diversity means people from a range of races/ ethnicities/backgrounds – including white people.

Engaging in our antiracist professional development program was sometimes the first opportunity that teachers had to recognize, to name, and to reflect on their white privilege. As Jan, a white kindergarten teacher stated in her final portfolio:

When I started the [program], I did not think I had biases that needed to be unpacked. I am a caring teacher from [the Midwest]. I don't have negative views on People of Color and love working with my Title 1 students. Some of the readings were offensive to me because they assumed I didn't understand what the struggle is like for People of Color. I have learned that white privilege is a real thing that negatively impacts our schools and culture.

She was operating under DiAngelo's (2018) third rule of engagement: "You must trust that I am in no way racist before you can give me feedback on my racism" (p. 124). Because we had two years to work with her to scaffold her experiences and to grow her understanding of antiracist teaching, she came to understand that white privilege "is a real thing" and that being colorblind was damaging to her students and not at all helpful. Starting with her identity set the stage for these valuable lessons.

As they were confronted with their white privilege, teachers often experienced feelings of guilt.. This guilt can present as anger, sadness, and in the case of the following teacher reflecting on her experience of creating the photo narrative, embarrassment:

At first I was almost embarrassed that I hadn't dealt with anything 'major' in my life, but everyone's perspectives are different. My experiences were still important to making me the person I am now.

Teachers can sometimes feel that they cannot relate to others if they themselves do not have similar experiences.

One of the tensions related to identity work was being mindful of and honoring the broad range of experiences of our teachers and therefore the reactions they had to engage in antiracist work. We cannot forget to give voice to the stories and struggles of People of Color whose participation in antiracist curricula is crucial yet is often overlooked. Antiracist curricula have typically been designed to allow members of the dominant white society to: increase awareness of self and others, challenge stereotypes, overcome prejudice, and develop relationships with people from different racial backgrounds (Goodman, 2011). Although several studies have focused on engagement and resistance patterns of whites to antiracist curricula (e.g., Boyd and Arnold, 2000; Donadey, 2002; DeMulder, Ndura-Ouédraogo, & Stribling, 2006; Sleeter, 1996), limited attention has been directed towards the experiences of People of Color. This is true even though there is evidence that they, too, find it challenging to engage in antiracist curricula (Ferber & Storrs, 1995). In our experience, feelings of discomfort were common for both white teachers and Teachers of Color. White teachers tended to describe discomfort with the content (e.g., relating feelings of cognitive dissonance between new understandings and long-held beliefs) and discomfort in discussions of racism as a sensitive subject. Many teachers responded to this discomfort with resistant behaviors that threatened to disengage them from the curriculum. We found, however, that discomfort often appeared to be a valuable component of a struggle that ultimately led to growth and change.

In contrast, for Teachers of Color, discomfort was not often expressed in terms of opening up or shutting down, but instead was experienced as frustration, anger, and disappointment with their white peers' resistance. Teachers of Color also described their "racial battle fatigue" and the discomfort of "speaking for" their race to help educate others (e.g., Franklin, 2019; Smith, 2008). Goodman (2001) argues that it is crucial that resistance is addressed if we are to effectively educate people from privileged groups and move them toward a social justice agenda. We argue that it is also crucial that People of Color have the support and encouragement of their teacher colleagues as allies so that they are not sacrificed in the service of this goal. As we advance knowledge about the struggles and challenges faced by Teachers of Color in multicultural education settings, this knowledge will enhance the capacity of educators to facilitate effective dialogue and to sensitively support and respond to People of Color so that they can sustain engagement in these crucial conversations.

CONCLUSION

Antiracist teaching starts with an examination of the self in relation to others. Who am I? What do I value? How has my identity shaped my experiences? And how have those experiences subsequently continued to shape my identity? What do I believe about the world? Knowing answers to these questions sets the stage for helping us unpack assumptions…the next important element of antiracist teacher professional development.

REFERENCES

Boyd, D., & Arnold, M. L. (2000). Teachers' beliefs, antiracism and moral education: Problems of intersection. *Journal of Moral Education, 29*(1), 23–45. doi:10.1080/030572400102916

Briggs, S. (2014, November 1). How empathy affects learning, and how to cultivate it in your students. *InformEd.* https://www.opencolleges.edu.au/informed/features/empathy-and-learning/

Brookfield, S. (2012). *Teaching for critical thinking: Tools and techniques to help students question their assumptions.* Jossey-Bass.

Carter Andrews, D. J., Brown, T., Castillo, B. M., Jackson, D., & Vellanki, V. (2019). Beyond damage-centered teacher education: Humanizing pedagogy for teacher educators and preservice teachers. *Teachers College Record*, *121*(6), 1–28. http://www.tcrecord.org/LIBRARY/Abstract.asp?ContentId=22737

Center for the Advancement of Well-Being. (2014, July 16). *Through students' eyes*. https://wellbeing.gmu.edu/research/projects/the-through-students-eyes-project-seeing-youths-perspectives-on-school-and-their-peers

Cook-Sather, A. (2006). Sound, presence, and power: 'Student voice' in educational research and reform. *Curriculum Inquiry*, *36*(4), 359–390. doi:10.1111/j.1467-873X.2006.00363.x

David, E. J. R. (Ed.). (2015). *Internalized oppression: The psychology of marginalized groups*. Springer.

DeMulder, E. K., Ndura-Ouédraogo, E., & Stribling, S. M. (2009). From vision to action: Fostering peaceful coexistence and the common good in a pluralistic society through teacher education. *Peace and Change*, *34*(1), 27–48. doi:10.1111/j.1468-0130.2009.00532.x

DiAngelo, R. (2018). *White fragility: Why it's so hard for White people to talk about racism*. Beacon Press.

Donadey, A. (2002). Negotiating tensions: Teaching about race issues in graduate feminist classrooms. *NWSA Journal*, *14*(1). https://www.jstor.org/stable/4316872

Eryaman, M. Y. (2007). From reflective practice to practical wisdom: Towards a post foundational teacher education. *International Journal of Progressive Education*, *3*(1), 87–107.

Ferber, A. L., & Storrs, D. (1995). Race and representation: Students of color in the multicultural classroom. In B. A. Goebel & J. C. Hall (Eds.), *Teaching a "new canon"? Students, teachers, and texts in the college literature classroom* (pp. 32–47). National Council of Teachers of English.

Franklin, J. D. (2019). Coping with racial battle fatigue: Differences and similarities for African American and Mexican American college students. *Race, Ethnicity and Education*, *22*(5), 589–609. doi:10.1080/13613324.2019.1579178

Goodman, D. L. (2011). *Promoting diversity and social justice: Educating people from privileged groups*. Sage Publications, Inc.

Gorski, P. C. (2009). Cognitive dissonance as a strategy in social justice teaching. *Multicultural Education, 17*(1), 54–57.

Hayes, C., & Juarez, B. (2012). There is no culturally responsive teaching spoken here: A critical race perspective. *Democracy & Education, 20*(1), 1–14. http://democracyeducationjournal.org/ home/vol20/iss1/5

Heick, T. (2015, February 10). Teaching empathy: Are We Teaching Content or Students? *EduTopia*. https://www.edutopia.org/blog/teaching-empathy-content-or-students-terry-heick

Howard, T. C. (2003). Culturally relevant pedagogy: Ingredients for critical teacher reflection. *Theory into Practice, 42*(3), 195–202. http://www.jstor.org/stable/1477420

Kendi, I. X. (2019). *How to be an antiracist*. One World.

McDermott, V. (2017). *We must say no to the status quo: Educators as allies in the battle for social justice*. Corwin.

Mendes, E. (2003, September). What empathy can do. *Educational Leadership, 61*(1), 56–59. https://www.asce.org/publicaitons/educational-leadership/sept03/vol61/num01/What-Empathy-Can-Do.aspx

Mezirow, J. (1990). How critical reflection triggers learning. In J. Mezirow (Ed.), *Fostering critical reflection in adulthood* (pp. 1–20). Jossey-Bass.

Milner, H. R. (2003). Teacher reflection and race in cultural contexts: History, meanings and methods in teaching. *Theory into Practice, 42*(3), 173–180. doi:10.120715430421tip4203_2

Racial Equity Tools. (2020). *Summary of stages of racial identity development*. https://www.racialequitytools.org/resourcefiles/Compilation_of_Racial_Identity_Models_7_15_11.pdf

Rimm-Kaufman, S., & Sandilos, L. (2018). *Improving students' relationships with teachers to provide essential supports for learning*. American Psychological Association. https://www.apa.org/education/k12/relationships.aspx

Robin, B. R. (2008). Digital storytelling: A powerful technology tool for the 21st century classroom. *Theory into Practice*, *47*(3), 220–228. doi:10.1080/00405840802153916

Schön, D. A. (1984). *The Reflective Practitioner: How Professionals Think in Action* (1st ed.). Basic Books.

Skouge, J. R., & Rao, K. (2009). Digital Storytelling in Teacher Education: Creating Transformations through Narrative. *Educational Perspectives*, *42*, 54–60.

Sleeter, C. E. (1996). *Multicultural education as social activism*. State University of New York Press.

Smith, W. A. (2008). Higher education: Racial battle fatigue. In R. T. Schaefer (Ed.), *Encyclopedia of Race, Ethnicity, and Society* (pp. 615–618). Sage Publications.

Townsend, J. C. (2012, September 26). *Why we should teach empathy to improve education (and test scores)*. https://www.forbes.com/sites/ashoka/2012/09/26/why-we-should-teach-empathy-to-improve-education-and-test-scores/#11ac76c71a0d

View, J. L., DeMulder, E., Stribling, S., & Kayler, M. (2009). Cultivating transformative leadership in P-12 schools and classrooms through critical teacher professional development. *Journal of Curriculum and Instruction*, *3*(2), 39–53. doi:10.3776/joci.v3n2p39-53

Warford, M. (2011). The zone of proximal teacher development. *Teaching and Teacher Education*, *27*(2), 252–258. doi:10.1016/j.tate.2010.08.008

Williams, B. (2016). Radical honesty: Truth-telling as pedagogy for working through shame in academic spaces. In F. Tuitt, C. Haynes, & S. Stewart (Eds.), *Race, equity, and the learning environment: The global relevance of critical and inclusive pedagogies in higher education* (pp. 71–82). Stylus.

Wink, J. (2011). *Critical pedagogy: Notes from the real world* (4th ed.). Pearson.

Zimmerman, C. R., & Kao, G. (2020). Unequal returns to children's efforts: Racial/Ethnic and gender disparities in teachers' evaluations of children's noncognitive skills and academic ability. *Du Bois Review*, 1–22. doi:10/1017/S1742058X20000016

Chapter 3
Critical Reflective Practice, Critical Pedagogy, and Culturally Relevant Pedagogy:
Unpacking Assumptions and Taking Action

ABSTRACT

This chapter describes the frameworks of critical pedagogy, culturally relevant pedagogy, and related experiences that teachers engage in as part of the authors' antiracist professional development work. Critical reflective practice is at the core of these pedagogical approaches and is central in offering effective antiracist teacher professional development, with these frameworks having the potential to help teachers become aware of the ways that institutional racism pervades schools and society and the ways we are all complicit in perpetuating racism; shift the focus of oppressive educational challenges from individuals—including self as teacher, parents, and students— to systems of oppression; support teachers to develop the knowledge and skills to advocate and take action for antiracist attitudes, policies, and practices, both in society and in their own classrooms; support teachers' antiracist teaching that positions students to develop as critical, antiracist, and engaged citizens; and ensure that teachers and schools recognize and support the optimal development of every child.

DOI: 10.4018/978-1-7998-5649-8.ch003

THEORETICAL FRAMEWORKS

In the recent and ongoing assault on public education, teachers have experienced a profound shift in the ways in which others view them and their work. School reformers have unquestioningly adopted the factory metaphor for schooling, positioning teachers as technicians tasked with following the mandates handed down to them by others (Giroux, 2020; Giroux, 2012). Teachers who had formerly embraced their knowledge and their responsibility of extending curriculum topics and creating innovative learning experiences are now "torn between their sense of what constitutes good teaching and the constraints of a bureaucratized and isolating system that does little to encourage initiative and experimentation" (Levine, 1995, p. 53). Relatedly, and not surprisingly, there is decreasing interest in entering the teaching profession and increasing numbers of teachers are leaving the profession, discouraged and dissatisfied (Learning Policy Institute).

Critical pedagogy and culturally relevant pedagogy are frameworks teachers can use to reclaim their agency and to examine their curriculum and the relationships they develop in their own classroom settings with their students, colleagues, and school communities. Researchers and educational theorists have challenged the notion of teachers as technicians whose sole responsibility is to transfer information to less-knowledgeable students (Adams, Blumenfeld, Castaneda, Hackman, Peters, & Zuniga, 2000; Brookfield, 2017; Giroux, 2020; Hooks, 2014; McLaren, 2015; Schön, 2017; Shor, 2012). Rather, teachers are encouraged to be critically conscious of the relationships between theory and their practice (Duncan-Andrade, Reyes & Morrell, 2008; Wink, 2011), to consider the moral dimensions of their profession (Hansen, 2017; Sockett, 2012), to create learning opportunities that are meaningful and liberating (Darder, 2015; Freire, 1970), and to create curricula that are culturally relevant to the diverse student population (Ladson-Billings, 2013; Ladson-Billings, 1995; Scherff & Spector, 2010).

Critical Pedagogy

Teacher professional development efforts that emphasize critical pedagogy, including critical reflection, dialogue, and collaboration (e.g., Brookfield, 2017; Schön, 2017; Wink, 2011) can support teachers in transforming their classrooms into democratic, empowering, antiracist learning spaces. As teachers develop the skills of critical reflection and as they discover the power of their own voices, they are able to re-envision their roles as critical educators who empower their own students. Such efforts offer on-going professional development that is cross-disciplinary, that combines the wisdom of P-12 classroom teachers along the age-grade spectrum, and offers experiential learning, as well as hands-on practice. Teachers design and implement action research, based on their lived experiences and drawing on academic and popular literature to contribute to our collective knowledge of teaching and learning. Teachers examine macro-level policies and systems, including the cycle of socialization (Harro, 2000), to actively seek openings for making change in schools and at the community level.

Critical pedagogy includes the practice of critical literacy, an instructional approach that encourages examination of the power dynamics inherent in "texts" (Janks, 2000; Ciardiello, 2004; Lewison, Flint, & Sluys, 2002). Perhaps the most helpful explanation of critical literacy was offered by Freire when he emphasized the power of not only reading the word, but reading the world (Shor & Freire, 1987, p. 135). He stressed the importance of critically examining the world in which we live and work in order to name existing inequities and begin to transform oppressive structures through the power of words (spoken, read, and written). The connection between literacy and liberation is at the core of critical literacy.

Culturally Relevant Pedagogy

Culturally relevant pedagogy is an educational approach that not only supports academic achievement and cultural competence, but also supports the freedom to change the system. Ladson-Billings (1995) contends that culturally relevant pedagogy has three criteria:

- Students must experience academic success.
- Students must develop and/or maintain cultural competence.
- Students must develop a critical consciousness through which they challenge the status quo of the current social order.

As Richard Shaull reminds us, "There is no such thing as a neutral educational process" (as cited in Freire & Macedo, 2000, p. 16). Education is a political act that either emphasizes conformity to the system or supports the freedom to change it. Within the critical frameworks described above, there is an expectation that teachers shoulder personal responsibility to shift their focus from deficit perspectives of students and families to engaging in antiracist practices in their classrooms. While these individual classroom efforts are necessary, they are not sufficient. Kendi (2019) suggests that "Americans have long been trained to see the deficiencies of people rather than policy. It's a pretty easy mistake to make: People are in our faces. Policies are distant. We are particularly poor at seeing the policies lurking behind the struggles of people" (p. 28). Teachers therefore can and should have a crucial leadership role in identifying and confronting racist structures and policies that limit students' opportunities for optimal educational support.

The connections among critical pedagogy, critical literacy, and culturally relevant pedagogy are best illustrated in the words of Gloria Ladson-Billings (1995). She writes, "Culturally relevant teaching is about questioning (and preparing students to question) the structural inequality, the racism, and the injustice that exists in society" (Ladson-Billings, 1995, p. 18). In conjunction with the values and practices embedded in democratic and critical approaches, these theories of teaching and learning provide an important foundation on which to frame the professional development of teachers.

Teachers and teacher educators who are prepared for a future that promotes educational equity for all children will be those who maintain a critical stance, who are creative and flexible, who use their voices in the public square, and who teach children to have a critical stance, to uplift their voices, and to engage in civic action. We define such teachers as artists, intellectuals, and citizens (View & DeMulder, 2009). A teacher as artist honors the practice of imagination, is a creative problem-solver, and uses artistry to bring learning alive for ALL children, including those who are marginalized and those who are placed at risk (e.g., Duncan-Andrade, Reyes & Morrell, 2008; Saranson, 1999). Teacher intellectuals understand the relationship between text and context, are inquisitive and courageous in pursuit of the unknown, risk being wrong or unpopular, and seek understanding through intellectual discourse, debate, and conversation (e.g., Freire, 1970). A teacher-citizen functions as an agent of change by promoting active critical thinking and engagement in civic life for self and students, understands hierarchies of power, and understands the necessity of student freedom in the context of adult authority (e.g., Beane & Apple, 1995; Dumas, 2014; Kincheloe, 2008; Ladson-Billings, 2009; Shor, 2012). A P-12 classroom teacher who is prepared to be a transformative leader insists on seeking answers to difficult questions in collaboration with peer educators, administrators, parents, and most importantly, students, regardless of grade level or discipline. It is possible to become such a teacher even years after entering the classroom, and professional development can be the catalyst for this transformation. It is through conscious practice with professional peers that teachers can transform themselves into leaders within and outside of their classrooms.

While learning and significant professional development processes are complex and thus not simple to describe, our ongoing work with teachers involved supporting the development of their critical reflective practice and critical consciousness and offering tools to understand and infuse critical pedagogy and culturally relevant pedagogy into their thinking and into their teaching practice. Some of the tools we used to offer this ongoing support were readings and discussions to foster critical reflection and critical dialogue, exercises to consider multiple perspectives and to unpack assumptions about teaching and learning, and extensive school-based action research projects that involved collecting and critically analyzing data. These projects included an equity audit that teachers conduct in their schools, school and community-based teacher action research projects, and a curriculum-based culturally relevant teaching project. These experiences and teachers' reactions to them are described below, starting with initial and ongoing efforts to build skills that foster critical reflective practice.

Critical Reflective Practice

As Faust argued, "You can't know anything with certainty" (Goeth & MacIntyre, 1957). If we can't know with certainty, we can certainly come to deeper understandings about ourselves, others, and the world. From a constructive-developmental perspective on adult development, creating scaffolded learning opportunities for adults to grapple with complex ideas and to learn to appreciate, or at least tolerate, ambiguity supports transformative learning (Kegan 1982; Kegan, 1998: Mezirow, 2000). In the context of teacher education and professional development for emerging antiracist critical educators, crucial steps toward deeper understanding and more complex meaning-making include systematically and continually seeking to discover and unpack assumptions and implicit biases, moving beliefs from the subjective realm to the objective realm (Kegan 1982, Kegan, 1998). As teachers develop critical attitudes toward received knowledge (Belenky, Clinchy, Goldberger & Tarule, 1997), they build a foundation for constructivist meaning-making using a critical lens. Brookfield's (1995) critical reflection process (Figure 1) offers a way to do so.

Figure 1. Stephen Brookfield's (1995) critical reflection process

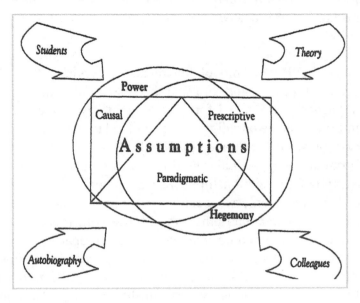

We used this model as a foundational exercise to carry forward throughout our work with teachers. Evidence from our teachers suggest that these efforts served to help them develop a critical stance, priming them to ask critical questions of the status quo and to begin to root out and address racist attitudes, practices, and policies, including the myth of "color-blindness" (Brown & Carnoy, 2005). An example serves to demonstrate this shift in thinking: At the beginning of the program, Lesley, a Biracial Latinx female Kindergarten/1st grade teacher, who identifies herself as white, wrote about the connections she made to the racial identity development materials. She wrote:

I agreed with one of the examples given: 'I'm just a person.' While I know my race is white, I also feel that my color doesn't define me. I am just a person, and others around me are just people, too.

Later in the program, she had developed a more critical lens:

My assumptions about teaching and learning were truths for me...Now, I am questioning my beliefs [and] my overall understanding of who I am as a teacher and as a member of society... I entered this school year with an assumption I now know is unjust: parents were not doing their best in teaching their children to be good listeners and to be respectful. (As I write this, I cringe...after all I have learned this year) ...this is not a "one and done" thing...it's an ongoing process; a shift in thinking. It's a practice that we... turn into a habit.

As the Brookfield (1995) model illustrates, teachers enter their classrooms with many assumptions and implicit biases about teaching, learning, children, relationships, and so forth that inevitably guide their practice; these assumptions can be paradigmatic (grounded in particular paradigms or world views), prescriptive (guided by beliefs about expected behaviors that are often grounded in a particular world view), or causal (guided by beliefs about cause and effect relationships). These assumptions are influenced by issues of power and hegemony; society is organized in such a way that some people have more power than others, and those with more power are able to decide what is considered normal and natural in regard to how the world operates and how the people in that world are expected to act. For example, a teacher may assume that a student's failure to earn good grades is a direct result of his not putting enough effort into his learning. This prescriptive assumption may stem from the belief that hard work is directly correlated with success, an idea perpetuated through the tale of the "American Dream" and by the more recent introduction and popularity of the concept of "grit" (Gorski, 2016; Mehta, 2015; Stitzlein, 2018). But if the teacher critically reflects on the student's struggles through multiple lenses, such as theory, the experiences of colleagues, the experiences of students, and the teacher's own autobiographical experiences, a greater understanding of the struggling student could emerge along with greater understanding of the systemic barriers standing in the student's way. This deeper and more complex understanding can lead to insights and efforts to find more effective ways to support his/her learning. In this scenario, critical reflection can help the teacher deconstruct the "myth of merit" (Generett & Olson, 2020) through considering the role that a system of racial hierarchy might play in understanding the student's struggles and listening to the experiences of students, as well as of other colleagues, in order to determine curricular practices that would enhance the student's learning experience. This systematic examination of our assumptions helps us learn, relearn, and unlearn (Wink, 2011) what we believe to be true, and that deeper understanding also gives us confidence to articulate new knowledge and perspectives. Brookfield (1995) suggests that "the discovery of one's authentic voice is at the heart of the critically reflective process" (pg. 47). This authentic voice has power and authority to not only communicate well-supported beliefs about teaching and learning but to take informed antiracist action. Susan, a white female Kindergarten teacher, described her growing confidence in her own voice: "Prior to this program, I would be very hesitant to speak up when I disagreed...Now, I... question their [administrators'] reasoning."

As teachers used critical reflection to develop deeper and more complex understandings of their classroom practice and the multiple contexts in which their classrooms are embedded, they became more able to meet the needs of their students. Through critical reflection, teachers asked questions such as: What knowledge is privileged in my classroom? Who is benefiting from my instruction? Whose voice am I hearing? Whose voice is silent/silenced? How can I include the voices, knowledge, and experiences of all of my students? Teaching, therefore, became more than just developing strategies for instruction; it became a process of critically questioning the teaching and learning cycle and the contexts in which these are embedded while building effective relationships with students that are grounded in real experiences and needs. Teachers were empowered in their own classrooms and schools then to model this critical reflective stance and to support their own students and colleagues to engage in healthy skepticism, to ask critical questions, and to recognize and critique the power dynamics in schools and society. The dual focus was on the development of teachers' critical consciousness and on building skills to foster their own students' critical consciousness to be change agents in the world they live in.

Dustin, a Biracial male high school math teacher, reflected on the ways that the critical reflection process helped him to identify broader structural barriers that impacted his classroom and students:

The first step of Brookfield's Critical Reflection Process is to "hunt for assumptions." There are a few assumptions I make about my teaching. First: that the current structure of schooling – from the macro of federal policy to the micro of my own classroom – is designed to meet the needs of global neoliberal hegemony, rather than the needs of students and communities. For my students – mostly low-income immigrants of color – the purpose of school is to make them believe that if they are socio-economically marginalized as adults, this is their fault rather than the effect of a structural flaw. In my immediate orbit, the capitalist power structure is codified as the algebra exam – an exam that all students in the state must pass to graduate high school. Theoretically, this exam is an assessment of [a] student's algebra skills. Practically, it is an assessment of their test-taking skills. Before they can show their math knowledge on the assessment, students must be able to focus for a 3-hour exam, switch back and forth between different unrelated skills, decode large blocks of text, etc. These ways of doing come naturally to students from dominant communities – in fact, these ways of doing originate from these communities. However, they don't come naturally for my students. Many of my students best show their math skills when investigating connected real-world problems generated from their own lived experiences. These investigations are often oral, tactile, and/or visual, as well as written.

In its mission to develop justice-oriented antiracist citizens, critical approaches to education rely on problem-posing methods. Freire (1970) introduced the idea of problem-posing education, describing it as a process in which "people develop their power to perceive critically the way they exist in the world with which and in which they find themselves; they come to see the world not as static reality, but as a reality in process, in transformation" (p. 64). Problem-posing emphasizes an educational process where value is placed on the problems that students pose related to their own life experiences rather than an educational process where students are required to regurgitate answers to questions asked by more powerful others (Kincheloe, 2018; Quintero, 2004).

Problem-posing teaching methods in the P-12 classroom are necessarily grounded in the lives and experiences of the students. Due to the growing diversity of cultures and experiences of students in the United States (Rabinowitz, Emamdjomeh, & Meckler, 2019), the problems posed have the potential to raise complex social justice issues as students grapple with how to negotiate dominant ideologies, maintain their sense of self, and seek more equitable social structures. Of course, critical and culturally relevant pedagogical approaches and curricula require more than fostering skills and relaying information to students. In order to co-construct meaning and ground learning in students' cultures and experiences, caring and trusting relationships between teacher and students need to be fostered, as described in Chapter 4.

This critical reflective process – hunting and unpacking assumptions – can be reinforced in many ways in other aspects of the work with teachers, including with research prompts, in discussions, and in feedback on written work (e.g., "How do you know this?", "What assumptions do you have related to this research question/ claim/argument?; What evidence do you have to support this claim/argument? What power dynamics are at play here?) Over time this critical reflection process becomes a persistent, helpful habit that reveals flaws in our own thinking as well as subtle and not so subtle oppressive attitudes, policies, and practices around us. Teachers become more aware of oppressive attitudes that are fueled by deficit perspectives and we have seen that they consciously shift their thinking using a strengths-based perspective, more fully appreciating the funds of knowledge students bring to school (Moll, Amanti, Neff, and González, 1992; Vélez-Ibáñez, 2018).

As Arundhati Roy (2001) wrote, "The trouble is that once you see it, you can't unsee it. And once you've seen it, keeping quiet, saying nothing, becomes as political an act as speaking out. There's no innocence. Either way, you're accountable" (p. 7). As Robin, a white female middle-school orchestra teacher lamented:

I can't read a newspaper article, listen to a news report, read a book or a magazine, have a conversation........none of that, without thinking, "Whose perception is that, through what lens is that information filtered, how do you know, why is that your position?" and on and on and on. It's driving my husband crazy!!! I will never again be able to simply accept something out of hand without critically examining it and reflecting on it. That's a huge change for me, and one I really needed... I'd never even really thought much about social justice in my classroom, school, and community before. Things just were what they were... I cannot look at my students and our school community ever again without considering the social justice aspect of what we do every day and the power we hold as teacher leaders.

As mentioned above, substantial experiences were offered as part of our curriculum to engage teachers in ongoing critical reflection, data collection, and critical analysis, including an equity audit, teacher research projects, and a culturally relevant teaching project. Examples of curricular experiences are described below.

Critical Inquiry – The Equity Audit

Many educators continue to underestimate the degree to which opportunity gaps/education debts are present in their schools and districts and often avoid discussing the structural causes of inequity, instead attributing achievement gaps to students' home lives or their genetics (Dodman, DeMulder, View, Swalwell, Stribling, Ra, & Dallman, 2019; Gorski, 2016; Ladson-Billings, 2006; Pollock, 2004; Rodriguez, 2012; Skrla, Scheurich, Garcia, & Nolly, 2004). Such attitudes, expectations, and behaviors persist despite the use of data (Gannon-Slater et al., 2017). Teachers are often underprepared and under-encouraged to recognize disparities in educational conditions affecting their students' schooling experiences. The idea that teachers can and should be aware of school inequities is rooted in Cochran-Smith and Lytle's (2009) idea that teachers should have an "inquiry stance" in which they "(1) have comprehensive, insightful understandings of equity and inequity relationships; (2) can critically question current accountability policy, and (3) work for true equity-positive outcomes in their local school contexts" (p. 86).

This definition has a political dimension that critiques power relations and describes teachers' habits of mind. It is insufficient for teachers to question their practice or to engage in culturally relevant practices; they must also examine the underpinnings of what they are asked to do and interrogate what will best bring about deep equity, rather than mere compliance with an initiative. This stance cultivates teachers' capacity for "equity literacy": the knowledge and skills to recognize inequity, respond to it, redress it, and sustain systems that help build equitable learning communities (Gorski & Swalwell, 2015). When applied to teachers' data analysis, an inquiry stance helps to make connections between teacher practice and data and promotes critical analysis of the data through an equity lens, rather than using data to perpetuate the status quo.

Our adaptation of an equity audit tool (e.g., Bustamante, Nelson, & Onwuegbuzie, 2009; Groenke, 2010; McKenzie & Skrla, 2011) supported the development of this critical stance by helping teachers to connect with issues of equity in the early stages of learning how to conduct teacher research, using critical data- driven decision-making (CDDDM), a counter to the blaming and shaming common to data-driven decision-making (e.g., Au, 2007, 2009; Mandinach, Friedman, & Gummer, 2015; Osei-Kofi, 2005). Teachers identified and analyzed disproportionality across six identities such as social class, (dis) ability, etc.; explored the literature related to one of the equity issues; and created and monitored an action plan (Scheurich & Skrla, 2003).

The use of an equity audit can do several things: (1) encourage critical data- driven decision-making that re-skills and empowers teachers; (2) expose deep-seated structural inequities in schools; and (3) help teachers address inequities through collaborative action. With the appropriate supports, teachers can learn to conduct equity audits as a strategy for creating more expansive data sets that include all members of the school community and that hold great potential for helping to orient educators towards equity as the driver for pedagogical and institutional decision-making.

Similar to school culture audits, an equity audit collects data related to the many possible inequities within a school and/or classroom: race, class, gender, (dis)ability, sexual identity, language, etc. Data sources typically include achievement data (e.g., standardized test scores, course grades, failure or dropout rates), discipline data (e.g., expulsions, suspensions, office referrals), extracurricular data (e.g., participation rates in athletics and the arts, student council membership), and staffing (e.g., teacher licensure, class size, etc.). Much like an action research cycle, the conductor of an equity audit selects an area for examination and collects disaggregated data about that area, identifies a pattern of inequity if it is occurring and analyzes why, collaboratively works to devise a solution, implements the solution, and monitors the results.

Our research (Dodman, et al., 2019) suggests that, as a result of scaffolding with relevant readings (e.g., Harry & Klingner, 2014) and conducting equity audits in their schools, teachers expanded their awareness of inequities, increased their understanding of and skill with data, and developed an empowered sense of change agency. For example, below are equity audit revelations described by Devi, a South Asian female who was an elementary advanced academics (AAP) resource teacher:

As I completed my Equity Audit, I felt the urgency to remedy my findings. Across the data, I could see that our students identified for the higher levels of advanced academic services are primarily white and Asian, which is a trend that we see across the country. What was more concerning to me was the data on students identified for AAP and also identified as receiving ESOL services –we have only one student who is a Level 4 ESOL and also receiving the highest level of our AAP services. We have a few students who are at further levels of English Language proficiency who are included in our AAP Level IV classes, but only one who is still receiving ESOL services. When I looked closer at the other data, I saw that students receiving ESOL services also did not participate in the extracurricular activities I tallied, such as patrols, afterschool enrichment classes, and Student Council.

Amanda, a white female high school Latin teacher, described her changing attitudes toward data as a result of her equity audit experience:

In the end review that I wrote for the first fall semester, I said, "Data can be powerful. I still, however, hold to a lot of original disdain towards the way we use data to drive decisions in education. There are so many factors that we cannot fit into a number, and I think that we still rely too heavily on data in policies and administration." I now have a deeper understanding of what data is, and I would now have said that I have a disdain towards the way we use the wrong kind of data to drive decisions in education.

In studying the impact of the equity audit experience on teachers' practice, we have learned that without established collegial, school-wide and system-wide supports, long-term systemic improvements are more challenging. An example of teachers' frustrations related to the equity audit experience is expressed by Nancy, a white female 6th grade teacher:

I can still understand why we have to use data and feel that there is significance when utilized properly. We have to endure a reflective process and cycle in order to effectively use data and follow through with creating action plans and actually acting upon them and then diving back into the reflective cycle. I have found that I, as well as even my school, have good intentions of doing things but seem to come to a standstill after making an action plan. We have to push on and pursue the action and continue to follow the cycle or the data just become a bunch of numbers that become meaningless to teachers and disturbing to administrators.

Nevertheless, for many teachers, the equity audit research experience profoundly impacted their thinking and practice. Additional research opportunities reinforced their commitments to addressing inequities in their schools, as described in the next section.

Critical Inquiry – Teacher Research

In our work with teachers, the equity audit was conducted during the first full semester of the two-year program, and teachers had several concurrent and subsequent opportunities to engage in semester and year-long teacher research projects informed by their equity audits, usually focused on their classroom or school. Readings that help teachers develop research skills (e.g., Booth, Colomb, Williams, Bizup, & FitzGerald, 2016; Caro-Bruce, 2007; Hinchey, 2008) and data collection and analysis exercises prepared teachers to identify research questions that they then chose to pursue.

In our program one of the first of several teacher research projects followed the equity audit data collection and analysis. Teachers designed and implemented an equity audit action research plan to address, in some way, one area of inequity that they identified through their equity audit.

These research efforts supported teachers to unpack assumptions, examine structural barriers, and take action when their equity audit identified unequal representation on academic assessments, in extracurricular activities, in special education and gifted programs, and/or in disciplinary referrals. Research projects focused on racial inequities included studying the source of the inequities and taking action to, for example:

- initiate restorative justice processes in schools where there was disproportionate suspension of Students of Color;
- identify barriers in schools where there were disproportionately fewer Students of Color participating in higher-level math courses and advocate for policies and practices that increase their identification and participation.

Claire, a white female high school instructional coach, described ways that her equity audit action project led her to unpack common assumptions and to reach out to immigrant families:

I am so pleased with the direction this project has taken my office when it comes to the way we are supporting our secondary ELL parents during the summer. This project is actively challenging the old, stereotypical adages of "ELL parents don't show up for school functions" and "They don't care about their kids", and I'm proud to have had a small part in that. I am looking forward to kicking off our first parent session in July and seeing where this project takes us.

The research process engaged teachers in ongoing critical reflection and dialogue using multiple perspectives of knowledge and experience, including those that help teachers to examine and challenge oppressive hegemonic structures of power and privilege (in both current and historical contexts) and those that offer opportunities for developing commitments to social justice. This critical reflection and dialogue helped teachers to develop their critical consciousness and to use critical pedagogical approaches – to challenge dominant discourses – with their students. Scaffolding the critical reflection process with reflection prompts supported teachers to pose questions that arose for them as they went about their work, as exemplified by Karen, a white female 2nd grade teacher, as she wrote a problem-posing narrative in response to the prompt, "How does critical pedagogy come into play as you develop and explore your research topic?":

The first ethical dilemma that comes to my mind is the question of equity in race/ethnicity in my classroom. Because my class was grouped the way it was, 15 of my 18 students are Hispanic. There is very little diversity in my room. Is this fair? At the beginning of the school year, I had a sign outside my door with each child's first and last name(s) on it, just like I have done every other year; yet this year I was told to take it down before our Open House because parents would not want to see that their child was in a class of primarily Hispanic students. Similar comments have been made to me by many staff members in my school and by many parents in the community, and it causes me to want to do something about it. Critical pedagogy has been in my mind since the start of this school year, as I have wanted to challenge the dominating beliefs and practices held by others in my school community. Why is it that a class of primarily Hispanic students should be looked at as the "low" class by a school? Why is it surprising when they make astounding progress? How could these viewpoints from adults cause students to doubt themselves and feel self-conscious about themselves as readers?

Feedback by faculty on teachers' research reflections offered another opportunity to examine assumptions. An example of the feedback questions we posed to teachers was this (partial) response to the narrative above:

When you say, "There is very little diversity in my room," what do you mean by that? Are all the Hispanic students from one particular culture, or is the term "Hispanic" used to describe students from a wider range of Spanish-speaking countries? What is it about being in a class predominantly made up of students with Spanish-speaking heritage that is assumed to concern parents? You say that your class was "grouped the way it was." What were the considerations that went into grouping these students for this class? We know schools sometimes do this based on ability. Is that the case here? If so, are there issues to explore here related to problems with conflating race/language/ethnicity with ability?

Through engagement in the teacher research process, teachers gained a more informed voice; they began to trust what they know about providing appropriate instruction to their students despite the pressures they feel from state mandates. Teachers responded with insights about the profound impact their research experiences had on learning and significant insights about their own practice as a result of the experience. Their own empowering professional development experiences led teachers to then create empowering experiences for their own students. By carrying out research with (not on) their students as research collaborators, teachers built connections with their students and supported students' own capacities for critical reflection and critical consciousness. As Maxine Greene emphasized:

Rather than posing dilemmas to students or presenting models of expertise, the caring teacher tries to look through students' eyes, to struggle with them as subjects in search of their own project, their own ways of making sense of the world. Reflectiveness, even logical thinking, remains important; but the point of cognitive development is not to gain an increasingly complete grasp of abstract principles. It is to interpret, from as many vantage points as possible, lived experience, the ways there are of being in the world. (Greene, 1988, p. 197)

Angelo, a white male 1st grade teacher, wrote a reflection at the end of the program that demonstrates the way teacher research can inspire new understandings and new efforts toward equity:

My inquiry stance is centered on creating more equitable learning conditions for English Language Learners. It was through the process of completing the research project this year that I developed the stance. Looking at cooperative grouping strategies to engage ELLs was really just a starting point. Observing students, interviewing them and conducting my own various forms of research and journaling led me to caring about and addressing issues far beyond just getting these students engaged in everyday instruction. This guided me to look at more systemic issues they faced and is what ultimately piqued my interest in working with city government. The work I was doing for the research project became the basis for other projects so that I could continue working on understanding the multiple perspectives of my extremely diverse groups of students and doing my best to address them through the culturally relevant framework.

While the tools of critical reflection (including the teacher research process) can be time-consuming and may well be a significant shift in the ways that teachers go about their daily practice, teachers on the whole have found the tools to be valuable assets in their teaching practice, as exemplified by Dustin's reflective feedback:

This program has forced me to reflect on my practice in ways that are genuine and take me back to the social justice roots of my practice. It is a lot of work but it is not busy work; it has made a visible impact on my practice. It forces me to pause, reflect, and think deeply instead of constantly running from one day, lesson, or class to the next.

The culturally relevant teaching project was another example of a specific teacher research experience that teachers engaged in to hone their critical and culturally relevant pedagogy skills related to their curriculum.

Culturally Relevant Teaching Project (CRP)

We designed this project to encourage teachers to be creative with their curriculum content in designing meaningful, culturally relevant learning opportunities for the students in their classroom and/or school. The curriculum design had to address the five themes identified in Brown-Jeffy and Cooper's (2011) conceptual framework of CRP: identity and achievement, equity and excellence, developmental appropriateness, teaching the whole child, and student-teacher relationships. The design also had to address the three culturally relevant pedagogy criteria that Ladson-Billings (1995) identifies: academic success; cultural competence; and critical consciousness.

Of course, many teachers have specific content or units that "must be covered," so this project offered opportunities to reconfigure the content into a broader culturally relevant framework that moved beyond "covering content" for the test; the project challenged teachers to consider how to teach students through the teaching of content. We asked teachers to do this work in their classroom/school/community – to puzzle out how they could move students beyond "covering the content" to ways of "uncovering the content" within a culturally relevant framework. For example, teachers could redesign a unit that created opportunities for students to grapple with broader social and cultural issues that impacted their own lives in ways that would help them make sense of and connect personally to the curriculum. The project required that teachers 1) identify the content and/or learning goals of the project; 2) create a lesson that fit within one or more of the following frameworks: multicultural, culturally relevant, and/or anti-bias; and 3) assess student learning formatively (collecting student data about the learning process and their learning throughout the project). Teachers self-assessed their projects using the Cain rubric (Table 1 in chapter 1) and a culturally relevant pedagogy rubric that we created to assess Ladson-Billings' criteria (Table 1).

Table 1. Culturally Relevant Pedagogy Through a Critically Race Theory Lens Rubric

	Rudimentary	**Proficient**	**Exemplary**
Academic Achievement	Proficiency is expected of and encouraged in most students, defined by a range of assessments	Proficiency is expected of and encouraged in all students, defined by a range of assessments	Excellence is expected of and demonstrated by all students, defined by a range of assessments
Cultural Competence	Teacher acknowledges that all students have culture and incorporates authentic and nuanced examples of home-community cultures/ languages/ race-ethnicity in the classroom	Teacher learns from students to make regular and explicit connections between home-community and school cultures/ languages/ race/ ethnicity that honors multiple ways of being	Teacher and students engage in regular and explicit critiques of privilege, including in classrooms that are presumed to be "all white"
Critical Consciousness	Teachers create opportunities for students to develop and/ or deepen awareness of root causes of inequality	Teachers create opportunities for students to develop ideas for eliminating root causes of inequality	Teachers create opportunities for students to take actions for changing root causes of inequality

Note: Created for classroom use by View, J.L., Stribling, S.M., & DeMulder, E.K.

After reading about and discussing different frameworks for understanding culturally relevant teaching (e.g., Souto-Manning, Llerena, Martell, Maguire & Arce-Boardman, 2018; Brown-Jeffy & Cooper, 2011; Banks, 2007; Gay, 2010), we asked teachers to reflect in writing on how they would explain 'culturally relevant teaching' to a colleague over lunch in the teachers' lounge. As this white female high school family and consumer science teacher's reflection indicated, this was a more difficult task than one might think:

It's funny you should ask this, because my husband asked me the same thing a couple of weeks ago, and I stumbled over an answer. I think my answer was something along the lines of, "Well, you know.... it's teaching.... that's culturally relevant." It is such a tricky question to answer, that I'm not sure any of the texts we read this semester offered a straightforward answer to the question. Instead, each author just provided lots of examples. To put it simply, I would explain that culturally relevant pedagogy is teaching and learning that values and incorporates students' multiple identities into the classroom. It is a pedagogy that helps students make stronger connections between their lives outside the classroom and the content we teach inside the classroom.

When it came to designing and implementing their culturally relevant teaching projects, teachers chose one or more texts to read and discuss with classmates that were more specific to their classroom context and research question (e.g., Barton, Ermer, Burkett & Osbourne, 2003; Bintliff, 2011; Campano, Lytle & Cochran-Smith, 2006; Cowhey, 2006; Gutstein, 2005; Helguera, 2011; Levstik & Barton, 2010; Quintero, 2004, Schmidt & Lazar, 2011; Selwyn & Maher, 2003; Teaching Tolerance, 2014). As a result of their reading, equity audit, and research experiences, many teachers became more attuned to the limited ways their curricula connected to their students' lives, and they worked to take a more student-centered, culturally relevant approach in their teaching practice, as described here by Angelo:

The change in structure for the way instruction is received by ELL students was probably the biggest success that came out of this project, as it relates to the culturally relevant framework. Removing myself from a position of power and sharing that space with students enabled me to acknowledge, validate, and understand their individual perspectives and experiences that they bring with them to school. This was compounded by the fact that, when they were the teachers, they essentially took the stage to – for the very first time – share knowledge and experience that was important to them. This was done while still learning the content objectives. I did struggle internally at times to allow the conversation to develop and continue organically. I fought my instincts to remove myself from the level field and chime back in as the teacher in order to move through the content quicker – to keep the lesson going. The outcomes of this lesson are proof that it was necessary for me to hand over some of the power to the students.

TENSIONS AND DILEMMAS

In our experience, both faculty and teachers were challenged by some aspects of our antiracist professional development approach related to critical and culturally relevant pedagogy. Sometimes teachers' written reflections and participation in class discussions (facilitated by faculty) were somewhat superficial, and we pressed teachers to dig deeper into examining the issues, particularly around race/racism and other oppressive structural barriers in schools and society. When teachers persisted with unexamined assumptions in their writing or in comments during discussions and/or teachers diverted the discussion to other "safer" topics, we attempted to address what seemed to be resistance, and for white teachers, some degree of white fragility (DiAngelo, 2018) by encouraging continued engagement through critical reflective processes. Our scaffolding of more complex meaning-making opportunities did not always result in deeper understandings, and we can imagine that our scaffolding efforts might not have always been as effective as we would have liked. We also wondered whether, in some cases, the teacher's current meaning-making capacity was not yet conducive to full engagement with these complexities – that having difficulty with ambiguity, engaging intellectually as a "received knower" (Belenky, et al., 1997), and/ or having a deeply entrenched and unmoving set of assumptions and beliefs may have limited individuals' deeper participation. When we moved the program mostly online, more opportunities for written discussions created space for preliminary contemplation, since the discussion forums were designed to take place over a 2-week period. However, the opportunities for faculty to facilitate discussions in real time (in the earlier face-to-face version of the program) had allowed for careful scaffolding and "in the moment" support for staying engaged and on topic, and the online space limited these opportunities. The synchronous online sessions opened up these reflection/ discussion spaces to some extent, but these sessions were not ongoing and not without technological challenges. The online discussions and reflections did create more opportunities for faculty to respond individually to teachers who were struggling with an idea or who wanted more support.

In a few instances over the years, teachers confronted us on what they perceived to be our biases toward particular antiracist perspectives, and it was suggested that we should offer a more balanced set of perspectives – discussing "both sides" and giving equal time to all the ways one might view the issue (e.g., on the topic of immigration). In response, we offered some version of Robert Jones, Jr.'s quote (2015), advocating for an antiracist world: "We can disagree and still love each other, unless your disagreement is rooted in my oppression and denial of my humanity and right to exist."

Despite the growing knowledge and awareness that an antiracist professional development experience might offer, teachers must often contend with isolation, lack of support, and even resistance to their perspectives and antiracist efforts. Teachers are members of professional learning communities in their schools. Those who begin to reflect on and question the power dynamics operating within schools may not find support among peers (particularly in non-unionized settings) and may not easily practice the skills of critical pedagogy and teacher activism. At worst, professional learning communities may impose conformity and "group think" disguised as shared vision, that works against the kind of systemic critique essential to critical pedagogy. As Schön (1984) suggests:

Reflection in action is both a consequence and cause of surprise. When a member of a bureaucracy embarks on a course of reflective practice, allowing himself to experience confusion and uncertainty, subjecting his frames and theories to conscious criticism and change, he may increase his capacity to contribute to significant organizational learning, but he also becomes, by the same token, a danger to the stable system of rules and procedures within which he is expected to deliver his technical expertise. (p. 328)

CONCLUSION

In order for antiracist teacher professional development to be transformative, our experience suggests that it is crucial to establish and sustain a professional learning community with strong ongoing relationships of support – both faculty-teacher and teacher-teacher. The next chapter describes our efforts to create and sustain these relationships in our program.

REFERENCES

Adams, M., Blumenfeld, W. J., Castaneda, R., Hackman, H. W., Peters, M. L., & Zuniga, X. (2000). *Readings for diversity and social justice*. Psychology Press.

Au, W. (2007). High-stakes testing and curricular control: A qualitative metasynthesis. *Educational Researcher*, 36(5), 258–267. doi:10.3102/0013189X07306523

Au, W. (2009). *Unequal by design: High-stakes testing and the standardization of inequality*. Routledge.

Banks, J. A. (2007). Approaches to multicultural curriculum reform. In J. A. Banks & C. A. M. Banks (Eds.), *Multicultural Education: Issues and Perspectives* (6th ed., pp. 247–269). Wiley.

Barton, A. C., Ermer, J. L., Burkett, T. A., & Osborne, M. D. (2003). *Teaching science for social justice*. Teaching for Social Justice Series. Teachers College Press.

Beane, J., & Apple, M. (1995). The case for democratic schools. In M. Apple & J. Beane (Eds.), *Democratic Schools*. ASCD.

Belenky, M. F., Clinchy, B. M., Goldberger, N. R., & Tarule, J. M. (1997). Women's Ways of Knowing: The development of self, voice, and mind (10th Anniversary ed.). Basic Books.

Bintliff, A. V. (2011). *Re-engaging disconnected youth: Transformative learning through restorative and social justice education*. Peter Lang.

Booth, W. C., Colomb, G. G., Williams, J. M., Bizup, J., & FitzGerald, W. T. (2016). *The craft of research* (4th ed.). University of Chicago Press.

Brookfield, S. D. (1995/2017). *Becoming a critically reflective teacher*. Wiley.

Brown, M. K., & Carnoy, M. (2005). *Whitewashing race: the myth of a color-blind society*. University of California Press. https://www.jstor.org/stable/10.1525/j.ctt1pn8hj

Brown-Jeffy, S., & Cooper, J. E. (2011). Toward a conceptual framework of culturally relevant pedagogy: An overview of the conceptual and theoretical literature. *Teacher Education Quarterly*, *38*(1), 65–84.

Bustamante, R. M., Nelson, J. A., & Onwuegbuzie, A. J. (2009). Assessing schoolwide cultural competence: Implications for school leadership preparation. *Educational Administration Quarterly*, *45*(5), 793–827. doi:10.1177/0013161X09347277

Campano, G. (2007). Immigrant students and literacy: Reading, writing, and remembering. Teachers College Press.

Campano, G., Lytle, S. L., & Cochran-Smith, M. (2006). Immigrant students and literacy: Reading, writing, and remembering. Teachers College Press.

Caro-Bruce, C. (2007). *Creating equitable classrooms through action research* (1st ed.). Corwin.

Ciardiello, A. V. (2004). Democracy's young heroes: An instructional model of critical literacy practices. *The Reading Teacher*, *58*(2), 138–147. doi:10.1598/RT.58.2.2

Cochran-Smith, M., & Lytle, S. L. (2009). *Inquiry as stance: Practitioner research for the next generation*. Teachers College Press.

Cowhey, M. (2006). *Black ants and Buddhists: Thinking critically and teaching differently in the primary grades*. Stenhouse.

Darder, A. (2015). *Culture and power in the classroom: Educational foundations for the schooling of bicultural students*. Routledge.

Darling-Hammond, L., & Carver-Thomas, D. (2017). Teacher turnover: Why it matters and what we can do about it. *Learning Policy Institute*. https://learningpolicyinstitute.org/product/teacher-turnover-report

DiAngelo, R., & Dyson, M. E. (2018). White fragility: Why it's so hard for white people to talk about racism (Reprint ed.). Beacon Press.

Dodman, S. L., DeMulder, E. K., View, J. L., Swalwell, K., Stribling, S., Ra, S., & Dallman, L. (2019). Equity Audits as a Tool of Critical Data-Driven Decision Making: Preparing Teachers to See Beyond Achievement Gaps and Bubbles. *Action in Teacher Education, 41*(1), 4–22. doi:10.1080/01626620.2018.1536900

Dumas, M. (2014). 'Losing an arm': Schooling as a site of Black suffering. *Race, Ethnicity and Education, 17*(1), 1–29. doi:10.1080/13613324.2013.850412

Duncan-Andrade, J. M. R., & Morrell, E. (2008). *The art of critical pedagogy: Possibilities for moving from theory to practice in urban schools*. Peter Lang.

Freire, P. (1970). Pedagogy of the oppressed. *Continuum*.

Freire, P., & Macedo, D. (2000). *Pedagogy of the oppressed, 30th anniversary edition* (M. B. Ramos, Trans.). *Continuum*.

Gannon-Slater, N., La Londe, P. G., Crenshaw, H. L., Evans, M. E., Greene, J. C., & Schwandt, T. A. (2017). Advancing equity in accountability and organizational cultures of data use. *Journal of Educational Administration, 55*(4), 361–375. doi:10.1108/JEA-09-2016-0108

Gay, G. (2010). *Culturally responsive teaching* (2nd ed.). Teachers College Press.

Generett, G. G., & Olson, A. M. (2020). The stories we tell: How merit narratives undermine success for urban youth. *Urban Education, 55*(3), 394–423. doi:10.1177/0042085918817342

Giroux, H. A. (2012). *Education and the crisis of public values: Challenging the assault of teachers, students, & public education*. Peter Lang.

Giroux, H. A. (2020). *On critical pedagogy*. Bloomsbury Press.

Goethe, J. W., & MacIntyre, C. F. (1957). *Goethe's Faust, part 1: New American version*. New Directions.

Gorski, P. C. (2016). Poverty and the ideological imperative: A call to unhook from deficit and grit ideology and to strive for structural ideology in teacher education. *Journal of Education for Teaching, 42*(4), 378–386. doi:10.1080/02607476.2016.1215546

Gorski, P. C., & Swalwell, K. (2015). Equity literacy for all. *Educational Leadership, 72*(6), 34–40. http://www.ascd.org/publications/educational-leadership/mar15/vol72/num06/Equity-Literacy-for-All.aspx

Greene, M. (1988). *The dialectic of freedom*. Teachers College Press.

Groenke, S. L. (2010). Seeing, inquiring, witnessing: Using the equity audit in practitioner inquiry to rethink inequity in public schools. *English Education, 43*(1), 83–96. https://www.jstor.org/stable/23017086

Gutstein, E. (2005). *Reading and writing the world with mathematics: Toward a pedagogy of social justice*. Routledge.

Hansen, D. T. (2017). *The Teacher and the world: A study of cosmopolitanism as education*. Routledge.

Harro, B. (2000). The Cycle of Liberation. In M. X. Zuniga (Ed.), *Readings for diversity and social justice* (pp. 618–625). Routledge.

Harry, B., & Klingner, J. K. (2014). *Why are so many minority students in special education?: Understanding race & disability in schools*. Teachers College Press.

Helguera, P. (2011). *Education for socially engaged art*. Jorge Pinto Books Inc.

Hinchey, P. H. (2008). *Action research primer* (Vol. 24). Peter Lang.

Hooks, B. (2014). *Teaching to transgress*. Routledge.

Janks, H. (2000). Domination, access, diversity and design: A synthesis for critical literacy. *Educational Review, 52*(2), 175–186. doi:10.1080/713664035

Jones, R. [@SonofBaldwin]. (2015, August 18). *We can disagree and still love each other unless your disagreement is rooted in my oppression and denial of my...* [Tweet]. Twitter.com.

Kegan, R. (1982). The evolving self: Problem and process in human development (Illustrated ed.). Harvard University Press.

Kegan, R. (1998). in over our heads: The mental demands of modern life (4th ed.). Harvard University Press.

Kendi, I. X. (2019). *How to be an antiracist* (1st ed.). One World.

Kincheloe, J. L. (2008). *Critical pedagogy primer*. Peter Lang.

Kincheloe, J. L. (2018). What are we doing here? Building a framework for teaching. In E. B. Hilty (Ed.), *Thinking about schools* (pp. 227–248). Routledge., doi:10.4324/9780429495670-20

Ladson-Billings, G. (1995). Toward a Theory of Culturally Relevant Pedagogy. *American Educational Research Journal*, *32*(3), 465–491. doi:10.3102/00028312032003465

Ladson-Billings, G. (2006, October). From the achievement gap to the education debt: Understanding achievement in U.S. Schools. *Educational Researcher*, *35*(7), 3–12. https://www.jstor.org/stable/3876731

Levine, D. (1995). Building a vision of curriculum reform. In D. Levine, R. Lowe, B. Peterson, & R. Tenorio (Eds.), *Rethinking schools: An agenda for change* (pp. 52–60). The New Press.

Levstik, L. S., & Barton, K. C. (2010). *Doing history: Investigating with children in elementary and middle schools*. Routledge.

Lewison, M., Flint, A. S., & Van Sluys, K. (2002). Taking on critical literacy: The journey of newcomers and novices. *Language Arts*, *79*(5), 382–392. https://www.jstor.org/stable/41483258

Mandinach, E. B., Friedman, J. M., & Gummer, E. S. (2015). How can schools of education help to build educators' capacity to use data? A systemic view of the issue. *Teachers College Record*, *117*(4), 1–50.

McKenzie, K. B., & Skrla, L. (2011). *Using equity audits in the classroom to reach and teach all students*. Sage Publications.

McLaren, P. (2015). *Pedagogy of insurrection: From resurrection to revolution*. Peter Lang.

Mehta, J. (2015, April 7) *The problem with grit*. Harvard Graduate School of Education. https://www.gse.harvard.edu/news/15/04/problem-grit

Mezirow, J. (2000). Learning as Transformation. In *The Jossey-Bass Higher and Adult Education Series*. Jossey-Bass Publishers. (Manuscript submitted for publication)

Moll, L. C., Amanti, C., Neff, D., & Gonzalez, N. (1992). Funds of knowledge for teaching: Using a qualitative approach to connect homes and classrooms. *Theory into Practice*, *31*(2), 132–141. doi:10.1080/00405849209543534

Osei-Kofi, N., Shahjahan, R. A., & Patton, L. D. (2010). Centering social justice in the study of higher education: The challenges and possibilities for institutional change. *Equity & Excellence in Education*, *43*(3), 326–340. doi:10.1080/10665684.2010.483639

Pollock, M. (2004). *Colormute: Race talk dilemmas in an American school*. Princeton University Press.

Quintero, E. P. (2004). *Problem-posing with multicultural children's literature: Developing critical early childhood curricula*. Peter Lang.

Rabinowitz, K., Emamdjomeh, A., & Meckler, L. (2019). How the nation's growing racial diversity is changing our schools. *Washington Post*. https://www.washingtonpost.com/graphics/2019/local/school-diversity-data/

Rodriguez, M. (2012). "But they just can't do it": Reconciling teacher expectations in Latino students. *Journal of Cases in Educational Leadership*, *15*(1), 25–31. doi:10.1177/1555458912442605

Roy, A. (2002). *Power Politics* (2nd ed.). South End Press.

Saranson, S. (1999). *Teaching as a performing art*. Teachers College Press.

Scherff, L., & Spector, K. (2010). *Culturally relevant pedagogy: Clashes and confrontations*. R&L Education.

Scheurich, J. J., & Skrla, L. (2003). *Leadership for equity and excellence*. Corwin Press.

Schmidt, P. R., & Lazar, A. M. (Eds.). (2011). *Practicing what we teach: How culturally responsive literacy classrooms make a difference*. Teachers College Press.

Schön, D. A. (1984). *The reflective practitioner: How professionals think in action*. Basic Books.

Schön, D. A. (2017). *The reflective practitioner: How professionals think in action*. Routledge.

Selwyn, D., & Maher, J. (2003). *History in the present tense: Engaging students through inquiry and action*. Heinemann.

Shor, I. (2012). *Empowering education: Critical teaching for social change*. University of Chicago Press.

Shor, I., & Freire, P. (1987). *A pedagogy for liberation: Dialogues on transforming education*. Bergin & Garvey.

Sklra, L., Scheurich, J. J., Garcia, J., & Nolly, G. (2004). Equity audits: A practical leadership tool for developing equitable and excellent schools. *Educational Administration Quarterly*, *40*(1), 133–161. doi:10.1177/0013161X03259148

Sockett, H. (2012). *Knowledge and virtue in teaching and learning: The primacy of dispositions*. Routledge.

Souto-Manning, M., Llerena, C. L., Martell, J., Maguire, A. S., & Arce-Boardman, A. (2018). *No more culturally irrelevant teaching*. Heinemann.

Stitzlein, S. M. (2018). Teaching for hope in the era of grit. *Teachers College Record*, *120*(3).

Teaching Tolerance. (2014). *Critical practices for anti-bias education*. http://www.tolerance.org/sites/default/files/general/PDA%20Critical%20Practices.pdf

Vélez-Ibáñez, C. G. (2018). Language hegemonies and their discontents: History, theory, bilingualism, and funds of knowledge. *Association of Mexican American Educators Journal*, *12*(2), 20–43. doi:10.24974/amae.12.2.393

Wink, J. (2011). *Critical pedagogy: Notes from the real world* (4th ed.). Pearson.

Chapter 4
Teaching/Learning Relational Dynamic

ABSTRACT

The authors contend that relationships are the basis for the teacher transformation that can occur in antiracist teacher professional development. Because self-understandings are developed contextually in relationship with others, sensitive instructor attention created the trust that was essential for teachers to critically examine long held assumptions about race, themselves, and their students. Furthermore, instructors designed the program to build trust among the teachers as teachers additionally learned through interactions with each other. Intentional community building also developed the community of practice that allowed for teachers' gradual participation in the critical work of antiracist education both in the program and in their own classrooms.

I think the strength of the program, [was] hearing from people who were not in my school division, who grew up and were educated in different contexts, coming together under the common umbrella of the [master's degree] program. Because we are all there for different reasons, how we each interpreted and interacted in that avenue, and getting those different perspectives, was really eye-opening. It really gave me a greater sense of the commonalities of the struggle, and the differences of the struggle, that we were all trying to address. --Alumni interview

DOI: 10.4018/978-1-7998-5649-8.ch004

INTRODUCTION

They learned through their own self-reflection. They learned in dialogue with each other. They learned from the stories and writings of others, and, although they learned from us, we mostly acted as midwives guiding them to the next stage of their social development as P -12 educators. The relationships we shared with our teachers, and they with each other, were fundamental in the transformations that we endeavored to bring to life.

Although all teaching and learning is enhanced by the development of positive teacher-student relationships, transformative teaching and learning are dependent upon them. This is because transformation is radically more complex than the simple transmission of information. It is not the accumulation of facts but a change in perspective and behavior.

Philosopher Paul Holmer (1978), distinguished between knowledge "about" and knowledge "of." He lectured on esteemed experts who knew everything there was to know "about" love, i.e., how heart rates change when seeing a beloved, how love may wax and wane, how love can be categorized as romantic, platonic, etc. They may even know all there is to know about great lovers and love poetry. But, alas, these experts did not know how to love, how to feel love or how to give love. They had no knowledge "of" love. This is not to imply that knowledge "of" is a simple matter of application. Instead, knowledge "of" a subject means that it becomes part of who one is; it becomes part of one's psyche and one's way of being.

The goal of our professional development program was not only to make our teachers knowledgeable "about" racism and inequity, but to impart knowledge "of" racism and inequity (particularly for the predominantly white teachers), such that their stance toward these issues was constitutive to who they would become and informative to how they would relate to others. It would change the way they understood themselves and others. Additionally, these changed beliefs and perspectives would result in new behaviors and stances toward the world.

Mezirow (1990) contends that such transformation is a result of critical self-reflection in which one critiques the assumptions that underlie belief and behavior. Critically examining these assumptions can lead to transforming one's perspective and way of being. The apex of adult development for Merizow is to be able to engage in such reflection, and then change one's perspective to see and accept differences, be more inclusive and accepting of others' perspectives, and be able to hold all of these differing views together in an integrated understanding of oneself and of one's relationship to others.

Mezirow (1990) cautions, however, that such critical self-reflection can be threatening to one's sense of identity. Identity is not a static, genetically determined construct. Instead, identity is developed in relationship to others and is constantly being renegotiated as individuals interact with their physical and social environments (Siegel, 2012). When an experience or new idea is too different from, or contrary to, fundamental self-beliefs, one's sense of self is challenged. To avoid the existential discomfort such new knowledge can elicit, people tend to ignore, deny, or manipulate the alternate view in such a way that it preserves current self-understandings. They organize their thinking and perception in a way that preserves their current sense of self, therefore relieving cognitive dissonance.

This is where the importance of relationships and the communities they constituted came into play. For our program learning *was* self-creation, co-creation, and transformation. It was knowledge "of", not simply knowledge "about."

This unique learning objective required unique teaching methods. Traditional, didactic pedagogical methods did not suffice. Teachers were not transformed on the basis of facts regarding differences, nor did they own such an "other"-oriented perspective simply because they were told to do so. Instead, their process of transformation was facilitated by participating in a critically reflective community of practice (Lave & Wegner, 1991, Wegner, 2011).

Several terms required emphasis as we applied them to our program. First, a community of practice must have a "shared practice" (Wegner, 2011). All our teachers were currently practicing educators at the time they learned with us. Together, we shared a teaching practice.

Beyond our teaching practices, however, our program's practice was even more specifically defined. We were a community of *critically reflecting* teachers. Together we critically examined issues of race, inequity, and social justice. We considered how these crucial issues affected us as educators, how they affected our classrooms and educational systems, and how they affected the students we taught. Our program "practice" was critical reflection.

In describing communities of practice, Wenger (2011) explains that a community of practice "shares [a] repertoire of resources: experiences, stories, tools, ways of addressing recurring problems." (p. 2). Our program repertoire included critical readings and exercises such as the equity audit, identity web, and student research; and experiences (field trips to the legislature, local museums, our teaching practices).

The most influential component of our repertoire, however, was our sharing our reflections in conversation. When asked how she changed through the program, Charlotte, a white high school foreign language teacher, commented:

The main influence of the program...[was that it] allowed for a lot of conversations and a lot of reading and delving into topics that I hadn't really spent a lot of time in before. Just having open and honest conversations about different things like privilege, the equity gap, and really having an active role. Participating in that.

Charlotte highlighted the second essential characteristic of learning in a community of practice. Learning and, in our case, transformation occurred through gradual *participation* (Lave & Wegner, 1991). Knowledge "of" is realized only through active engagement. Teachers must do the work. Each of them must participate in a continual process of critical reflection. As they were exposed to new material regarding race and (in)equity, they had to reflect on that material, work to apply it to their practice, then reflect again on its application. It is this engagement, this participation in our shared practice, that enabled our students to be transformed and learn our program's language; discourse; and stories of antiracism, equity, and social justice.

Finally, this "learning/transformation" was a collaborative project facilitated by supportive trusting relationships in a community. These relationships provided the safety and confidence – yet challenge – to critically self-reflect and develop a more inclusive and other-oriented perspective. Transformative teacher educators had to be facilitators of learning and of development, rather than disseminators of knowledge.

Some have referred to this type of teaching as "mentoring" (Dyson & Plunkett, 2014; Southern, 2007) – a term that suggests a more personal engaged relationship. Unlike traditional teaching relationships in which teachers have all the power (i.e., they determine the curriculum, the appropriate response, and the standard for success), a mentoring relationship is based on shared authority. The mentor does not exert power over her students but instead asserts her authority as a knowledgeable guide, responsive to the mentee's unique needs and shared goals. To be effective, the relationship must be built on trust – trust that is earned through regular non-judgmental conversation and support. Using sensitive questioning within the safety of the relationship, mentors can challenge mentees to critically examine their perspectives and assumptions. This safety and connectedness enables the mentee to risk an honest assessment of self and minimizes the threat to the mentee's identity.

The relationship to the trusted mentor gives confidence to the newly emerging self as it struggles to integrate new understandings and points of view.

This kind of mentoring relationship was not the only learning relationship our teachers experienced. They also learned from each other. As the opening teacher quote suggests, they journeyed together as a cohort, exploring the boundaries and foundations of self, of others, and of society. Also, like the mentoring relationship, cohort relationships had to be built on trust and a mutual commitment to work together on their transformative project. In an end-of-term reflection, one teacher commented:

Another necessity for me [was] the daily phone communication that continued to volley between various members of our cohort. It was helpful to hear from others who had questions or thoughts about the projects or just a word of encouragement. It was rare that a group text re: one of the two projects wasn't showing up in my texts. The support and encouragement that this group lent to one another was amazing.

Although our program goal was the transformation of our teachers, we endeavored to enlighten and embolden our teachers for the sake of their P-12 students. Just as our work with teachers was relational, so was their work with their students. As our work influenced teacher identity and self-understanding, so their relationships influenced student identity and self-understandings.

The relationships our teachers formed with their students was fundamental to their students' development and academic outcomes. These relationships played an integral role in many aspects of children's development, including their academic, motivational, and social-emotional development. Student outcomes were also affected, as students who have positive teacher-student relationships perform better academically than students who do not enjoy such relationships (Briggs, 2012; Mendes, 2003; Heick, 2015; Rimm-Kaufman & Sandilos, 2016; Townsend, 2012).

Student identity development is another outcome that is influenced by the teacher-student relationship. In his meta-analysis, Cornelius-White (2007) found that positive secure teacher-student relationships formed the basis for the development of healthy self-concepts. Teachers are the key to this process, as their relationships with students are the most influential school resource for student learning, social-emotional development, and identity development.

School-aged children come to school with a sense of self as influenced by their early childhood relationships and experiences (e.g., Derman-Sparks & Edwards, 2009; Reschke, 2019; Swanson, Cunningham, Youngblood &

Spencer, 2009). Then, in time, they develop other selves in response to their expanding experiences, differing relationships, and various social roles. Eventually, students must integrate these various selves into a harmonious, coherent identity for healthy development.

At first glance, such identity integration might appear to threaten students' multiple identities for fear of collapsing the various selves into a homogenous whole (Tate, 2012). Integrating identities, though, is not the same as homogenizing them. In this case, "integration" does not mean that students must give up certain dimensions of their identity for the sake of other aspects, or assimilation. For example, a student need not surrender his understanding of himself as Latinx in order to understand himself as American. Instead, individuals must integrate their multiple self-understandings into a coherent whole or, as Tate (2012) urges, they must integrate their self-understanding into a "universal, complex, subtle, considered adult" identity (p. 209).

Because self-understandings are developed contextually in relationship with others, integrating one's senses of self may be more challenging for students who come from cultures that are in the numeric minority at their school. Instead of encouraging integration, the differing cultures may result in a clash among students' multiple identities, possibly leading to cultural dissonance and the invalidation of a student's unique cultural background.

Pearce (2015) describes the goal of "identity integration" as one in which a student's unique cultural identity becomes joined with the prevailing school culture.To accomplish this, students need educational experiences that value both their unique cultural background and the local culture within which they live and learn (p. 186). They need relationships with teachers who are appreciative of their cultural differences.

Teacher-student relationships and classroom environments that become the basis for such positive identity development and integration are characterized by "a high degree of agency and communion" (den Brok & van Tartwijk, 2015, p. 311). Teachers show empathy for their students and seek a friendly understanding connection to them. These teacher-student relationships and environments are characterized by warmth and sensitivity to student needs and characteristics. Teachers are "attuned" to the child as they caringly respond to each child's unique requirements and individualities (Siegel, 2012).

Being attuned and responsive in this manner is a challenging requirement. Even if the teacher and student share similar cultural backgrounds, creating such environments and establishing sensitive relationships is demanding, as teachers must navigate their own internal cultural contexts, the external context of the school and classroom, and the differing internal contexts of their students. The process becomes even more complicated when the teacher is not aware of her students' internal contexts because of the cultural differences between them. Unaware that they lack an accurate understanding of their students, teachers relate to students on the basis of their assumptions and cultural misperceptions. Lacking this cultural understanding and sensitivity, teachers cannot create learning environments or establish teacher-student relationships that value the unique characteristics of each student. Thus, they put the successful integration of students' identity with the prevailing local culture at risk.

This, then, was the ultimate goal of our program: the transformation of teachers who were able to negotiate their own internal context as they developed an awareness and empathy for the unique backgrounds and identities of their students. We endeavored to create sensitive, appreciative teachers who could establish growth-enhancing, positive identity-developing relationships with their P-12 students.

BUILDING RELATIONAL LEARNING DYNAMICS WITHIN OUR PROGRAM

Brown's (2004) research indicates that the method one uses to structure and deliver transformative curricula is more influential in developing cultural awareness than the curricula's content itself. The primary structural imperative for our transformative program was building a learning community of practice in which teachers felt safe, supported, and invested in their learning and that of their colleagues.

Feeling Safe

Because our program intended to be transformative, teachers had to feel a degree of "safety" as members of the community. They had to feel able to risk honest critical self-examination. They had to feel free to disclose their thoughts to program instructors and cohort peers. Even before that, they had to feel psychologically safe to accept new insight for themselves. Critically examining self can be a vulnerable experience. Without proper psychological priming and reassurance, teachers might avoid consideration of uncomfortable social inequities and retreat to the comfortable, familiar way of looking at self and others.

To increase our teachers' sense of security when confronting diverse perspectives, we first checked our own assumptions and acknowledged that our teachers had varying levels of, and capacities for, self-understanding. Each began their transformative journey from a different starting point and with differing background experiences and perspectives. We tried not to judge them on where they were in the self-reflection process: our goal was growth. We equally applauded a teacher who moved from a 3 to a 5 on a hypothetical ten-point scale of critical consciousness, as we did a teacher who moved from an 8 to a 9.

As importantly, we also expressed this reality to teachers at the program's outset. "Where you are and what you think is okay. Let's talk about this." Explicitly expressing our acceptance was essential and communicated that teachers were safe in sharing their experiences and perspectives – whatever they were. We did not want the instructor-teacher relationship to be endangered by a sincere expression of teacher thought.

Similarly, when asking teachers to engage in potentially identity-intimidating exercises, we first primed their experience with appropriate expectations. We cautioned them that some of the program exercises and conversations would be discomforting. Again, we reassured them that the possible uneasiness was normal and that each teacher's response was uniquely personal and equally valid. There were no right or wrong answers – just an honest reflection of where one was. When interviewed about her experience in the program, Claire, a white ESOL instructional coach, remarked:

That's what the work is. We were always being reminded that it's messy. There's no one answer. As much as it's personal, it's also trying to figure out how it translates into interactions that you have outside of [the program]. So it was just the reassurance that the uncomfortableness was normal. .... And it's okay that you are feeling a certain way or you're not. Your thinking doesn't look like anybody else's thinking.

Deemphasizing grades and grading was another way that we tried to reassure our students and also focus them on the program's priority of critical self-reflection and growth. Everyone could earn an A. When asked, "how do we get a high mark in this course?" we repeated the mantra of sincere reflection. When asked, "how long should our paper be?" we responded, "long enough to answer the prompt." The goal was critical self-reflection – not "right" answers or fitting a standardized rubric.

Being Challenged

Making our teachers feel safe and supported, however, did not mean that we helped them avoid uneasiness. Instead, we strove to provoke them throughout the program. Critical reflection is meant to challenge self-understandings (Merizow, 1990). We expected it to be uncomfortable, and we continually challenged our teachers to confront assumptions and perspectives. Michelle, a white female elementary school teacher, remembered an instructor saying, "It's going to be uncomfortable. You have to be uncomfortable to talk about it [race]". She also recounted that:

They kept us on our toes. You never quite knew what they were going to ask, but I always anticipated that they were going to ask me something to make me squirm. I felt like that was the learning part. Asking me a question that I knew the answer to wasn't their purpose. Their purpose was to push us into that uncomfortable [space] and talk about things that we might not normally talk about.

Integrating diverse and perhaps contrasting perspectives into current self-understandings was hard work. Claire, the white ESOL instructional coach, commented on the difficulty:

The hard part of having to look at some things, some folks in your life, the way you were raised...and things you surround yourself with...Just knowing that all of these things over the course of your last 30 years have gone into creating your identity. This [integration] is not work that can be done overnight. It's a process. Each time you question something, you put yourself into a place to reflect [on] whether you changed your mind or not. That's what it is. That's what the work is...." and, "I think a lot of the teachers in my cohort, myself included, are fixers. We want to just come in and fix something. We want that easy solution. Like, what's the answer? I know [inequity] is an issue. I just need to know what to do. This process of becoming more responsive and equitable is not an easy fix. It's not a quick fix.

Challenging existing assumptions and perspectives was an essential curricular feature, but, as Claire's comment makes clear, supporting teachers through such challenges was equally important. Without careful guidance and coaching, exposure to diversity can lead to intolerance (Skelton, 2015). Unsettled and unsure how to integrate differing perspectives – in the absence of a "quick fix" – teachers may deflect recognition of such important issues as inequity, racism, and social responsibility. Then, attempting to justify the deflection, they may insist on the primacy of their own orientations, thus reinforcing their prejudice. In diabolical contrast to program goals, the possibility of this retrenchment made support through the critical process urgently vital.

We provided practical in-the-moment guidance to our teachers as they navigated the unease of critical reflection. Again, Claire commented,

You don't want to offend. You don't want to say something that is misrepresenting what you're trying to communicate. All of that makes you uncomfortable.... And if somebody said something that was not as sensitive as it could have been or just needed to be rephrased to have a better understanding among the group, our professors were really quick to step in and say, 'so what you're saying is this', or 'what I hear you saying is this', 'is that what you're trying to communicate' or 'this is completely normal and this person has written about it, here's a video that we can watch about it'. It [the guidance] really helped that unease that - that uncomfortableness.

Trust

Engaging in the critical process *with others* had both individual and relational consequences. The stated intended outcome was confidence in reformed teacher identities that enabled social action on behalf of students and the education establishment. But the shared experience of challenge, reflection, and response – going through the process together – also had fundamental essential consequences for the relationships that supported that change. It built trust.

Trust was fundamental to our program and fundamental to our teachers' development. Teachers needed to trust to risk deep assessments of self. Teachers needed to trust that the challenge was fair and worthwhile. They needed to trust that their community would support their journey without qualms or expulsion from the group.

Risking vulnerability, but then experiencing its resolution with the guidance of others, engenders trust in those others (Gillespie & Mann, 2004). Our confidence in their ability to handle the unsettling learning opportunities we created enabled them to risk the discomfort that their honest reflection might have caused. Our reassurance as they struggled with new questions encouraged them to continue. Finally, the confidence they developed by having gone through the process showed that they could trust us to guide their learning. In response to, "What did you most appreciate about the program?" Charlotte, the white high school, foreign language teacher, said:

The support of the program...a sense of feeling supported and being able to accomplish all these things." The process of sensitive challenge, responsive guidance, and new confidence helped create trusted relationships in which teachers came to know that they could risk and grow.

Instructor-Teacher Relationships

At its most individual and practical level, providing support through the unsettling discomfort required responsive availability, sensitive feedback, and knowing each student. We all taught every class, participated in online discussions, regularly met one-to-one with teachers, but encouraged teachers to contact us with questions and concerns and responded with a personal message.

We worked as a team – at everything. We taught as a team, planned as a team, provided feedback as a team, and discussed teacher needs and progress as a team. This team approach allowed us to be more sensitive to, available for, and in tune with each teacher.

The benefit of our team approach is that each of us, of course, has a unique personality and brought different abilities, experience, and perspectives to bear on our interactions with teachers. As a result, teachers might have been naturally drawn to one of us or another. It also provided multiple models for teachers to observe. Although this required more time and effort, the presence of our entire instructional team allowed students access to whichever instructor they felt they could most relate to.

Our team approach also allowed us to know and work with all teachers throughout the entire program. There were no gaps in knowing what happened last semester or in other classes. We walked the entire program with our teachers and were able to facilitate their progress, course by course, term by term. In addition to teaching every class together, we also met at least weekly to discuss teachers, their work, their growth, and their needs. Altogether, this helped provide a unified and consistent set of expectations and communication for our teachers.

Although we taught all classes together, we rotated the mentor role each semester. This allowed for a closer relationship between mentor and mentee and enabled each of us to provide more focused attention and detailed feedback to our own group of teachers. Lesley, a Biracial Latinx elementary school teacher, who identifies herself as white, commented:

I started to read their comments and read their feedback, and I tried to model or mimic what they were doing, so that I could get that practice. I think, by the end, all of us had grown a lot and we all were doing a much better job.

The rotating mentorship also allowed each of us to know teachers in a one-on-one relationship – and them to know us. Many factors and personal characteristics would have been influential in how teachers related to us. Some teachers may have been drawn to an instructor's calm demeanor, another to an instructor's, "Tell it like it is" approach. Some may have connected to an instructor because they both had been elementary school teachers or because they shared other background experience.

Despite the multiple reasons one is drawn to another, we did observe some consistent patterns in how our teachers related to each of us based on our race. First, we observed that teachers tended to prefer a mentoring relationship with a same raced instructor. On one occasion, a white teacher requested not to be paired with the Black instructor. The teacher had had many positive encounters with the instructor, and appeared to have a genuine liking for her but feared saying the wrong thing and being misunderstood.

Similarly, we observed that teachers expected us to "get them" when our races matched and to make exceptions for their lack of insight based on our presumed common understanding. This was an assumption that we had to consider. Were we too sympathetic in understanding a shallow reflection because we personally related to a teacher's race and background experience? Did we push *every*one enough?

At times this caused friction, as in the case of a teacher who was in conflict with her same-raced mentor. She resented that her lack of growth was not excused by this mentor. As she did not express the same frustration with instructors of a different race, it was sensed that she thought she should be given a pass based on belonging to the same racial group.

These same- and mixed-race relationships became their own source of learning. Teachers were not excused from uncomfortable relationships nor did they receive special exceptions based on background. Growth was the goal. They were expected to develop an antiracist, more inclusive perspective. "More" was more, regardless of where their background started them.

Teachers reported that our team approach made them feel supported. Charlotte, the white high school foreign language teacher, said:

I always felt supported. When I found out that all three professors taught every single course, I wasn't sure how that was going to work, but I really enjoyed it because they have such a good – really good – relationship. It [their relationship] broadened the vibe for the whole class.

As Charlotte's comment suggests, we too were supported by the team arrangement. Our relationships with each other mattered. Not only did we share our work as a team, but we also shared our passion for this work. Collaborating with each other helped keep that passion vital, as we mutually guided teacher and program development. Our work together also nurtured each other's development, as our own diverse backgrounds allowed us to check each other's assumptions with caring consideration of each other's thought and action.

Cohort Relationships

Ours were not the only relationships that challenged and encouraged. Cohort members also played a significant role in one another's growth. The program was structured using a cohort model. Teachers were admitted as a group. They took each course as a group, and they graduated as a group. They were an enduring community of practice.

As a cohort, they challenged, encouraged, and guided each other, but at its most basic level, they provided a sense of belonging. The importance of belonging to a community is highlighted by a teacher in the hybrid online program reflecting on our face-to-face meetings. She commented on the motivational impact of belonging:

If I hadn't met and interacted with others, I wouldn't be participating in this relationship. Without a relationship and a face, I would be signing in, completing the minimum requirements of the assignment necessary to get an 'A', and signing off. Having a face changed everything for me. It changed me. And that had an inherent impact on my students.

Belonging was also reassuring. When interviewed, Lesley, the Biracial Latinx elementary school teacher, remarked:

The face-to-face sessions... really appealed to me because, as much as it felt like I was learning on my own (when online later), I never felt isolated. Having the community built into the program was outstanding.

In addition to a sense of belonging, teachers also extended each other's understanding through the provision of feedback and questioning. A teacher experience illustrates: "I enjoy hearing from the others and them giving me feedback or asking me questions that help me to further my understanding". Indicating the weighty nature of their critical practice, Michelle, a white elementary school teacher, commented:

It [talking about race] was a difficult process to engage in. I think [the cohort] was very comforting. It was valuable in that, if I was thinking, 'oh, I'm in over my head' and just mentioned it, the same feeling would come out from across the room. Most people probably felt the same way ['I'm in over my head']. If they didn't feel the same way, they could give you hints on how to go along...It was a tight-knit group.

On occasion, teachers would recognize qualities and growth in each other and bolster them with recognition and encouragement. When interviewed, Lesley reported on such an experience:

Almost everyone in the class...said that they appreciated my leadership. I was like, 'I'm not a leader.'...That was a really big growing moment for me. ... So, for the past two and a half years, I've been actively seeking leadership positions at my school.

Teachers also invested in each other's growth. From the beginning, we pushed them to talk to each other - not just with us. Charlotte, the white, high school language teacher remarked: "We progressed together. Everyone was in it together."

Community of Practice Development

Each of the hybrid online cohorts met for a week of face-to-face meetings during the first and second summers of the program. Developing our community of practice was the weekly objective. Our goals were to build teachers' sense of belonging and trust and to create a critically reflective cohort identity.

To foster camaraderie and cohesion, we filled the weeks with community-building activities. For example, when the program was fully face-to-face and the summer sessions were two weeks long, we put the cohort through a ropes course requiring teamwork. In later years when the program was hybrid online and the face-to-face summer sessions were one week long, we had teachers organize themselves as teams for a campus-wide scavenger hunt. In both versions of the program, we required teachers to go on "read-the-world" field trips with classmates to visit local galleries, museums, historic sites, and government offices.

Teacher reflections indicate the intended outcome and benefit of our effort, as one of our teachers stated:

Throughout the week I became more and more comfortable with sharing and asking questions in front of my peers. ... I was surprised at how quickly I established a rapport, and even a basic trust, with several of my classmates.

Another commented: "I now have formed relationships with everyone, including my professors, and will not be afraid to take risks and to learn from everyone else." Finally, a teacher expressed the propitious purpose of the first week of the program when she commented: "I am excited to engage in deep conversations with my peers who I have come to know and respect. I look forward to watching all of us grow." Teachers felt safe, connected, and motivated to grow together.

We also began critically reflecting and sharing on day one. Brown's (2004) research indicates that critical self-reflection and conversations regarding race must commence from the start. We did this for several reasons. First, it was important to define our practice from the start. We were not just a collection of well-meaning teachers enjoying time together. Our community had a purpose: personal transformation. Our community had a practice: critical self-reflection toward antiracist behaviors.

Second, as described earlier, going through the vulnerable experience of self-reflection and disclosure together engenders trust. An end-of-term reflection described the dynamic: "In the five days we were together, the content we discussed was challenging and it was personal/sensitive at times. Both of these elements caused our group to open up and begin to build trusting relationships."

Embedded Cohort of Practicing Teachers

Another structural feature of our program was that all of the participants were practicing P-12 teachers, P-12 administrators, or educators who worked closely with P-12 classroom teachers. This allowed us to create a community of practice niche within their larger teaching communities of practice. This feature was invaluable to teacher growth.

Teachers want professional development that they can use. In our survey, *How Does Teacher Professional Development Matter?*, we asked teachers how they defined high-quality teacher professional development. The most frequent response was that the taught material had immediate applicability to the classroom. Teachers wanted professional development that they could use.

Although the practice of our community was critical reflection, our ultimate purpose was to create antiracist teachers who could form identity-enhancing relationships with their own students. Through our curricula, we could expose teachers to new diverse perspectives. We could insist that they critically reflect on their teaching practices. But to *become* critical educators, they had to actually do it. It was not enough for them to only imagine themselves so. This was not meant to be only a theoretical exercise. Belonging to a larger teaching community allowed them to enact their newfound insight and, thus tried, provided fodder for further reflection.

Being practicing educators also provided our teachers with a context upon which to reflect. Not only were they able to analyze specific actions they took or did not take, but they were also able to critically reflect on the organization and practice in their classrooms, schools, and educational divisions. Optimally, having done so, they could consider how they might influence structural inequities and injustices. Relationships within their wider communities were also influential in teachers being able to manifest their transformed identities. Interviewed teachers cited supportive administrators and colleagues as facilitative in their efforts to change.

OUTCOMES

As already described, our relational effort had the benefit of building a critically reflective community of practice. We were able to create a group in which our teachers felt safe to ask hard questions of themselves and share what may have been uncomfortable responses with each other. Our community supported each other and helped each other grow. But how did being a member of this community grow them? Were they transformed? Did their transformative insight influence their relationships with their students?

Although we had some teachers every term who did not make the transformative growth we expected, most of our teachers made observable and significant changes in their perspectives, relationships, and ways of being. Some even reported being a "different, better person." When interviewed, Michelle, a white elementary school teacher, commented that:

The program was made to change the way people teach. ... [It] changed the way I look at my kids, the way I looked at my coworkers. It changed the way I look people in the grocery store. ... I feel like [the program] made me a better teacher, a better person.

Many reported continuing to use a student-centered approach to their teaching. Marianne, a white elementary school teacher, shares an account of her changed teaching:

My students were not only very diverse, but also came from very different backgrounds and experiences. I used those differences as the heart of all of our classroom lessons, reflections, and discussions. I changed my way of teaching to better meet the needs of those learners. I feel like for the first time in my teaching profession I really met the needs of my students and not just the requirements of the state standards.

Others changed their stance toward their students, enabling closer, more positive connections with them. When asked about the experience of making his culturally relevant framework transparent, Angelo, a white male high school ESOL teacher, commented:

The change in structure for the way instruction is received by [English Language Learning] students was probably the biggest success that came out of this project. Removing myself from a position of power and sharing that space with students enabled me to acknowledge, validate, and understand their individual perspectives and experiences that they bring with them to school.

Donna, a white high school science teacher, shared her experience of trying to be less formal and friendlier toward her students. She reported:

To address disruptions in my class, I felt I needed to be more of a strict disciplinarian to maintain control. But after beginning the research process and developing some strategies to develop warmer relationships based on student and colleague comments, I decided to adopt a less formal, friendlier demeanor while still requiring adherence to our established rules and procedures. The day I first tried this strategy, I heard one student saying to another, 'I like this version of Mrs. [Name] today.' That was the first day I began to see a turnaround of more engagement and fewer disruptions in this class. As time went on, I saw improvement in more time engaged, less time off topic.

In an end-of-term reflection a teacher reported:

I realized that I needed to look at each student individually. I was going to embrace my students and try to reach them not only academically, but emotionally. I realized that I needed to spend personal time with my students, getting to know them and doing more to help them makes a difference.

Lesley, a Biracial Latinx elementary school teacher, reported a different stance toward the parents of her students:

I came from a really tough school. We just had a lot of very needy students who experienced lots of trauma at home. We tried to help them with that at school. I loved it, but I realized that I had been making assumptions about students and families and thinking like, 'well, his parents are just, you know, they just don't know how to parent' or 'they don't know how to do this.' And like, 'who am I to say that?' I have sort of learned through this program to really step back and think about all of the possibilities for why a student or a parent or a colleague might be doing something. I really feel like my relationships with my students and their families have grown a lot, which has so many impacts.

Other teachers also tell of their students' changed behavior based on changed relationships. In an interview Lesley shared that she was, "not having as many behavioral concerns in the classroom. [Her] students feel more connected to me because I'm showing that [I'm] really genuinely interested in what's happening in their lives."

Angelo, a white male high school teacher, reported that his new student relationships were what he most valued about his year-long teacher research project:

I most valued the relationships that I built with students during this project because it is something that I have been missing. I work diligently at a lot of things. I work hard at being efficient, at time management, at detailed planning, at progress monitoring and at producing results. I realized along the way that when I operate as a machine and not as a human being, I lose a little bit of my humanness in the process. I think that I've probably treated my students as such, and so I value the experience and the reflection that this has prompted.

Interestingly, one teacher learned about the importance of the teacher-student relationship from her students. When Donna, a white high school science teacher, interviewed her students for her research project, she found that "having a positive relationship with the teacher" was the most prevalent theme that emerged from her work.

Not only did the program change teachers' relationships with their students, but it also influenced how they interacted with colleagues. Marianne, a white elementary school teacher, reported: "It opened my eyes to what leadership really is and showed me who I am as a person....It helped me develop as a teammate and a leader with my peers." After the program Lesley became the leader of her school's new equity program.

CHALLENGES

Developing a sensitive responsive community of practice is not without its challenges. First, it is time consuming. Even though our cohorts were small, for each of us to teach every class, respond to students, and plan together took a lot of time. Second, we were fortunate to admire, respect, and genuinely like each other. Good working relationships were essential to the success of our program. Students commented on how the fact that we got along so well, positively influenced the class and enhanced the effects of our modelling. Moreover, we spent a lot of time together. This would be hard to do if we did not appreciate each other as much as we do.

Our teachers also expressed some challenges enacting their changed perspective once they left the shelter of our community of practice. One teacher commented, "What is still a challenge for me is calling out things I find that are inequitable or a problem, as it is hard to point out issues when you don't feel like you are in any position of power yourself." Claire also expressed a struggle to manifest a critically informed perspective and a need for a community of practice:

Now that I've been away from the program, I'm starting to get more ingrained in some of the big operational procedures of the division. Equity is still something that I'm very passionate about, but it's harder for me to see and effect change on a larger scale. We have only two years in the program and it may seem like a lot of time for some, but for me, I could be a continuing student in this program and I would be fine.

Change to Hybrid Online

In 2014, our program was changed to a hybrid online course from one that exclusively met face-to-face. We were surprised by the transition, as we feared a loss of community, connection, and depth of content. Meeting face-to-face for the program's first week, however, was essential. Those initial face-to-face meetings laid the foundations for the community of practice we were constructing. A teacher summarized its importance:

I was surprised at how quickly I established a rapport, and even a basic trust, with several of my classmates. I'm glad we started out face-to-face, so when we work together online, we won't have the typical problems that arise with a virtual class, e.g., misreading of someone's tone.

Our teachers, too, were ambivalent. Many expressed a desire for more face-to-face time together but acknowledged the convenience of online instruction. They recognize that they probably would not have had enough time to participate in our program if it had been fully in-person, particularly for those teachers who lived in other states. Working online freed them from the commute to campus and afforded flexibility to work when they had the time. Charlotte expressed her ambivalence:

Every time we got together for face-to-face interaction was always preferable. ...We wish we had more face-to-face interactions, but at the same time, we all chose the program because it was online. We decided to do the online portion, because of our busy schedules. We were able to do [the program] that way. But I did like the hybrid, being able to meet with people. Whenever we had projects or did group things, we had to [meet]. Probably nine out of ten times we chose to get together to work on it. I liked that flexibility of being able to work together, but if it couldn't happen, we could always do a video or phone conference.

CONCLUSION

Creating a community of practice was essential in the critical development of our teachers. We worked to create safe and supportive relationships with our teachers and among them. These relationships were built on trust and became the context in which teachers could personally wrestle with critical challenges to self-understandings. Creating and sustaining a critical community of practice required a dedicated faculty willing to contribute additional time and effort to be personally available and attentive to each cohort member.

This program was about a lot more than just getting a master's degree for me. I have made more personal growth over the last two years than you could possibly know. It's also the first time in my life that I knew what it felt like to be successful at school. It's the first time I believed that I was intelligent after a lifetime of seemingly always falling short. I grew up with a very high level of ADD that was undiagnosed and it impacted, and continues to impact, every day of my life. It makes everything I do difficult, and it's taken a lot of work to learn how to manage it over the last few years. Undertaking this program seemed like a very tall task for me, but I felt supported and nurtured –the entire way through–and that allowed me to flourish. I came in tired, scared, and ready to leave the profession. I'm leaving confident, optimistic, as a grant winner, as a city council commissioner, and for the first time since about the 1st grade, as a straight A student. In essence, transformative teaching transformed me. (Angelo's final reflection)

REFERENCES

Briggs, S. (2014, November 1). How empathy affects learning, and how to cultivate it in your students. *InformEd.* http://www.opencolleges.edu.au/informed/features/empathy-and-learning/

Brown, E. L. (2004). What precipitates change in cultural diversity awareness during a multicultural course: The message or the method? *Journal of Teacher Education, 55*(4), 325–340. doi:10.1177/0022487104266746

Byram, M., & Feng, A. (2005). Teaching and researching intercultural competence. In E. Hinkel (Ed.), *Handbook of research in second language teaching and learning* (pp. 911–930). Erlbaum.

Cornelius-White, J. (2003). Learner-centered teacher-student relationships are effective: A meta-analysis. *Review of Educational Research, 77*(1), 113–143. doi:10.3102/003465430298563

Den Brok, P., & van Tartwijk, J. (2015). Teacher-student interpersonal communication in international education. In M. Hayden, J. Levy, & J. Thompson (Eds.), The SAGE Handbook of Research in International Education (2nd ed., pp.309-324). SAGE Knowledge.

Derman-Sparks, L., & Edwards, J. O. (2009). *Anti-bias education for young children and ourselves*. National Association for the Education of Young Children.

Dyson, M., & Plunkett, M. (2014). Enhancing the interpersonal relationships in teacher education through the development and practice of reflective mentoring. In D. Zandvliet, P. den Brok, T. Mainhard, & J. van Tartwijk (Eds.), *Interpersonal relationships in education* (pp. 37–56). Brill Sense. doi:10.1007/978-94-6209-701-8_4

Gillespie, N. A., & Mann, L. (2004). Transformational leadership and shared values: The building blocks of trust. *Journal of Managerial Psychology, 19*(6), 588–607. doi:10.1108/02683940410551507

Heick, T. (2015, February 10). Teaching empathy: Are We Teaching Content or Students? *EduTopia*. https://www.edutopia.org/blog/teaching-empathy-content-or-students-terry-heick

Holmer, P. (1978). *The grammar of faith*. Harper & Row.

Lave, J., & Wenger, E. (1991). *Situated learning: Legitimate peripheral participation*. Cambridge University Press. doi:10.1017/CBO9780511815355

Mendes, E. (2003). What empathy can do. *Educational Leadership, 61*(1), 56–59. http://www.ascd.org/publications/educational-leadership/sept03/vol61/num01/What-Empathy-Can-Do.aspx

Mezirow, J. (1990). How critical reflection triggers transformative learning. *Fostering Critical Reflection in Adulthood, 1*(20), 1-6.

Pearce, R. (2015). Culture and identity: A method for exploring individuals within groups. In M. Hayden, J. Levy, & J. Thompson, J. (Eds.). The SAGE Handbook of Research in International Education (2nd ed., pp.185-199). SAGE Knowledge. doi:10.4135/9781473943506.n13

Reschke, K. (2019). Who am I? Developing a sense of self and belonging. *Zero to Three*. https://www.zerotothree.org/resources/2648-who-am-i-developing-a-sense-of-self-and-belonging

Rimm-Kaufman, S., & Sandilos, L. (2018) *Improving students' relationships with teachers to provide essential supports for learning*. American Psychological Association. https://www.apa.org/education/k12/relationships.aspx

Siegel, D. J. (2012). *The Developing Mind*. Guilford Press.

Southern, N. L. (2007). Mentoring for transformative learning: The importance of relationship in creating learning communities of care. *Journal of Transformative Education*, 5(4), 329–338. doi:10.1177/1541344607310576

Swanson, D. P., Cunningham, M., Youngblood, J., & Spencer, M. B. (2009). *Racial identity development during childhood*. GSE Publications. http://repository.upenn.edu/gse_pubs/198

Tate, N. (2012). Challenges and pitfalls facing international education in a post-international world. *Journal of Research in International Education*, 11(3), 205–217. doi:10.1177/1475240912461219

Townsend, J. C. (2012, September 26). Why we should teach empathy to improve education (and test scores). *Forbes*. Retrieved January 15, 2020, from http://www.forbes.com/sites/ashoka/2012/09/26/why-we-should-teach-empathy-to-improve-education-and-test-scores/#11ac76c71a0d

Wenger, E. (2011). *Communities of practice: A brief introduction*. Academic Press.

Chapter 5
Teacher Leadership and Collegial Relationships

ABSTRACT

The authors assert that P-12 classroom teachers are and should be leaders in the teaching and learning of children. The strongest teacher leadership is shaped by co-constructed knowledge and collaborative practices. The change that is required to help classroom teachers be better advocates for antiracist education can come from the leadership of teachers themselves, with the support of administrators and professional development designers. The authors examined teacher reflections on a variety of teacher leadership experiences and efforts to engage in equity-based initiatives at the school or district level to create antiracist policies and practices. The examination included an anonymous survey of school- or district-based equity initiatives, and how the goals are defined, what teachers perceive to be the impact (on students, teacher colleagues, their school, their district), and whether and how teachers are taking leadership in the initiatives.

Not everything that is faced can be changed. But nothing can be changed until it is faced. --James Baldwin

DOI: 10.4018/978-1-7998-5649-8.ch005

If you are neutral in situations of injustice, you have chosen the side of the oppressor. If an elephant has its foot on the tail of a mouse and you say that you are neutral, the mouse will not appreciate your neutrality. --Bishop Desmond Tutu

You cannot, you cannot use someone else's fire. You can only use your own. And in order to do that, you must first be willing to believe that you have it. -- Audre Lorde

INTRODUCTION

An article of faith that has governed our work doing teacher professional development is that K-12 classroom teachers are and should be leaders in the teaching and learning of children. The change that is required to help classroom teachers be better advocates for antiracist education can come from the leadership of teachers themselves, with the support of administrators and professional development designers. Too often, education policy and the professional development that in-service teachers receive in schools is driven by people who are not educators, and who are not expressly antiracist. In the history of public education in the U.S., teachers have not been treated as professionals in the same way as other professionals, so that their leadership is muted, if not actively denied as has happened with teacher strikes, especially since 2012. We support antiracist professional development that amplifies the voices and leadership of teachers because teachers have the greatest opportunity to build relationships with children and families and to connect children with liberatory academic content.

Over time, we have come to recognize that teacher leadership is shaped by the degree to which teachers innately possess and/or come to develop critical consciousness. In addition, there is a spectrum of approaches to their own leadership and their exercising of critical consciousness that goes from "small p" policy change to "big p" policy change. In this chapter, we describe some of the ideas and experiences that can shape leadership development among K-12 practicing teachers.

Teachers as Professionals

The history of teaching as a profession has been contested since the formation of public education in the U.S. Educational historians declared that all professions shared the characteristics of having a discrete body of knowledge that stems from the university, a moral commitment to service, autonomy (Hatch, 1988), and specialized expertise, which is the centerpiece of professional authority (Bledstein, 1978). Medical doctors, engineers, lawyers are professionals and are granted social and economic authority because they are presumed to know something that their clients do not (Larson, 1979; Abbott, 1988). Teachers, on the other hand, are perceived as "semi-professional" – part of neither a full-fledged profession nor a trade (D'Amico, 2015; Etzioni, 1969; Lortie, 1975; & Ingersoll & Perda, 2008). Everyone presumes to know what teachers do or should do, and teacher work is highly regulated and managed, depriving them of the authority and autonomy that other professions claim (e.g. Porter, 1989). According to policymakers and school leaders, the purpose of teacher professionalization is to improve the nation's public schools (D'Amico Pawlewicz, 2020) without necessarily increasing teacher power and leadership. Even among families and communities of color that historically understood the professional teacher as an agent of change and a force of liberation and disruption, the professional teacher labored on behalf of the community's evolving definitions of antiracist policies, rather than as an autonomous leader (D'Amico Pawlewicz & View, 2020).

Change as a Collaborative Process

In our own practice, we insisted on team teaching all of the courses because of a belief that knowledge is co-constructed and that collaborative instructional leadership creates better learning environments. The constructivist nature of teacher professional development allowed us to change course materials, experiences, assignments and expectations as part of our ongoing debate about instructional goals in light of the varied composition of the cohorts.

In the program and course design we understood the power of teachers working collaboratively to make change, even in cases where there were no pre-formed organizational structures, such as teachers' unions. At a minimum, school-based teaching teams, at the level of grade or subject matter teams, especially regarding critical data-driven decision making (e.g., Christensen,

2005), can provide professional strength to change school policies. Comments from teachers suggest that their learning was heightened by the ethic of collaboration:

So I think with teacher learning, if we could learn more from each other and hear from colleagues and share and build a collaborative process, that probably would be the best, the best avenue teacher learning could take coupled with area experts in resources that can help us make meaning for it in our own context. (Alum interview).

I would consider myself a strong teacher when I was in the classroom, but for a lot of us, because we were doing things that may have been outside of the norm of the operating system, of the context of our department or whatever, we kind of isolated ourselves a little bit. So you don't realize that what you're doing is unique until you have an opportunity to go and see other classrooms or hear from other teachers and realize, okay, not everybody is doing what I thought everybody was just doing. Um, so in the program there was a lot of empowerment of teacher leaders to share these ideas with colleagues to provide the lessons that they were planning and curricula they were planning with other people as evidence of this is good practice. ... Because the program got you thinking about your own practice to build confidence in the repertoire that you had and then gave you the opportunity to share out with colleagues, it fostered teacher leadership in a way that I thought works really well in a school context (Alum interview).

I really liked hearing from people who were not in my school division and who grew up and were educated in different contexts coming together under the common umbrella of the [graduate] program and exploring how we each interpreted and interacted in that avenue and why each of us was there. 'Cause we're all there for different reasons. Just getting those different perspectives was really eye-opening. Hearing from one of my colleagues who worked in [another state] and what she was experiencing versus the account of another colleague in the cohort who was in [a nearby district] was fascinating. And then couching that within my experience in [my own county] really gave me a greater sense of the commonalities of the struggle and the differences of the struggle that we were all trying to address (Alum interview).

In one example, Linda, a white music teacher who admitted early on to being challenged by the early and frequent discussions of race and equity,

117

discussed in her end-of-program portfolio the steps she was taking to collaborate more to educate herself:

This graduate program has helped me become a more collaborative teacher. Examples include:

- I routinely reach out to parents to discuss their child when I have a concern. Previously, I only called parents when there was a serious problem. Now, I involve the families early and often.
- I have become much less afraid to reach out to other teachers and administrators in my building if I have questions. Before this program I never advocated for myself and I tried to solve all of my problems alone.
- During my culturally relevant teaching project, I invited the parents to come in and share if they had any drumming experience from their home country.
- I am trying to get a community dance group to perform at my school's Heritage Festival.
- I go to the classroom teacher for help if I see a student struggling in my class. Recently, [a graduate school colleague] helped me create a behavior plan to help engage an autistic student who was having trouble participating in music class. He now participates regularly and well.

HARNESSING TEACHER LEADERSHIP

We advocated for our teachers in terms of developing their voices as capable and knowledgeable leaders. To that end, we designed several learning experiences to support the expression of teacher leadership over the course of the two-year program. These included teacher research, a schoolwide equity audit, a culturally relevant pedagogy project, and policy leadership work in the second summer that included personal leadership profile, simulation, power mapping, a visit to legislature, and a policy brief.

Teacher Research

The teacher research experiences that teachers engaged in in the first and second years offered opportunities to use classroom instruction as a setting for gathering data about teaching practices and student learning. They also provided teachers with new insights and resources to share with colleagues and administration at their school and beyond. The teacher research projects serve the purposes of nurturing teacher collaborations and of deepening the individual teacher's leadership capacities.

The research process remind[ed] me that we don't teach in isolation. I can't imagine a day when I would close the door and no longer rely on my teammates for ideas and inspiration. The ONLY reason I have been able to experience the successes I have is because of the village of excellent teachers who work with me every day (Alum interview).

In one example, Angelo, a white special education teacher made a determined effort to collaborate with his cooperating teacher to document whether collaboration made a difference in the learning of his English language students. In his end-of-program portfolio he stated:

I learned that collaboration is not only possible, but necessary....My data revealed that In the weeks when my cooperating teacher and I met more frequently the cooperative groups worked more efficiently with the students. During the weeks when perhaps we missed meeting up for one reason or another, my observations had more instances of students being off task – perhaps because we were not as much on the same page and not being as efficient as a result. Our collaboration helped us to build a relationship and the relationship became contagious it appears, to the students. As students reported over time feeling more welcomed and a part of the fabric of their classroom, I realized that I felt similarly.

In another example, Dawn, a veteran white science teacher expressed her hopes for the outcome of her teacher research project on cooperative classroom management:

I hoped that my research might help establish an opening for constructive dialogue between teachers and administrators on the topic of classroom management and discipline. While I didn't think it likely that the veterans would change their views based on my research, I believed my research could help these newer, more open-minded teachers become successful. I believed that many administrators see the type of classroom problem I researched as a shortcoming on the teacher's part, which makes it difficult for most teachers to seek their advice. When teachers feel they will be judged, rather than receive constructive assistance, they feel defensive and won't ask for help for fear that their admission of inadequacies will show up on their evaluation.

Equity Audit

The equity audit was another opportunity for teachers to gather, analyze, and use data to address racism in their classrooms and schools. The equity audit tool generated data for teachers to examine the ways and places in the school where inequities occur as a result of practices and policies that are racist. Table 5 shows the kinds of data that were collected. The important analytic tasks for teachers came when they were asked to compare the proportion of Students of Color in one category with the overall proportion of Students of Color in their classrooms and school and when they were asked to make meaning of the racial data and to analyze the strengths and areas of improvement for serving Students of Color. Reflections regarding teacher leadership and the uses of the equity audit are included in Chapter 3.

One high school teacher in particular, Barb, is a white high school teacher of early childhood and family studies at a school with a large Latinx population. She co-authored a research article about her experience of using the equity audit and how it shaped her subsequent leadership. She discovered that English Language Learners at her affluent school had disproportionately high dropout rates and low graduation rates and she sought to build stronger interpersonal relationships to create more academic success strategies. She joined her school's monthly equity committee and when she observed the data showing that Latinx students were slipping farther behind on standardized measures of academic achievement, she shared her research data with colleagues on root causes and potential mitigation strategies. She stated:

At times, I have found engagement in the political process to be the best strategy to target a root cause of issues identified in my research. When it became clear to me through my research that a major driving force behind the high ELL drop-out rate is SOL testing requirements, I spent time at Capitol Hill sharing my findings and concerns with my congressional representatives. When I discovered that my state board of education has the power to make beneficial changes to the implementation of testing requirements, I created and sent a policy briefing to a board member I hoped would be sympathetic to the plight of ELL high school students. Although this activity has met with mixed results, my experiences with the process have found application in my teaching beyond my research. Most notably, when my students have become

Table 1. Equity Audit Data Collection and Analysis Tool. Section 3. Race & Ethnicity

Section 3. Race & Ethnicity Calculate for your school and your classroom as available and where relevant		
	Number	**Fraction & Percentage**
a. Students of Color. (Insert numbers from Sect. 1c: For purposes of calculating "Students of Color," add up all but "white.")		
b. Students labeled for special education. (Insert numbers from Sect. 1d)		
c. Of the number of students identified for special education, what fraction and what percentage are Students of Color?		
How does the response to Item 3c compare to Item 3a in this section?		
d. Students identified as "gifted" who are Students of Color.		
How does the response to Item 3d (percentage) compare to Item 3a (percentage)?		
e. Students identified as economically disadvantaged in your setting who are Students of Color.		
How does the response to Item 3e (percentage) compare to Item 3a (percentage)?		
f. Certified staff who are People of Color in your school.		
How does the response to Item 3f (percentage) compare to Item 1i (percentage)?		
g. Uncertified staff who are People of Color in your school.		
How does the response to Item 3g (percentage) compare to Item 1i (percentage)?		
h. People of Color serving on the school board.		
i. Report two pieces of academic achievement data in your setting as they relate to race and/or ethnicity. (Examples: student of color participation in honor society, robotics club, chess club, etc.)		
j. Collect racial comparison data on at least two other areas in your school/setting (Examples: parent-teacher organization participation, student council, safety patrol, band).		
What do these racial data mean? In your analysis, include the strengths and areas of improvement for serving Students of Color.		

impassioned about political issues such as federal nutrition assistance programs for young children or local school board policies affecting students with chronic illnesses, I have been able to guide them in their own engagement in the political process. In various situations my students have done their own research, identified decision makers, and taken action through petitions, social media, congressional letter-writing campaigns, and even spoken at a local school board meeting to advocate for the issues important to them. I am both a student and a teacher – and as I have honed my skills as a researcher and a change- maker, I have been able to share what I learned with my students in immediate and authentic ways. I fight for a better education and a better world for my students, and I model for my students how to advocate for the changes they wish to see in their own world.

Culturally Relevant Pedagogy

In the culturally relevant pedagogy assignment, teachers are asked to take a piece of curriculum that is familiar and to reengineer it using the rubric described in Chapter 3. The teacher leadership insight that can emerge from this experience is expressed by Barb:

One thing that I have learned during my experiences in the classroom is that my students bring a breadth and depth of background knowledge and cultural viewpoints that I am, even now, only beginning to grasp. The racial, cultural, and linguistic diversity in my classroom provides a rich –and sometimes daunting –tapestry of perspectives to draw upon as we work and learn together. This diversity is likewise mirrored in the preschool children my adolescent students work and interact with each day. This complexity provides an opportunity for building bridges and increasing cultural understanding, yet also poses a danger of slipping into cultural misunderstandings and discord if not intentionally and mindfully managed.

Policy Leadership Work

It was during the second summer residency that teachers were expected to demonstrate public policy leadership in very specific ways. Teachers were expected to analyze and articulate differing policy arguments and perspectives regarding education; develop a critical understanding of collaboration and cooperation in working with stakeholders; and exercise teacher agency and voice in efforts to enhance student learning in multiple domains and across multiple need levels. They did this through several experiences and assignments described below.

Personal Leadership Profile

On the first day of the second summer residency, teachers began to complete a leadership profile that focused generically on the skills and dispositions they sought to develop over the course of the coming academic year. From their reflections teachers created a specific action plan, that included accountability partners and outcomes for making personal changes.

Making Change Happen Simulation

This simulation helped teachers explore their skills-building for leadership and advocacy. Beginning in 2011, we used a hard copy of the Making Change Happen game that is specific to school settings and equity. The three-hour board game allowed teachers to struggle through a change process over the course of "two academic years" and helped shed light on some of the tactics, strategies, relationships and challenges that are important in helping to make systemic change. Some of the outcomes of the Making Change simulation included new insights into the pace and the nature of the change-making process. Kathy, a white 4th grade language arts and social studies teacher stated that, "The Change Game helped to provide concrete examples and action steps that I can use as a leader to advocate for change." Donald, a white high school social studies teacher stated, "A deep insight I had was during the change game, which showed how we can have power and make real change even without the full support of our administration."

Jessica, a white 2nd grade teacher perceived that:

The Change Game and all of our work this summer inspired me to be brave and build relationships as a means to help solve issues in my school community. I'm inspired to get outside of my classroom and continue to develop school-wide leadership roles and relationships.

Maria, a Latinx science teacher, summed up the sentiments of many of the teachers regarding the simulation:

I learned that persistence produces change. That it is necessary to speak to people who have the power and that if those people do not respond to your request, you must continue talking to other people who can listen to you. The learning of the game and the purpose of the visit to the [legislature] demonstrated that power is in the unity of those who believe that advocating produces change.

Power Mapping

The second experience of the summer residency was an exercise adapted from community organizing that helped teachers visualize and analyze power structures in their schools, communities and beyond (Figure1. Micro Power Map, and Figure 2. Macro Power Map). Here teachers began to explore their local environments and how to advocate or organize for positive change on an issue of concern. The issues tended to be very specific to the teacher and school, and/or to the policy exercise described below. None of them spoke directly to antiracist policies, but the skill of developing a power map was easily transferrable, for example to an equity committee action plan to increase resources for school or district based antiracist teacher professional development.

Teacher Smith Goes to the Legislature

The third experience of the summer residency was a daylong visit to the legislature, in some years to the U.S. Capitol offices of their elected federal

Figure 1. Micro Power Map

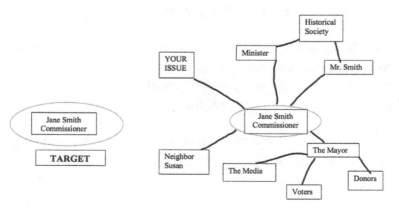

Figure 2. Macro Power Map

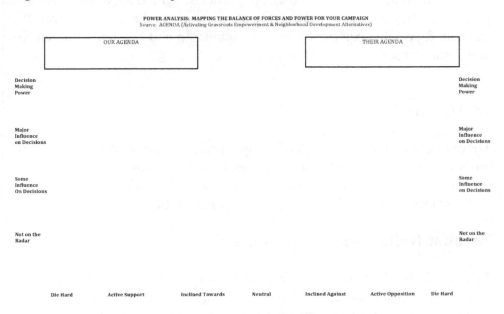

officials, in some years to the state legislature. The venue changed depending on the composition of the student body and the policy issues that were poised to shape the upcoming school year. To prepare for these legislative visits, teachers reached consensus about which policy issue to discuss with their elected official and what their collective position was on the issue. The day of the legislative visits was often the first time that the K-12 classroom teachers had encountered their elected officials face to face while advocating for an education issue. In nearly every case, the experience was eye-opening. Specific outcomes are described in greater detail in Chapter 6.

Policy Brief

Following the legislative visits, teachers were expected to create a policy brief advocating for an educational issue of concern. It could be the issue they addressed the day before at the legislature, the issue they addressed in the power mapping activity, or another issue. Their three tasks were to research the positive and negative impacts the issue had on their local community, citing 8 or more sources; to write a 2-3 page brief articulating their position on the issue and proposed solutions; and to email the policy brief to a policy maker. The policy maker could include entities teachers identified in the

"Power Mapping" activity, their elected official, or their superintendent and principal. They also were required to send a copy to the faculty. Typically, teachers found the experience to be enlightening and heartening about the democratic process.

OUTCOMES

The outcomes from the teacher leadership experiences included their reflections on their personal and professional changes, insights from the process of sharing their action plan with others, and efforts to engage in equity based initiatives at the school or district level to create antiracist policies and practices.

Teacher Reflections on Leadership

Teachers defined their own functional leadership as a range of transformations from interior perceptions or behavioral changes, to a change in professional position to grade or subject matter leadership, or to in-school administrative leadership. For some, it meant pursuing additional credentialing, as it did for this program alum, "After I left the program, I [decided that to] use this leadership capacity in a school would be really powerful. So then I just got a [teacher leadership] certification." For others the change was at the level of self-perception as a leader:

Not only do I see myself as more of a leader, it is how I am being viewed by the administration. My view on school leadership has expanded as well. While I once had a limited "us vs. them" mentality of teachers vs. administrators, speaking with so many administrators has helped me enlarge my world and take into account another key player, the school board...I feel like I have more self-efficacy in my teaching skills (Alum interview).

This program didn't directly impact my teaching, exactly. I feel like it helped me develop as a teammate and a leader with my peers more than with my students. I know that I have a bossy, loud, and selfish personality. This program showed me how to dial it all back and use them in a more positive manner with others. .... I learned the importance of building relationships, following the powerline up to make real change, and the value of listening in order to be a better teacher leader. It opened my eyes to what leadership really is and showed me who I am as a person (Alum interview).

I feel like a more confident leader than I was before….By choice, I haven't taken on any leadership roles per se, like any formal leadership roles, just because, like I said, there's a lot going on, and that's not something that I'm interested in right now. But I feel like my role is like activators in the department… if I'm excited about something, like getting people on board or really drumming up the excitement about something or getting teachers to join, I feel like my role as activator and leader in the department has shifted in a good way and I'm more vocal, not in a bad way…. I feel like I can be a teacher leader in my department and not necessarily be the head of a committee … I am a teacher leader even though I don't have a title (Alum interview).

Other teachers sought the kind of formal leadership that extends beyond securing more credentialing; they pursued action to change policies, as in these examples:

I volunteered to be the leader of our school equity committee, based on my new degree. And, I felt like it was something that I could do (Alumni interview). The [new leadership] job functioned one way before I came to the position and through just the different interests and things that I've done, [the job has] changed so it's not necessarily outside of my job description, but it [has become something that I would not have done before] …I've kind of been able to shape the direction that my particular position has taken because of the types of things I was doing in the [graduate] program (Alum interview).

I can facilitate leadership qualities and provide some limited opportunities for teachers that I work with to show growth and leadership capacity in the division. For me as just, again, a small cog in a very big wheel. Figuring out how that looks and what I can do to lift others up is where my work is now, what I'm trying to do in my professional life (Alum interview).

We have summer reading programs in the elementary, middle and high school level …. It's this whole convoluted system, but it's not truly equitable because especially the students that I deal with want to engage in additional reading. But their level of language proficiency is not at a level to command independent practice yet. So they're locked out of the opportunity. So one of the things that has been a continuing process from that initial paper that I started in 2015 is working with our supervisor of library and media research to make that a more equitable practice for all students, including students with a disability and students who may have dyslexia. How can we find a different format to allow students to be able to succeed in the summer without having direct instructional support? (Alum interview).

Teacher Sharing Insights and Outcomes With Others

An important part of exercising leadership is to share what they have learned with colleagues, administrators, and policy makers. On the issue of asserting classroom level leadership, one teacher stated:

So I'm not going to say I'm a successful grant writer now, but I have done a few more since [the first grant writing assignment]. So it kind of broke the ice and this unattainable thing that's out there and I'm like, 'Oh, I can write these,' like 'I can do this.' (Alum interview).

Another teacher discussed a conversation about race that emerged in the workroom at school and referenced a specific conversation that occurred a year prior with graduate school colleagues:

I'm thinking back to a specific conversation that happens a little less than a year ago … when we were trying to figure out what the difference was between ethnicity and race. And it was like something that I was doing for a project and it was something that I then brought up to the work room conversation. And I just remember starting that conversation and sparking that conversation. And people really digging into it and something that we wouldn't have been discussing otherwise. It was just a really productive and really honest and open conversation that we had. I remember that being sparked by the program (Alum interview).

Claire, a white teacher who became an instructional coach in the course of her participation in the program, shared that her own learning helped reach English Language Learners in her school through her work with their teachers:

Finally, this project helped me show teachers that the strategies I promote in the Level 1 training really are the best practices for our ELs by combining a PD filled with research-based techniques with individualized, classroom-embedded coaching. While my time with the five teacher-volunteers focused on instruction for their EL-only classes, each teacher went on to apply the strategy we developed in their other classes, as well. These educators used the data collected in their classrooms to show that targeted instructional techniques and an increased focus on ELs can be the rising tide that raises all ships. This project has created a PD experience that sets a high bar for future sessions… and I hope that through these efforts I can begin to shape the reality of what quality PD looks like.

Teacher Leadership in School/District Based Equity Initiatives

In the last several years, school districts nationwide have been engaged in equity initiatives, driven by an understanding that persistent opportunity gaps are observable in standardized achievement data. The initiatives have tended to define "equity" in multiple ways including curricular changes, access to specialized programs, school based policies such as dress codes and discipline, and budget changes (Samuels, 2019). In the next chapter, we discuss these initiatives as part of larger policy implications, but here we focus on the impacts on teacher leadership formation.

The action steps our teachers took to engage in equity initiatives are still emerging, as many of the efforts are relatively new and only have provisional funding. We conducted interviews and an anonymous survey with alumni to discover the extent to which the equity initiatives are providing leadership opportunities for classroom teachers to make a difference in their own classrooms and in their schools:

"I'm not a leader." That's not who I am, [I thought, but] that experience was a really big growing moment for me. From then on, now for the past two and a half years, I've been actively seeking leadership positions in my school. …I also invited teachers to come observe in my classroom, which is something I never felt that I wanted to do before. Then, my principal had approached me about this new county position at central office. And she was like, "I think you can do it", you know, so I applied. I didn't get it, but it was a really big eye opener for me. Now I'm actually the equity lead at my school. I'm just really actively pursuing those opportunities.…I feel like I've really grown as a leader, but also I've just seen the value in having teacher leaders in the school. I think it's really important that as a staff we see each other leading the learning and sort of taking on the role of leader instead of everything just coming from the principals. and luckily my current principal does a great job of offering lots of opportunities for teachers to become leaders for different situations (Alum interview).

One alumni from our program expressed their perceptions of teacher leadership within these initiatives as follows:

When I finished the program in 2017, my school division was just starting a big rollout of trying to increase cultural awareness throughout our school division.... it's a struggle. We're trying to get everything there, but I felt like I was in the program with the right people at the right time to be able to advise my division on some of the things that I had just learned in the program and would apply to the work. So I've been able to kind of continue the through line of the activities that I had seen in the program, in my current instructional capacity as well as in division leadership. I work with teachers who are trying to do the best they can for English learners. We have over 120 different countries and languages represented in our division, so figuring out how to have your curriculum be a window and a mirror and a door for specific people has been really a big part of my practice and I also work with high school students, middle school and high school students (Alum interview).

Another stated that "There is no accountability and simultaneously not enough people are moved to taking action either." This same respondent seems to be among the rare identifiable Teachers of Color in the survey and also someone who functions as an "equity lead" in her school district. She stated:

Equity leads are supposed to deliver PD provided by the county and from what I gather from whole group meetings, we are also supposed to lead some sort of equity- related work in our school buildings. There is no follow-up, though, to see if we are actually doing so. There is no accountability with principals to see if they are meeting regularly with equity leads. Another challenge is that if you are one of the only People of Color in your building, you're looked at like the equity evaluator.

In many ways, her assessment of the initiatives seems to be the most damning, in that she is hard-working, tokenized, held solely responsible for equity outcomes in her school, and isolated from colleagues who are experiencing success. This teacher's experience as equity lead in her school is consistent with the experiences of full-time chief diversity officers in Kentucky, Missouri, Nebraska, Nevada, North Carolina, and Oregon interviewed by Education Week:

[Equity efforts] can also be isolating, difficult, and a magnet for hostility, both inside and outside the school system. It's profoundly unsettling for school staff and some members of the community to hear that their own beliefs and practices are contributing to the intractable gap in achievement between white affluent students and students who are Black, Hispanic, or from low-income backgrounds. "One of the ways we see institutional racism is the casual acceptance of the gap," said Dani Ledezma, the senior adviser for racial equity and justice for the Portland, Oregon school district. "We have to build a culture that doesn't accept that." (Samuels, 2019, p. 3).

TENSIONS AND DILEMMAS

Teachers who were introverts or who did not perceive themselves to be leaders were sometimes challenged by expressions of leadership that were public or that required speaking in front of other adults. We encouraged those teachers to understand leadership broadly to include sharing with other teachers any successful curricular changes, raising critical questions with colleagues and students, and deepening their relationships with students and families. By working in teams, each person can play to their strengths and offer silent or behind-the-scenes leadership by engaging in tasks such as data collection, conducting one-on-one interviews with key stakeholders, designing marketing and outreach materials, paying attention to group dynamics, offering guidance, and so on.

Despite this encouragement some teachers perceived that leadership outside of the classroom was "not my job" – that the most profound leadership they could and should offer was with their students. In one cohort we offered intensive scaffolding that included the strategies described above (e.g., power mapping, Making Change game, etc.) and offered small group opportunities to insert more teacher voice in the policy discussions about education reform and to engage in specific teacher-designed and teacher-led "extracurricular" group projects. Some of the resulting projects included plans for political action, writing articles in teacher research journals, producing videos, creating a blog, creating an action group, and examining ways that their own practice could deepen connections to family and community. However, six of the 42 teachers, given the option to join a small group, refused to engage in any kind of individual or group action project, despite written statements about the value of power mapping for their practice.

There are many reasons why a K-12 classroom teacher might resist school-wide or district-wide leadership including personal family circumstances, insufficient skills, the perception of being tokenized in an indifferent or assimilationist environment, or the fact of working in a toxic environment where individual leadership is penalized. Such teachers who prefer to use their gifts only for the children and families in their classroom in a given year may still be offered leadership opportunities by serving as mentors to newly inducted teachers, as cooperating teachers for pre-service teachers, and as models of instruction for colleagues to observe.

What We Lost With Online Instruction

In the application to the original program, one teacher stated, "Fortunately, a co-worker is taking the courses with me. We can bring our newfound knowledge and ideas back to school to share." With the shift in format from a fully face-to-face program to a hybrid online program, we were not able to recruit teachers from the same school to enter as school-based teams. An advantage of such teams was that teachers had a built-in network of people who were familiar with the school culture, who could support the individual growth and development of team members, and who could navigate the school structure to gain information and resources that were mutually beneficial. Another important advantage was that school-based teams could more easily conduct collaborative research projects that impacted the entire school, something a solitary teacher would have more difficulty executing. A teacher who entered the program as the only person from her school stated:

I never felt like [faculty said], "you're racist or you have bias against this particular group, so you're a bad person." The way that the conversation was structured and formulated gave me a model for how to replicate that in additional conversations down the road. One of the biggest challenges is how to take the work that took me two years to kind of process through and do the same types of thinking and allow the same types of development opportunities for folks who may or may not be ready to have that conversation. So, this program in my mind gave me a lot to think about and it gave me a lot of research and things to show that this work is necessary and it's very important. It's then you're left after the program with the burden of, "okay, how do I take this and expand it beyond just my little sphere of influence? How can I help with a greater understanding and exposure to those kinds of ideas?" (Alum interview)

Other solo teachers expressed the challenges of carrying into their schools the skills and insights gained during the graduate program, especially regarding race. For example, one such teacher stated:

[Activism] is one thing that I am trying to navigate myself. The thing that's been interesting now is that, because I am a part of a larger organization, harnessing that in a way that is still true to my own predilections of trying to advocate and use my privilege to provide seats at tables where they may not have been previously while still navigating the waters of, I don't always get to speak for myself in a room where I know I need to speak for some, for someone to allow them to come in and be a part of that process. ... I work in a pretty conservative division as much as we are forward thinking in some programmatic things...we're not as progressive as I am in my own personal journey. And there are some times where I want to say something to shine light on an inequity that I may see, but I always have to feel like I ask myself, "Is this the right time and do I have enough time to collect my thoughts so that they seem constructive and not aggressive? 'Cause the questions that I raise sometimes are, may come off as accusatory or may have somebody go into that uncomfortable space of having to think about their own type of biases and things like that. And sometimes it is appropriate to do that in the moment and sometimes it's not. And that's the struggle that I have where it's like, how do I share this understanding that I have in a way that is not going to isolate or, um, derail a conversation. And it's also a struggle because I am like lowest man on the like power totem pole and the division; sometimes it's like how forcefully do you speak experience to power? Like that's the part that is also a little bit tough to navigate as well because in this program I felt really empowered to do thinking and to find ways for me to bring in some of my colleagues who have different experiences to create a more holistic narrative of what's happening in our division around equity, around justice, around activism. But is it appropriate for me to do it? That's the part that I still struggle with in my professional career. ... knowing whether it is appropriate for me to make a particular comment about making a situation more equitable for students. Considering the way that the conversation is going, can I be free to say that this is my opinion? If I'm trying to leverage my position as a division representative to push a particular idea, that that's where I have to be very clear about what role, in what lane I'm currently in, so that I'm not burning bridges that I may need to cross later on by asking somebody to push their thinking in a way that they're not ready to do yet. But they may, with some persistence [on my part?] be able to do it a few

days, a couple months later. (Alum interview) At the end of the program, I was more skilled in having conversations about equity and race and other topics than I was at the beginning. But now two years after that, I feel like I've developed a little bit further, but I'm not 100% sure. So I'm going back to the coursework just to double check, but I'm kind of in the unknown. As teachers are going through their careers after they have left the classroom, some may be in a leadership role; how do you transfer those skills that were based on student study, lesson study, curriculum study, policy focus? How do those skills translate as you grow in your trajectory? (Alum interview)

Nevertheless, solo teachers seemed to carry with them an understanding of the importance of collegial relationships and teacher leadership, even when they were not connected with their graduate school cohort.

I should be paying attention to these things rather than just putting blinders on ....I focus on my classroom and that's all, capacity wise, I have so many responsibilities and things inside and outside of school that it's so hard to have the time to do [policy advocacy] when you know you're not getting graded. So this is not like a project, like go write this policy brief or go research this new law that's coming out. But I will say that I do pay more attention to policy coming down the line and really being interested in what's going to happen, how I'm going to be affected by this. And starting those conversations with colleagues about like, 'did she know that this is why this is happening?' (Alum interview)

The tensions expressed, especially by the teachers who entered the program without school-based colleagues, reinforced the idea that antiracist teacher leadership is not intended to be a heroic solo endeavor. Barb, the high school family sciences teacher, reminded us that this work is rooted in strong relationships between teachers and their students:

Students are crying out to be known, to be understood. They have vast potential to become the leaders of the next generation, bridging the gap between cultures and languages. To realize that potential, they need the assistance of empathetic and responsive educators. They need our support to build and maintain strong interpersonal relationships with teachers, peers, and the wider community. They need thoughtful teachers who provide them with the tools they need to develop their potential to make change in the world.

And they need us to be responsive to their growing abilities and push them to discard those supports when they are ready.

REFERENCES

Abbott, A. (1988). *The system of professions: An essay on the division of expert labor.* The University of Chicago Press. doi:10.7208/chicago/9780226189666.001.0001

Bledstein, B. (1978). *The culture of professionalism: The middle class and the development of higher education in America.* W.W. Norton.

D'Amico, D. (2015). "An old order is passing": The rise of applied learning in university-based teacher education during the Great Depression. *History of Education Quarterly, 55*(3), 319–345. doi:10.1111/hoeq.12124

D'Amico Palewicz, D., & View, J. L. (2020). Social justice and teacher professionalism in the United States in historical perspective: Fractured consensus. In R. Papa (Ed.), *Handbook on Promoting Social Justice in Education* (pp. 1279–1297). Springer., doi:10.1007/978-3-030-14625-2_130

D'Amico Pawlewicz, D. (2020). *Blaming teachers: Professionalization policies and the failure of reform in American history.* Rutgers University Press.

Etzioni, A. (1969). *The semi-professions and their organization: Teachers, nurses, social workers.* Free Press.

Hatch, N. (1988). *The professions in American history.* University of Notre Dame Press.

Ingersoll, R., & Perda, D. (2008). The status of teaching as a profession. In J. Ballantine & J. Spade (Eds.), *Schools and society: A sociological approach to education* (pp. 106–118). Pine Forge Press.

Larson, M. (1979). *The rise of professionalism: A sociological analysis.* University of California Press.

Lortie, D. (1975). *Schoolteacher: A sociological study.* The University of Chicago Press.

Porter, A. C. (1989). External standards and good teaching: The pros and cons of telling teachers what to do. *Educational Evaluation and Policy Analysis*, *11*(4), 343–356. doi:10.3102/01623737011004343

Samuels, C. A. (2019, October 24). The challenging, often isolating work of school district chief equity officers. *Education Week*. Retrieved January 27, 2020, from https://www.edweek.org/ew/articles/2019/10/23/the-challenging-often-isolating-work-of-school.html

The Elementary and Secondary Education Act Publ. L. No. 107-110 (2010). http://www2.ed.gov/policy/elsec/leg/esea02/index.html

The Network Inc. (n.d.). *Making Change Happen* [game]. The Network, Inc. http://www.thenetworkinc.org/games/leadership-series/mch/

Chapter 6
A Policy Manifesto for Antiracist Teacher Professional Development

ABSTRACT

The authors believe that the de-racialization of teacher professional development is as harmful to teachers as the deprofessionalization of teachers, leaving them without the tools needed to attend to the basic and unmet needs of Students of Color, immigrant students, low-income students, as well as of affluent white students. Teacher educators, administrators, and policy makers should invest in sustained and broadly applied antiracist practices and policies as a matter of public self-interest. To extend Kendi's notion of antiracist educational policies, the authors suggest a spectrum of small "p" and big "P" policies that address the uniqueness of schools as institutions of learning and human development, where children are sorted early by skin color and family income to their "assigned" school. The authors offer this chapter as both a call to action and an invitation to collaborate to create and broaden antiracist teacher professional development.

There is no such thing as a single-issue struggle because we do not live single issue lives. --Audre Lorde (February 1982)

DOI: 10.4018/978-1-7998-5649-8.ch006

Education...is the practice of freedom. The means by which men and women deal critically and creatively with reality and discover how to participate in the transformation of their world. --Paolo Friere (2000, pg. 34)

INTRODUCTION

To begin this chapter, we revisit Ibram Kendi (2019) on racism, assimilationism, and antiracism as related to schooling. White supremacy defined by the Merriam- Webster dictionary is the belief "that the white race is better than all other races and should have control over all other races. (Merriam Webster, 2019)." While there is no scientific support for the idea that there are differential "races" among humans (e.g., Gannon, 2016), there is ample evidence of the social belief in race as a descriptor of people. In the United States people who are defined as "white" are positioned as the dominant political and economic actors. Kendi (2019a) defines racism as support for policies, actions, inactions, and expressions that support these racial hierarchies. In his terminology, antiracism is manifest in support for policies, actions, inactions, and expressions that dismantle racial hierarchies (p. 9). Assimilationism positions "any racial group as the superior standard that another racial group should be measured against, the benchmark they should be trying to reach". (Kendi, p. 29). Racial inequity is evidence of two or more racial groups standing on unequal footing, such that one can predict and measure winners based on their racial assignment (Kendi, 2019 b). To Kendi's point, "every policy in every institution in every community in every nation is producing or sustaining either racial inequity or equity between racial groups" (Kendi, 2019 p. 18). These terms offer no clearer descriptions of schools in the United States, given the national, state level, and school district statistics on student academic achievement, school leaving, school disciplinary outcomes, college attainment, and so on as disaggregated by "race."

We believe, as Srivastava (2007), that antiracist education and professional development "enable us to see that racism is learned and therefore can be unlearned" (p. 302) and that it is possible to foster an influential association between knowledge and conduct. While we have witnessed teachers' capacities to be equity warriors (Rochmes, Penner & Loeb, 2017), we also believe that P-12 classroom teachers cannot and should not be left alone to do the work of dismantling 500 years of institutional racism. We argue that the de-racialization of teacher professional development is as harmful to teachers as the deprofessionalization of teachers, leaving them without the tools needed to attend to the basic and unmet needs of Students of Color, immigrant students, and low-income students, as well as of affluent "white" students. Antiracist teacher professional development may offer teachers the skills and tools for making progress if teacher educators, administrators, and policy makers invest in sustained and broadly applied practices and policies as a matter of public self-interest.

Teacher Response to Equity Initiatives

We know that teachers do not work in isolation of the larger world. They observe and experience racism that is both overt and covert. Ture and Hamilton (1967/1992) define the terms as being closely related:

We call these individual racism and institutional racism. The first consists of overt acts by individuals which cause death, injury or the violent destruction of property....The second type is less overt, far more subtle, less identifiable in terms of specific individuals committing the acts. But it is no less destructive of human life...When white terrorists bomb a black church and kill five black children that is an act of individual racism... But when in the same city – Birmingham, Alabama – five hundred black babies die each year because of the lack of proper food, shelter, and medical facilities, and thousands more are destroyed ...because of conditions of poverty and discrimination in the black community, that is the function of institutional racism (p. 4)."

P-12 classroom teachers are engaged in head work, heart work, and heart-to-heart work to battle against the racism they observe and experience. The development of critical consciousness is the thread that weaves this work together. ne cannot change policy if one does not recognize that the system that exists sorts and marginalizes students. While it is important to "just love children and youth," a teacher with critical consciousness comes to understand that love alone is insufficient for changing the conditions of racist schooling.

We also know that P-12 teachers value high-quality teacher professional development as a way of fixing a broken system by enhancing student learning. Such teacher professional development can afford collaboration and critical dialogue with professional colleagues, create greater awareness of student differences, and enable the practice of learner-centered instruction. It can also provide the opportunity for self-reflection as well as the opportunity to create culturally relevant curriculum.

Given these two realities, it may be appropriate to employ a range of practices and policies in the service of antiracist teacher professional development. At one end of the spectrum might be processes like the W. K. Kellogg Foundation Racial Healing Circle that foster appreciation/affirmation, belongingness, and consciousness change as pathways from trauma informed care to healing centered engagements (HCE). HCE is defined as being: explicitly political, rather than clinical; culturally grounded as a way to restore identity; asset-driven with a focus on well-being; and a support for adult providers (or in this case, teachers) in their own healing from racial trauma (Ginwright, 2018). In the middle of the spectrum might be the kind of accountability that Demar Pitman conducts through the Discriminology website to track school-level data (Stern, 2020). At the other end of the spectrum might be the kind of advocacy and political organizing that teachers' unions have typically conducted to change the material conditions of teaching and learning.

The professional development that could support this range of policies and practices might be found in the contemporary equity initiatives that school districts around the country are attempting (Samuels, 2019), which we began describing in Chapter 5. However, the alumni survey gives some insight to the possibilities and limitations of these initiatives to date.

The anonymous survey posed ten questions to discern whether there are school- or district-based equity initiatives, and if so, how the goals are defined, what teachers perceive to be the impact (on students, teacher colleagues, their school, their district), and whether and how they are taking leadership in the initiatives. Sixteen alumni responded. Four of the teachers indicated that there are no equity initiatives in their school or district, including one respondent who stated that "things are fine as they are." The other three respondents indicated no equity initiatives in their school or district, but they had ideas about what should be happening to improve equity outcomes for students.

My school needs to beef up their ELL program. They also should focus on our lower income population, we have poor attendance and increase in violence in our school.

There aren't any (equity initiatives). The students are all treated the same; there are no incentives or special things to look forward to. They receive punishments only, enforced inconsistently (anonymous survey on equity initiatives).

There seems to be a broken system for receiving students who are newcomers to our country and/or who are learning English. They don't seem to get the same level of "customer service" in getting an appropriate schedule in a timely manner. In such a large county, it's just so easy to fly under the radar. Everybody gets to pass the buck or say that's not their job. There's not a lot of transparency, so that an individual teacher has no idea what's supposed to be happening at central office (anonymous survey on equity initiatives).

Students with disabilities are sometimes left out of equity initiatives. The focus is on race or gender, but so many times students with learning differences are still left behind. This doesn't help close the achievement gap. Also, equity is a loaded word, and means different things to different people. Many times it becomes a political pawn for those who are in power to silence voices that should be heard (anonymous survey on equity initiatives).

Where teachers identified school- or district-based equity initiatives, they perceived that the goals are to improve student performance on standardized tests (50%); change graduation goals (58%); create systemic change (for example, changing policies or rules regarding access to certain programs) (50%); provide resources for families to help their child succeed (75%); improve teachers' data usage (33%); and/or improve teacher awareness of race, language, and culture (92%). Teachers believed that the greatest impact on students would be to help them and their families feel more engaged in school (92%) and help students be more academically confident and successful (66%)

The perceived impact of equity initiatives on teacher colleagues, schools, and school districts varied. Teacher colleagues might expect an improvement in their teaching practice as a result of the initiatives (82%). They also might experience improved connections with students and their families (82%) and with colleagues (36%). Nearly half (45%) of the teachers expected that the equity initiatives would help their colleagues be more connected with academic content.

Nine percent perceived that the equity initiatives would have no meaningful impact on their colleagues. One respondent reported that the county equity initiative is not supported by their school and so would have no school impact. Over one-third of teachers (36%) expected that the initiatives would improve school-wide test scores and improve academic content overall, but 92% expected that schools would become more engaged with students and their families as a result. One respondent perceived that the equity initiatives would have no impact on the school district, stating that "equity initiatives are not applicable in specific school change or improvement, e.g., redistricting of students from high poverty areas." Most other teachers perceived that the greatest district level impact of the equity initiatives would be to help county/district peers to be more connected with one another (64%), to help student develop pride in a district that supports their confidence and success (64%), and to help the district be more engaged with students and their families (64%). Some teachers indicated that their peers, schools, or districts would not be impacted in any meaningful way by the initiatives, but none of the respondents believed that the equity initiatives would fail to impact students in any meaningful way.

That all of the respondents perceive that the school- and district-based equity initiatives are intended to improve teacher awareness of race, language, and culture is striking. Without the details of each initiative, it is not certain the extent to which these initiatives are intended to move schools from an assimilationist approach to equity, toward an antiracist approach to equity. Yet half of the teachers perceived that the schools and districts intended to implement systemic change, such as changing policies or rules regarding access to certain programs such as Advanced Placement, gifted, honors, International Baccalaureate, and other programs.

Despite the intentions of the equity initiatives, we know that the size of the problems of educational inequity is larger than should be tackled by a single teacher or full-time school district chief diversity officer or a one-size-fits-all equity initiative. Working together, teachers, parents, administrators, teacher educators, and policy makers can craft and implement antiracist "laws, rules, procedures, processes, regulations, and guidelines that govern people" (Kendi, 2019, p. 18). The challenge is to figure out how to do so.

ANTIRACIST TEACHER PROFESSIONAL DEVELOPMENT

To extend Kendi's notion of antiracist educational policies, we suggest a spectrum of small "p" and big "P" policies because of the uniqueness of schools as institutions of learning and human development, where children are sorted early by skin color and family income to their "assigned" school (e.g., Anyon, 1981; Luke, 2010). Kendi offers eleven strategies for eliminating racial inequities in schools; we have adapted these in accordance with our research on our teacher professional development master's degree program and teacher outcomes. Table 1 matches Kendi's eleven strategies with small "p" policies at the classroom and school levels and with big "p" policies at the district, state, and national levels.

For a small "p" example, at the classroom and school level, a teacher can conduct an audit that reveals that her award-winning "blue-ribbon" school has inequities that have been hidden or ignored regarding newly immigrated students who are emergent bilingual. Her classroom-based action plan may be to build relationships with these students and their parents using the resources of the school's bilingual parent liaison. She may also try to work with her grade level colleagues to create a communications process with these parents using accessible audio technology that has been translated to the home language. This small 'p' policy change does not blame anyone at the school for the marginalization of the newly immigrated students and families and the presence of only one parent liaison; rather it names bad policy and examines the assets of the teacher, her colleagues, and her school for creating antiracist policies. At the big "p" policy level, this same teacher might work with others to expand the budget resources for translation, parent liaisons, and bilingual books for the school library.

In Table 1 the question marks indicate acknowledgement that gifted programs, charter schools, vouchers, and tracking have been controversial as programs, policies, and practices that can serve racist, assimilationist, and antiracist agendas, depending on how they are implemented. The task for supporters is to demonstrate how they can be consistently antiracist in the service of educational equity.

The following examples of teacher work and reflections align with the eleven strategies, including two extended reflections on small "p" and big "p" actions taken by P-12 educators. As will be evident, these strategies are not mutually exclusive and in many cases fold on top of and intertwine with one another.

Strategy 1. Admit Bad Policy, Not Bad People

Linda, an early career music teacher discussed her intention to transform her curriculum within her classroom and for the larger school district:

Since my new realization that my [school district] curriculum is Eurocentric, I plan to teach more culturally relevant music and composers. I will try out lessons with my students, and then I will contact the county to see if I can get the [curriculum standards] changed. I want at least one composer and piece of music on there that comes from somewhere other than Europe or America.

Table 1. Kendi, Small "p" and Big "p" Policies

Kendi	Little "p" Policy	Big "p" Policy
Admit bad policy, not bad people	Equity audit	Gifted programs? Charter schools? Vouchers? Tracking? Budget authority Fiscal policy
Identify racial inequality in all of its manifestations	Equity audit	Legal policies Regulatory policies Legislative visits
Investigate and uncover all racist policies	Teacher research Culturally relevant pedagogy Equity audit Critical literacy	Legislative visits Policy briefs @university and district levels Race/ethnicity not predictive of outcomes
Invent/ find anti-racist policies	Cain Rubric Alternatives to CO-GAT and other assessments CRT Project Representation in curriculum Critical literacy Asset-based Learner- centered/ "IEP" Restorative justice	Policy briefs Race/ethnicity not predictive of outcomes
Who has power to eliminate racist policies	Teachers Parents Administrators Deans Students Policy makers Voters	
Disseminate and educate about correctives	Use Cain Rubric in PD Publish teacher research Teacher grant-writing	Policy briefs Educational researcher publications
Work with anti-racist policy makers	PD @ school/district level Deans Philanthropists Teacher grant-writing	Policy briefs
Remove racists	Unions Administrators Deans Parents Philanthropists	
Monitor closely	Accountability	Enforcement
Start again, as needed	Accountability Teacher research	Enforcement
Vigilance	Accountability	Enforcement

Strategy 2. Identify Racial Inequality in All of Its Manifestations

Two teachers, Donna and Kelsey, described the outcome of their teacher research projects. Donna, a white high school science teacher, stated that:

Because of the current make-up of my class, I found Why Are So Many Minority Students in Special Education? (Harry and Klingner, 2014) to be the most valuable reading for me. I found myself connecting to every page and asking the same questions that the authors sought to uncover answers to about special education services. It made me wonder about the special education referral process at my school and how much equity is actually involved in it. It also led me to question my judgment about students I have brought to my Local Screening Committee in the past – did they truly have a disability, or was I missing something? This reading ... made me want to scream at the unfairness of the process and at the mistreatment of parents of minority students. This happens constantly at my school, and I can't stand it. Yet I don't do anything or say anything. Reading this book made me realize how important my voice can be in standing up for these parents who are talked down to, talked badly about in private, or assumed to be terrible parents by other "professionals" at my school. I know that I need to step up and do my part to defend my students and their families when they need defending, and this book proved it to me.

Kelsey, a white high school health and fitness teacher stated in her final project feedback:

Because of this program I have continued to push for access to the special education student's information from Individual Education Plans [IEPs; specialized instruction] and 504s [learning accommodations] for coaches that are also teachers (at the very least). I am now on an advisory committee for [coaches in my county], and at our last meeting I brought the issue up to the Director of the Office of Student Activities and Athletic Programs. Similarly, when I brought it up to my athletic director, he thought it was important for coaches to have access to that information. He was surprised that we didn't already have the information and is looking into ways that can be accomplished.

Strategy 3. Investigate and Uncover All Racist Policies

Here we offer reflections from two teachers, Linda and Paris, whose consciousness grew a great deal over the course of the two-year program. Linda, the white instrumental music teacher mentioned above, was a young teacher with limited life experience with Students of Color and lower income families. Initially resistant to changing her practice beyond what she learned in her pre-service teaching program, she identified "baby steps" that she began to take as a result of the two years in the master's degree program. Among the planned changes was to become "a more collaborative teacher." She also indicated an intention to continue to uncover racist policies through the use of her newly developed teacher research skills:

I plan to continue to use the research skills from this program to help me solve problems in my classroom. This has been my favorite part of the graduate program. Every day I see my research skills paying off in my students' achievement. I have realized that my students know what they need to learn. I just need to ask them what they need instead of assuming I know better than they do. I will continue striving to make my classroom more democratic and student centered.

Paris's reflections, while lengthy, present a sense of her evolution over the course of her second year, year-long teacher research project. Paris, is a white teacher who described efforts to involve Parents of Color in the school community in a more meaningful way. Initially, she had been one of the resistant teachers in the program, doubting her need to change her practices. In the middle of her teacher research data collection and analysis process, however, she recognized how cultural sensitivity might enhance engagement and began to realize her own power as a teacher. She reflected on her insights:

Over the past several weeks I've had a chance to go back through my documentation and data with a fresh perspective. I've changed the focus of my research from focusing solely on how an increase in cultural proficiency among teachers might lead to an increase in parental involvement, to a focus on the impact that someone outside of the classroom could have on the relationships teachers have with students, staff, and parents. In looking at my data through this new lens, I've come to three understandings that I'm hopeful will lead to solid claims as I wrap up my work with teachers. The first of these understandings is that working to provide teachers training on ways to support their ESOL students through an increased knowledge of culturally relevant pedagogy can lead to teachers striving to find out more about their students. Last semester I had a chance to take a group of teachers through a three-day intensive training focused on CRP as it relates to working with ESOL students. Teachers were given tools to use in their classrooms that they really latched on to. Through conversations with teachers since the training, I've noticed that they are using these tools, especially during their Social Studies lessons. One specific example of this was during a lesson on the reasons early colonists chose to leave their home country and start new in Jamestown. Teachers used connections to their students' lives, since our school is full of children who are immigrants themselves, to help bring this content to life. Teachers have expressed to me that they feel better equipped to have these conversations because of the skills they gained when learning about culturally relevant pedagogy.

The second understanding I've come to is that when teachers are given powerful tools that help them meet the needs of their students, they use those tools not only to enhance their classroom but to empower themselves to become leaders in their school. The same teachers who went through training with me have since become standouts among the staff. They've provided turn-around training with our entire staff and have sought out new and cutting edge ways to improve our school. They are partnering with administration to pilot programs in our school, such as one-to-one technology. As of yet, I'm not able to draw a direct connection between the training that teachers received at the beginning of the year to their increased leadership in the school, but I am confident that with a little more time with teachers this connection could become clear.

The final understanding that I've reached at this point is that those of us who are outside the classroom are capable of having as significant an impact on relationships with parents as classroom teachers. Last year a small team of support staff (reading and math specialists) began working on some after-school/evening activities for parents to attend. There was little turnout, and teachers were largely kept out of the loop. This year, in order to take what was started and really turn it into something fantastic, I and a few other classroom support teachers formed the Family Engagement Committee. Teachers have so much on their plates as is that I felt it was very important that those of us who do support the teachers take that further and use our resources to help increase parental involvement. We've held three events so far this year.

The Family Engagement Committee has been responsible for the planning and preparation of these events and we've partnered with teachers in the execution. We were strategic in the planning and wanted to make sure that the message parents received was that teachers are the experts and the ones they can rely on for their students' needs, so we made sure that all content at these events was presented by teachers.

I'm happy to report that after a meager turnout at the first event where only 8 families attended, we had over 100 parents attend our most recent night which focused on reading. This is a huge step in the right direction and many of the things I learned from my research last semester came into play in helping get these events off the ground and running. What might this all mean for the broader field of education? Well, I think that oftentimes there is an assumption that when you're out of the classroom you're on the sidelines of what is happening in schools and in the lives of students. I really don't believe this to be true. While I'm no longer working with students on a daily basis, my reach is actually much larger than it was when I was in the classroom. Partnering with a dedicated staff has allowed my passion to trickle down and reach students in many classrooms. This realization could have a huge impact on schools.

After the completion of the teacher research project, Paris reflected on the outcomes. She considered her own consciousness, her capacity for leadership, and the need to encourage collaboration with her colleagues to create antiracist policies for her school:

There is a vast difference between the race and culture of the teachers versus that of the students. This divide leads to a lot of misunderstanding and a general lack of understanding about the culture and race of the students who attend [my school]. I began to recognize my own lack of understanding surrounding the culture, race, and challenges faced by parents and families in the community I serve. As I talked with other teachers in my school, I realized that I wasn't the only one who felt that there was a lack of understanding that stood in the way of reaching students in a more powerful and impactful way. In my own studies I had begun to understand cultural proficiency and the way that it can influence what happens in the classroom.

With my shift from classroom teacher to instructional coach, I saw an opening to bring learning about cultural proficiency to my school in an attempt to grow the competency of teachers and ultimately increase parental involvement and relationships with families. I wondered what the impact on parental involvement would be if I were able to increase the cultural competency of teachers and I sought to answer this question. If I were able to find ways to decrease this cultural divide, there might be a shift in parental involvement at my school. As I began, I can't say that I had any concrete evidence that this issue was important for my school, but I did have observational evidence and had conversations with most of the staff about this issue. In the previous school year I'd noticed the low turn-out for open house and back-to-school night. I'd heard teachers complain about not getting to meet all of the parents in their class and the impact this had on their relationship with the students. I had also observed the school trying some new things to form better relationships with parents, such as offering back-to-school night in both English and Spanish. This was also the first year that teachers were sending interim reports home in the student's native language. This led me to believe that the school sees lack of parental involvement as a problem and is interested in coming up with a solution.

To begin this work, I was invited to participate in the county-wide leadership kick-off. It was at this kick-off that I was able to hear about special opportunities that would be held during the year.... Over the course of three days in September and October, there was the EL (English Learners) Innovation Cohort. Participating schools would receive specialized training to better help address the needs of the EL's at their school while developing a strategic plan on how to use these new resources and provide turn-around training for the entire staff. I approached the interim administration about taking a team of classroom teachers to participate and was given the go-ahead. The principal selected members for this team that she felt were strong leaders and had respect from colleagues. The team was made of a 2nd, 3rd and 4th grade veteran teacher, an ESOL (English Speakers of Other Languages) teacher, and me, one of the school's instructional coaches.

In early September we, along with our new full-time principal, attended our first day of training. This session was a full day's worth of information about culturally relevant pedagogy and how it impacts those who work with EL students. Upon completion of this session I conducted a survey to see where the teachers' thinking was after engaging in this new learning. Teachers indicated that the background information on culturally relevant pedagogy was interesting and informative, but they did not see the link to what was happening in their classroom. When asked the question "How does this new learning impact your daily classroom practices?" three of the teachers responded with answers that indicated it did not by saying things like 'This doesn't really apply to my classroom.' And 'I don't think it does right now.'

During our second session together we were given more hands-on materials and information that could be used within our school. We focused on looking at the whole child to determine educational strategies, much of which included a thorough understanding of the child's background and culture. After this session together teachers latched on to some of the ideas that were easily implementable in their classrooms, such as supporting EL students through an increased use of sentence frames and question stems. Two teachers offered to take this learning and present it to the entire staff during a professional development day. While it was great to see this type of leadership emerging from the teachers, this learning had little to do with an increase in their cultural competency and instead only showed an improvement in their instructional practices when working with EL students.

We also spent a good portion of the second session looking at data for our school to make sure that we had an accurate picture of who we serve. Teachers indicated in a follow-up survey that they were surprised to learn that the majority of the students at our school are native-born American citizens. One teacher in particular felt very passionate about this data as indicated in her response, 'I'm sick of being told our students can't perform when they've been in the United States their entire life! Why aren't my students functioning like their non-Latino friends? This is the question we need to answer instead of using the excuse that they weren't born here…yes, they were!' Other teachers indicated that the misconception that most of their students were foreign-born could play a role in how they are viewed and taught and felt it also could contribute to a delay in providing necessary services to students, especially those who require special education services.

Upon the completion of our second session, teachers still had a vast amount of questions about how to use their new learning to foster learning in a new way in their classroom.

As a result, we were able to partner with county support to work throughout the year, specifically in the area of providing interventions to our neediest students. However, there was a clear lack of connection between improved understanding of who our students are and parental involvement in our school. I was concerned that teachers were either not making a connection between their new learning and the need for increased parental involvement or that I wasn't providing them with the right way to support that connection.

While all of this work was happening at the EL Innovation Cohort, I began to partner with other support staff in the building; an assistant principal, a reading teacher, a special education teacher, and a guidance counselor to form the Family Engagement Committee.

This was a team of staff members who also saw the need for an increase in our family involvement and were passionate about finding ways to make improvements. In the early months of the year we began by looking at requirements for our school improvement plan that related to family engagement but had not been met in previous years. The formation of the Family Involvement Committee brought to light how little we do as a school to form relationships with families and how, in many cases, we are out of compliance with state regulations. We knew we had to have a clear vision statement on how we, as a school, would interact with parents, and we sought to have one. We also began looking at the calendar and planning events that would be held throughout the year to engage families in meaningful ways. There were plans to hold a 2nd grade parent night, a 3-6th grade SOL prep night for parents, and a round table discussion with parents to see what their take is on how they might be involved in the school more. At the end of these months it was very clear, as I ascertained from survey responses and observations, which teachers were internalizing the information they learned at the first meeting of the EL innovation cohort and which staff members had left themselves out of the equation (either as the problem or the solution). This helped me to understand which teachers might be used in future professional development plans and which might need more time before they were ready for something like this.

Strategy 4. Invent/Find Antiracist Policies

Stovall (2018) speaks of the "radical imaginary" that is required for teachers to commit themselves to a process of education that exceeds the traditional expectations of schooling. Christensen (2005) described teacher-designed and -led professional development strategies, similar to what Claire used in her transformation from being a classroom teacher to an instructional coach.

In her reflection on her year-long teacher research project, she described the outcomes of her efforts to create better professional development for teachers of English Language Learners:

Due to my [teacher research project which led to my] increased presence in schools, teachers I have never met before and who have never previously attended any of my PD sessions are now seeking support. This outreach has shown teachers and administrators that I am invested in the success of the teachers and students in our school division. In an age of individualized education plans, district leaders can no longer rely on a "one size fits all" approach to PD. When I am observing teachers in schools throughout our division, I am expecting to see them differentiate their lessons and acknowledge the individual learners in their rooms, so why should we accept any less when it comes to the way we train educators? Gradually, more and more educational leaders are beginning to acknowledge the undeniable truth that "teaching is inherently complex and nuanced" and that we must provide teachers with PD that recognizes this (Gulamhussein, 2013). While I was able to find many resources touting what quality PD should look like, the amount of reports that actually give specifics of successful programs were shockingly limited in number.

Strategy 5. Who Has Power to Eliminate Racist Policies?

It is certainly the case that principals and superintendents have the power and obligation to eliminate racist policies that impact all schools in their jurisdiction (Horsford, Stovall, Hopson, & D'Amico, 2019). Yet we also believe that teachers are and can be powerful leaders in this effort. Data from two teachers, Linda, the music teacher, and an anonymous alumnus interview, offer some evidence of small "p" abilities to eliminate racist policies. A program alumnus indicated that he or she might have embraced the "soft bigotry of low expectations" (Stoops, 2018, quoting Michael Gerson) when engaging with students, only to be pushed to act differently:

Challenging assumptions comes much easier, now that I've made it a habit. I remember going into my student case study during our first Fall session with a lot of assumptions about how stress was ruining the lives of our teenagers. Interviewing the students' parents helped me see multiple perspectives. They didn't feel that the stress in [our region] was a bad thing, per se, but instead gave our kids opportunities they wouldn't have elsewhere. I had never even considered a positive outcome of stress.

In her end-of-program portfolio, Linda, the music teacher, experienced tension between her small "p" policy victories outside her music classroom and her big "p" policy aspirations:

I challenged the existing [gifted program] screening process. I gave several examples of students who I felt were unfairly excluded from the gifted services. I talked with many other teachers in my school who agreed with me that the students I was advocating for should be receiving gifted services. ..... I have not found any evidence of my supporting my students' social justice awareness. I believe this is because I am still developing my own social justice awareness. Since I am not confident in this topic, I do not feel knowledgeable enough to guide my students in their own journey.

Yet at the level of her own music classroom, Linda felt empowered to make curricular changes that could be antiracist:

The first thing I am going to do is finish the [comprehensive music and movement] certification that I started years ago. This will enable me to better teach improvisation and composition so my students can create their own music. I would love for the day to come where I can put on a concert entirely with student created music. [The certification] will enable me to find ways to make music more culturally relevant to my students. Since they will be creating their own music, it will be relevant to their lives. They can create using themes from their own lives.

Kelsey, a white high school health and fitness teacher, sought to address the concerns of her students who are Latinx, many of them recent immigrants to the U.S., and who have experienced myriad challenges in the large, impersonal school setting. Starting with herself, Kelsey took on small and large "p" policy changes in her school:

The progress I made last year in understanding that making a connection and treating all students with respect and patience, instead of rushing through and trying to get everything done, has already made a big difference in my teaching. Of course, we all think we are good teachers, care about all students, and always treat students fairly. I learned that there was a lot more that I could give and therefore more I could get back from the students. Through the discussions, readings, and learning in this program, I can also easily recognize other teachers who are exhibiting behaviors on the nonexistent side of the Cain rubric. I don't think I am at the transformative level yet, but I can see myself growing (and therefore my students benefiting) to reach the progressing and advancing stages. Not restricted to just this project, for example, I am working on helping students in the "Committed to Students" section...and would say I'm in the advancing stages in trying to give one of my [Hispanic English Language] students, who has not only a language difficulty but also a hearing challenge, a voice by examining the factors that set him up for failure. I have spoken with an ESOL teacher and an administrator about a policy that would allow students to avoid being put into a class with a previous teacher from whom they had received a failing grade. Other students' cultural capital would have them removed by their parents from a repeat failing teacher, but this student doesn't have that knowledge or support. His counselor told him there weren't any options, and the student didn't know any other avenues for change. Hopefully, this policy will be changed so all students are treated equitably, regardless of their language skills or the amount of academic support provided by their parents.

Strategy 6. Disseminate and Educate About Correctives

Although an optional part of the legislative visits, most teachers worked together to create a policy brochure to leave with their elected officials that described their position on a public policy issue of deep concern to teachers. Figure 1 is an example of a brochure that focused on school safety and gun violence.

Strategy 7. Work With Antiracist Policy Makers

One of the few men in the program, Angelo, described in his end-of-program portfolio narrative the intersection between his growth as a more collaborative teacher and his growth into a big "p" policy actor at the school district level:

Teacher collaboration and relationship building was key in all of the shifts that took place. Teacher collaboration and relationship building created a space where the teachers felt supported and safe to try something new. Then the teachers were able to create the same space for students to feel safe enough

Figure 1. Policy Pamphlet

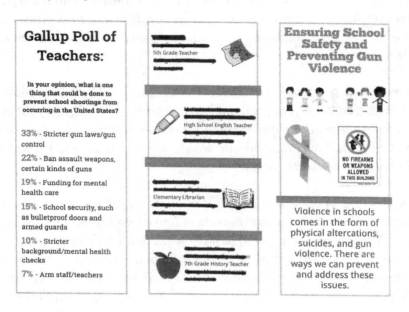

to try something new as well, although it took time for both relationships to blossom (both teacher relationships and student relationships). In 2016 there is much talk about teachers not feeling supported. That message is delivered from many different stakeholders. Sometimes it comes from school board members arguing for a bigger budget. Other times it comes from principals petitioning their superintendents for more resources. It even comes from teachers who say they are leaving the profession for that very reason. Teacher support means many different things to different people, all of whom are trying to be heard. What this research project demonstrated is that if teachers could just be given the time to collaborate – that is unstructured time without an agenda or an administrator overseeing the meeting – then they very well may be able to find the support that they are looking for on their own. Teachers may feel that support when they have had the opportunity to build a relationship with a colleague and they very well may be willing to try new and different strategies and techniques that break from the norm and that benefit all of their students in a holistic way.*

This year I partnered with one teacher whose classroom I supported through ELL services and I've already begun to plan for expanding on that for next year. I am now having conversations with teachers who would be interested in partnering in a similar way. I have data and students and a cooperating teacher vouching for how all forms of collaboration that took place this year led to more positive outcomes for students, which is always at the helm of everything we do.

[I learned] that as a teacher leader I am capable of effecting policy. The initial shift that took place for me was essentially realizing that being a teacher could actually empower me to push for changes in policy, whereas before I truly believed that no one would want to hear what I had to say, simply because I was a teacher.

The [legislative visit] was a defining moment ... for me in just one day. [I was initially] worried that my understanding of policy may not be as sharp as the politicians we were going to meet with, and I then reflected on how in many cases it seemed that we were actually more informed than they were. The empowerment that I felt through the experience [made me realize] that if I could go and discuss policy with such high-ranking officials, then engaging in similar conversations on a local level would be far less daunting.

I also reflect[ed] on what this experience meant for me as a leader and talked about how taking risks, which is something that I had tried to avoid, was not only necessary for leadership but could have a big payoff as well.

This experience was supplemented by the policy brief. I was brand new to [my city] as a home owner and as a school division employee and was nervous to put myself out there and be taking a stance on issues that I was only just beginning to get a handle on. However, like in the case of the [legislative visit], I was met with responses from local officials who at least appeared to be happy to hear from me and interested in what I had to say.

The combination of things I learned through the [legislative visit] and the policy brief piqued my interest in shaping policy in [my city] and ultimately led to my application to join the city council's Child, Youth and Families Collaborative Commission....My learning from the program immediately became applicable since being appointed in January. [I created a Power Map] as my commission chose to focus on affordable housing as one of its key interests. Our goal was to lobby the right groups in order to push the city council to allocate more than $5 million for increasing the affordable housing stock.

What I learned through power mapping and the change game is that one really does need to know how to leverage relationships and know the proper channels to go through in order to accomplish any kind of change. We took on this battle because it is an important equity issue that children and families face in this city, and I am proud to say that, although this was one of the first projects that I worked on as a commissioner, we were successful.

We continue to look at issues of equity, and I have my voice in all of those discussions. I recently emailed my mentors to solicit their opinion because the commission wanted to host community forums about equity and allow the community discussion to drive the direction of what equity issues the commission should focus on next. I recognized that, in a city where 87 different languages are spoken, many perspectives would be left out.

This is not something that I would have stopped to think about two years ago nor something that anyone else on the commission considered either. I've since thrown a wrench into those plans by voicing this concern, and through the process I realized that my perspective as a teacher leader matters, it's important, and it does afford me the opportunity to shape policy and help address equity in my city.

Strategy 8. Remove Racists

Using a "politics of interruption" (Stovall, 2016, p. 12), teachers can work with colleagues, parents, and policy makers to navigate power structures to demand quality education and equity for all students. In a critical reflection essay, Lesley, a Biracial Latinx early childhood teacher, wondered how to support in-service teachers and screen pre-service teachers in the hiring process for their dispositions toward children and Youth of Color:

I wonder what kind of professional development could be held that will help teachers adopt a growth mindset about their students? I wonder how the interview process for new teachers at a school could somehow pick up on the mindset of the teacher being considered for a new position? This is something that I will continue to explore in my classroom and at my school.

Strategy 9. Monitor Closely

In her end-of-program portfolio narrative, Charlotte, a white high school Latin teacher, reflected on the power of data and its use in schools:

I think challenging assumptions also means assumptions about what qualifies as data. I now understand that data means a lot more than numbers and statistics. It's taken a while for me to get on board, but I understand that anecdotes are legitimate pieces of evidence, and I now see bits of evidence in more places than before. In the end review that I wrote for the first Fall semester, I said, "Data can be powerful. I still, however, hold to a lot of original disdain towards the way we use data to drive decisions in Education. There are so many factors that we cannot fit into a number, and I think that we still rely too heavily on data in policies and administration. I now have a deeper understanding of what data is, and I would now say that I have a disdain towards the way we use the wrong kind of data to drive decisions in education.

Strategy 10. Start Again, as Needed

All of the teachers were forced to "start again," especially with their teacher research projects, partly due to the dynamic school environments in which they worked and partly because we insisted that they keep probing for more data and deeper analysis of the data. As stated in one of the alumni interviews:

[The professors] kept us on our toes. You never quite knew what they were going to ask, but I always anticipated they were going to ask me something to make me squirm because I felt like that was the learning part: asking me a question that I knew the answer, you know, that wasn't their purpose. Their purpose was to

push us into that uncomfortable space and talk about things that we might not normally, you know, talk about. I think that they did a really good job expecting more of us. .... 'No, we talk about this. It's something to talk about because the more we talk about it, the less uncomfortable we are.'

Strategy 11. Vigilance

An alumnus of the program expressed the need for antiracist vigilance in describing their abilities to act as an antiracist teacher:

At the end of the program, I felt like I definitely was more skilled at having conversations about equity and race and other topics than I was at the beginning. But now, two years after that, I feel like I've developed a little bit further, but I'm not 100% sure.

So I'm going back to the coursework just to double check, but I'm kind of in the unknown.

Um, so as teachers are going through their careers after they may have left the classroom, some may be in a leadership role. How do you transfer those skills that were based on student study, lesson study, curriculum study, policy focus? How does that translate as you grow in your trajectory? That may be hard to do, but it could even just involve looking at some different types of leadership styles ...

Another, when asked to discuss the graduate program experience of examining race, stated:

...I'm trying to think. Yes. I mean when we talked about race and [one of the professors] said, 'It's going to be uncomfortable. You have to be uncomfortable to talk about it.' And, I had a little one last year who, um, whose mom was white and his dad was Black and nobody else in the class was black. So [student name}, I don't know how he saw himself, but you know, he would bring it up quite a bit and the kids' heads would snap. 'Wa Wa he's being racist'. 'No, he's not' No he's not. you know, before I would have just kind of shoved it under the rug, but I felt more comfortable talking about it, and I used their words. It's not comfortable for people to talk about. White people think that talking about race makes you racist. No, we talk about this. It's something to talk about because the more we talk about it, the less uncomfortable we are. So, I mean that helped when I kind of channeled the instructors for that.

Yet this same alumnus, in response to the prompt, "Tell me your thoughts about race," stated, "It's difficult today to talk about and I feel like, of all of the areas, it's the area I'm least comfortable talking about, least comfortable dealing with, and have still the most to learn."

Another alumnus unwittingly made the case for vigilance in making regular equity discussions an acceptable and necessary discipline in schools by stating that "[This school district] is made up primarily of white females. I think that is reflective of the field of education in general, though. That's all I feel comfortable commenting on here."

WHAT TEACHERS WANT IN TEACHER PROFESSIONAL DEVELOPMENT

Our teachers have told us what they want from teacher professional development and what they valued from our program. Consistent with our national survey asking whether teacher professional development matters and the characteristics of high-quality teacher professional development, the data from program alumni indicates that they desire immediately applicable information and techniques that can enhance student learning, collaboration with professional colleagues, critical dialogue with peers, awareness of student difference/differentiation, the opportunity to learn about learner-centered instruction, the opportunity for self-reflection, and the opportunity to create culturally relevant lessons. In describing the master's degree program, one alumnus stated:

A lot of professional development that I have experienced does not consider my experience or expertise in an area. So I'm just talked at a lot and then it's up to me to kind of make meaning with whatever understanding I got out of the session. Whereas in the [master's degree] program, I was constructing my understanding as I was learning the process, so it was immediately relevant. I think I could have deeper levels of understanding and meaning-making from the time that I spent in that program versus other professional learning.

Other elements of the program were also highlighted in alumni interviews:

Equity

"So as far as the program materials, um, I thought that it was really interesting and relevant, and I felt like we were always one step ahead of like all the hard-hitting topics of the day. So it was talking about equity and for like two years we were talking about equity and then all of a sudden now in [my school district], the big buzzword is equity. But two years ago we were already talking about that and that's just one of the things that I noticed. I was like, 'Oh wow, you know, we've been talking ...' I liked that I got to try new things in my classroom, like flexible seating was a big project that I did and was actively able to incorporate into my classroom. Like as I was doing the project, um, I did a project, a research paper or project on parent communication. So I was able to, you know, actively try new things with parent communication. So, I don't know, what's the word I'm looking for. It was a really good way to like try new things but also be supported in that at the same time and do it all for credit."

Critical Pedagogy

I think especially the critical pedagogy piece where you're always supposed to be reflecting and thinking about what you're doing and how you could do it better. I think professional development is the way that you can go out and better yourself and learn tools and add more things to your classroom. I think that the in- school – like the mandated professional development – hasn't always been stewarded well."

Relevance

"It never felt like we were doing coursework for the sake of doing coursework. Like it was always an extra, really connected to my classroom, and I was always able to use everything that we did pretty immediately after we were talking about it.

Self-Reflection

...Everything we're learning as we're learning it, I was envisioning how it worked with the kids In my room. The projects that they had us do, um, pushed us to do things we might not normally do. I mean walking around Capitol Hill, talking to our Congress people; I thought that the trips were

amazingly valuable. I thought that [the professors] were respectful of our time, instead of reading this whole book 'Here, read this chapter.' I thought that everything they had us do project-wise, the collaborations, the, you know, they would regroup us so that we had access to all the different people within the cohort. It's just, it was seamless the way everything's designed and the way everything ran.

OUTCOMES TO DATE

An important component of antiracist teacher professional development is its "stickiness" (Baird, 2012; Gladwell, 2000/2002; Inglis, 2014), or the extent to which it fosters vigilance and an expanding network of people who act to create educational equity. We were also interested in the outcomes related to changes in the program design.

Program Stickiness

Excerpts from alumni interviews offer insights into the longitudinal impact of program experiences:

Antiracist Awareness

I really came into the program thinking like, 'you're either racist or you're not.' and I've learned a lot since then. But I learned that race is like so much more or less than what we think it is and that it is sort of this social construct, that is embedded in our history and our society and we're socialized to make these assumptions that people do about race. So I also met a big Aha for me and growing moment was that I sort of went in thinking like, "Oh, I, I'm colorblind, I don't see color in the classroom, we're all equal,' and I learned very quickly that it's actually worse to ignore a student's color or their culture or their background because it's just denying all of their history. And so that was a really big growing moment for me too. Realizing that, embracing and welcoming all of that and even talking about it when appropriate (which I have yet to do in my classroom, but I'm going to someday), is really important.

Antiracist Self-Reflection

"Speaking from a deficit perspective has been a habit for me. If I can continue to be aware of this bad habit and change my perspective, that can be a big step in the right direction. Negative words from a teacher is a sure way to destroy motivation. The research process has made me reflect. When I actively observe, talk with co-workers and students to gain more perspective, and act to change what I feel is not working, I apply the strategies of the research process on a regular basis. I feel that the more I consider the perspective of others and the more I learn about teaching, the more likely I will be to make the research process a habit. I have also learned that my critical consciousness has been awakened by not only the research process, but more so from the knowledge I have gained from this graduate program. I have learned to ask important questions, not assume that I know the answers. I have learned to view things through a more compassionate lens. I now know I am not the center of the class. I am not dictating as much as I am guiding. As I type this, I am remembering a less-than- proud moment when I reverted to dictator status with less-than-successful results. I created a standoff situation where no one could 'win.' Now, if I don't have the forethought to do what's right or best in the moment, I am able to reflect and try a better alternative next time. I am more mindful of my actions as they are happening and am more likely to step aside instead of confront or put a student in a power struggle situation where one of us will 'lose.' How can a child feel motivated to participate in such a negatively competitive environment?"

Antiracist Relationships With Students

This [program] changed the way I look at my kids, the way I look at my coworkers. It changed the way I look at the people in the grocery store. I think it had more impact. I feel like this made me a better teacher, made me a better person, as opposed to giving me tools to incorporate technology into learning. I feel like this program was made to change the way people teach.

[When probed to say more about how the alumnus sees things differently, the teacher responded:]

I have a boy in my class who is listed as homeless. He's Special Ed, he's ESOL. He has every label possible. When he shuts down, when he's working, instead of assuming, 'Oh, he's just being a pain in the butt,' if you've walked over and talked to him, you'll realize that you've said a word he doesn't understand or he doesn't hear the directions and is embarrassed to ask again. So just taking the time to listen. You know, I would not have, I would have just stereotyped him.

Antiracist Relationships With Families

I learned a lot. I learned what it really means to be responsive to students and families. Um, I learned sort of why this work is so important right now because, like I said, I even have a paper that I wrote about this. I went into the program thinking like, 'I'm, I'm not racist' or like, you know, kind of the big picture, but not really understanding what is diversity. And it's so much more than, you know, race, skin color or language or anything else. It's stuff that you can't see. Um, so that's a really big takeaway for me...

Antiracist Agency in Curricular Design

The cultural unit [I was assigned to create] supported my third-grade curriculum perfectly. While we spent the year learning about many famous Americans, we really didn't get a chance to dig deep into their lives, beyond just the basic facts. Through this unit my students were able to better relate to these individuals and were inspired to learn more on their own about them.

So I can still see, you know, the footprint and the fingerprints, the fingerprints of the program, like in my classroom now with the, um, just all the new things that I got to try. So we did a technology unit and I put it in, uh, like a bunch of new games and I wrote a grant, which I have done since then. So we wrote a grant for technology, which I didn't get, but it kind of broke that ice, although I haven't gotten one since then. So I'm not going to say, 'I'm a successful grant writer now,' but I have done a few more since then. So it kind of broke the ice and um, it's not like this unattainable thing that's out there and so I'm like, 'Oh, I can write these, like I can do this.' So that was, that was helpful and that was something that I definitely see I do now that I didn't do before. I've also got like yoga balls all over my classroom —some flexible seating stuff going on that I really tried to incorporate little-by-little each year. Uh, just attuned to things that help the students focus more, I guess.

Collegiality

This program didn't directly impact my teaching, exactly. I feel like it helped me develop as a teammate and a leader with my peers more than with my students.

Program Design Outcomes

Another set of outcomes relate to our design of the program. We were highly resistant to the pressure to shift a successful 20+ year fully face-to-face program to a fully online program. Our resistance was manifold. We enjoyed the personal interaction with students, the excitement that comes from co-creating curriculum, from entering those organic "teachable moments," and from the human emotions that are a natural part of teaching and learning. We perceived a very steep learning curve regarding the development of online instructional skills. Most important, we did not believe a fully online program would permit us to successfully and authentically build trust and community among cohort teachers, and between ourselves and the teachers. It was this sense of trusting community that allowed for the deep excavations of antiracist professional development.

Our resistance won the ability to create a hybrid program rather than a fully online program. We structured the program to begin with face-to-face meetings. The very first encounter was a full week of in-person instruction and orientation. This occurred the summer before the first academic year of online instruction and became the basis for meaningful shared reflection and communication during our online learning. We also added a second week of face-to-face encounters during the second summer session between the first and second years of online instruction. Outlined below are comments from two alumni who specifically commented on the outcomes of this hybrid design.

Flexibility

The online cohort format is much like the Career Switcher's format, which was a perfect fit for me, providing the flexibility I needed while supporting me in acquiring an excellent education. It also embodies the ideals of imparting research- based practices to which, as a scientist, I am firmly committed.

Depth of Instruction and Learning

I would say the professors [are the strength of the program]. Also I really feel like the assignments and the readings. I don't know that I speak for everybody, but I know for me, I really, I didn't do one project or assignment or reading that I felt was a waste of my time. I think the structure of it, like having it mostly online, some face-to-face, um, I think that made it more doable for people. Like I wouldn't have been able to do a face-to-face, like a full face-to-face master's program, but that said, I think the feedback they got revealed from our cohort was that we wish we could have more like Saturday sessions or more opportunities to meet in person. Other strengths? I think just the constant opportunities for reflection and growth is a strength. And then also just the way that they taught us was really modeling. Like from day one they were modeling for us how to have these [difficult] conversations, how to do this with our students, how to do this with other adults too.

TENSIONS AND DILEMMAS

As program designers and teacher educators, we may be proud of student outcomes, yet as researchers, we cannot ignore the disaffirming data that emerged from alumni interviews, as well as the praise. One alum stated that, "It's too 'frustrating' to do this work. Too few resources and pressures of testing." For another alum the course content was useful but did not take the place of professional power in making change for educational equity:

I think all that we learned in class was very powerful and thought-provoking. One thing that I learned since, though, is that seniority plays a larger role. As I've changed schools twice since class. I am realizing that how long you've been in a school and grade level is more powerful than who you are coming in. Your experience has some weight, but others' time in the school generally outweighs you.

Two other alumni noticed differences in the work experience between Title I schools and more affluent schools.

After teaching 6 years of Title I, I wanted to return to a school closer to what I grew up in personally. While I love all children, the parents and the challenges that came with Title I were reason enough to leave. The pressures of testing and the lack of resources were really frustrating to deal with on a daily basis. I am much happier at my new school. I used the [master's degree] program as a way to improve my Title I frustrations by networking with people in class, brainstorming ways to fix my situation, and learning about the surrounding counties. As a result, I left [one school district] on a pay scale 1, to a bordering county with a pay scale 6. (Alum interview)

There is definitely a divide [among schools]. I won't say that the teachers are better in one kind of school over another, but there is less transiency in non-Title I schools. Being at a 'non-Title I' school now, I notice that we have less funding. We have to buy more of our own supplies or we have to ask the parents for them. Less money is available to teachers and we have less technology. (Alum interview)

One alum expressed a primary concern that made the master's program very difficult for the university to "market," despite the accolades from many alumni:

The only thing I regret about this program was that I walked away with a degree that didn't really get me anywhere different. I got the pay bump that I wanted, but I don't have any specialized skills that will broaden my teaching abilities (in terms of a resume). I went in as a general education teacher and I am leaving/staying a general education teacher. The only change that I can really make is maybe becoming an instructional coach. Yes, I can be a lead teacher, but I could have eventually gotten that with experience and seniority anyway. There are times I wish I had done a special education or reading endorsement instead.

And, then, there are the alums whose "stickiness" was difficult to discern. Is the following teacher being respectful or disdainful of parental wishes? Is she preserving professional boundaries or dismissing parental concerns?

… I have two boys [students] that my pet peeve is that they don't go outside and play. They stay inside and play video games all afternoon. And I stopped harassing them, because I started thinking, 'well, maybe they're not allowed to go outside.' Maybe I don't live in a place where their parents want them to go, maybe, their parents aren't home and they don't want them outside until they get home and when they get home it's too late to go outside. So, just, you

know, taking a step back and thinking about things like that, is something I wouldn't have done in the past. Um, but I also have a parent who wants me to tell her kid not to play video games anymore, and that's not my job.

WHAT WE RECOMMEND FOR ANTIRACIST TEACHER PROFESSIONAL DEVELOPMENT

Ideally, investments in antiracist teacher professional development would be part of overall reforms in public school funding. Only 8% of funding for public schools comes from the federal government and the balance from states (48%) and from localities (44%) (Park, 2007). State funds, ideally, would be used to balance the inequities in spending and distribution that result from local property-tax-based educational resources. States would provide substantial per-pupil funding, distributed in such a way as to address the concentrations of poverty throughout the state with the generosity afforded by its wealthiest taxpayers, including those whose children do not attend public schools.

Yet only the states of New Jersey and Wyoming come close to equity on four measures of school funding equity: funding level, funding distribution, effort, and coverage (Baker, Farrie, & Sciarra, 2018). More often,, schools where 70% of the students qualify for free or reduced-price lunch (a standard measure of poverty) are severely underfunded, even those that are highly celebrated for student achievement and 100% graduation rates (Strauss, 2018). In New Jersey adequate funding was the result of 21 court orders forced by school districts on elected officials – an indicator that much of the decision-making about public school expenditures are within the policy framework of teacher organizations. Working with parent and community groups, in a practice of critical policy analysis (Horsford, Scott & Anderson, 2019, p. 210), teacher leaders can force the issue of adequate, if not generous, public school funding that can support critical teacher professional development.

Darden and Cavendish (2012) also advocate for the kind of non-money resource allocations controlled by school boards that can erase the education debt/opportunity gap in schools and school districts. Such policies include teacher assignment (assigning experienced high-quality teachers equally across schools); staff-based budgeting (making leftover salary funds available to the poorer schools for teacher training and to create financial incentives for recruitment of more seasoned higher-quality teachers); formal equality over equity (allocating resources according to the number of students in a school); assigning equal amounts of the general education funds to poorer schools, regardless of the amount of categorical funding they receive for programs like free and reduced lunch and English language support; parental involvement (welcoming the funds of knowledge that less-affluent parents can offer, in addition to offering their children the kinds of extracurricular and arts programs more affluent parents secure for their children); curriculum (making available to all children upper-level courses in science, mathematics, foreign language, etc.); and building maintenance costs (allocating funds according to the age and condition of the school building, rather than on a per-pupil basis).

As we have indicated in other chapters of this book, we believe that it is in our collective self-interest to change our educational policies – at the small "p" and the big "p" levels – even if we fail at changing the hearts of educators and policy makers. We also understand that the nature of a program such as described here is labor-intensive and could be unattractive to some potential graduate in-service teachers and/or some teacher education faculty, and expensive for universities to run. Policy makers may quake at the thought of organized and empowered teacher leaders with an antiracist policy agenda that places Children of Color, low income children, emergent bilingual children, immigrant children, and children with varying abilities on equal footing with their own children.

Policy makers, universities, state departments of education, school districts and accrediting authorities that embrace the task of creating antiracist education for all children will seek to create and invest in enduring and meaningful professional development that elicits quotes such as this:

I believe that I would have been another "check the box" [equity] trainee if not for the [master's degree] program. Because of the program I really understand the importance of the issue of equity. I believe most people want to do what's right but, I don't think the real understanding is there the way those in [our program] understand.

We embrace the idea that Kennedy (2019) proposes about the nature of strong professional development that has the ability to make a difference in the lives of teachers, students, and communities:

[There are] three ways of thinking about how to improve teaching: one focusing on teaching behaviors, one on increasing content knowledge, and one on strategic thinking...the third approach has had the greatest positive impact on

teachers' effectiveness...[there is] some evidence that this approach enables teachers to continue to improve their own practice independently after the formal PD is finished...due to its emphasis on purpose, which in turn helps teachers function autonomously after the PD providers are gone. (p. 157)

Schools and school districts lacking in strong and race-conscious teacher education and teacher professional development stand to continue to be embarrassed by the kind of news-worthy mistakes that well-meaning classroom teachers can make when using their imaginations (or assumptions) to create lessons they believe are culturally relevant or even antiracist (e.g., Garces, Ishimaru, & Takahashi, 2017). More importantly, these schools and school districts will be guilty of continuing the structural and cultural violence (Galtung, 1969; 1990) against children and teachers that perpetuate racism.

Team Self-Reflection

As teacher educators, our continuing challenge has been to help P-12 teachers – at all grade levels, in all subjects, and at varying stages of adult development – to translate antiracist theory into practice. At its core, this book highlights how difficult it can be to transform teaching practices, even in a two-year master's degree professional development cohort. After analyzing the myriad sources of data, we were sometimes disappointed by the teacher outcomes. What was most puzzling was that we thought that we had, over the course of the twenty years, scaffolded the theories and strategies leading up to the development of teacher products. The curriculum we designed had our teachers analyze video clips of P-12 educators focusing on academic achievement, developing cultural competence, and developing critical consciousness with their students; read and discuss articles and books; engage in simulations; create new curriculum; gather and analyze classroom and schoolwide data; engage with local, state, and national policy makers; and engage in endless self-reflection. In the early days of the program, there was evidence that teachers could identify antiracist teaching and critique the work of others, but that they sometimes struggled to translate those insights into their own practice. Later, we incorporated processes where teachers regularly and more fully analyzed one another's work as a way to illuminate gaps in their understandings and between their knowledge and their practice.

What seems clear is the need for continuing and intentional efforts to deepen the practice of P-12 teachers and of teacher educators to enact antiracist pedagogy. Toward this end, teacher educators need to develop knowledge and skills to support the convergence of theory and practice in P-12 teachers' work. This praxis must include more effective ways to reach and challenge all students to be successful, not merely as measured by standardized test scores, but as actualized in students' successful participation in our diverse and dynamic society.

We attempted to do this. Yet we became aware that in the multicultural, multilingual, multiclass classrooms where our teachers work, we wanted teachers to differentiate the antiracist lens they used: for Children of Color, we wanted their teachers to place special emphasis on high expectations of academic achievement and to name and address the root causes of inequity as a way to resist the null curriculum (Flinders, Noddings, & Thornton, 1986) and to validate students' experiences; for school settings that were all-white, we wanted teachers to demonstrate cultural competence through their critique of white privilege and of the myth of a hierarchy of human value and to demonstrate critical consciousness through specific and concrete actions to address the root causes of inequality with their white administrators, colleagues, students, and parents. After all, the world into which these students are entering is not all-white.

Early in our practice we were limited by a reliance on the theories and practices of constructivism and critical pedagogy, rather than on a full embrace of antiracist pedagogy. Constructivism demands that the curriculum be guided by the stories that people bring to the educational setting, rather than on the faculty driving the learning toward pre-set outcomes. One outcome that we sought was that our teachers improve their practice, and adult learning theories urge a developmental approach that meets people where they are, rather than attempting to impose an ideal outcome on their learning process. What that meant, however, was a discovery early on that we had walked on eggshells regarding explicit discussions of racism, either to avoid being pigeonholed as "progressive faculty with political agendas" or "the angry Black woman" who silences teachers in the early stages of racial identity development. Rather than saying outright to teachers, "Race is a social construct that upholds and sustains racism and white privilege; who are you as a racial being in your classroom setting and how can we subvert racism and acts of whiteness through the curriculum we design and use?" we instead said, "What are the cultures you see in your classroom, and how can you design curriculum that helps all students achieve academically, attain and share cultural competence, and consider the structural inequities that exist in our society?" In the more recent online iteration of the program, we attempted to employ antiracist pedagogy to compensate for the inadequacy of the earlier scaffolds we prepared for teachers.

Below is an example of the kind of extensive feedback we offered to a cohort that engaged in an online discussion of their own teacher research, including what they took from the book by Harry and Klingner (2014) about race and disability in schools:

Feedback on Discussion #2

We have enjoyed your posts regarding the Harry and Klingner text and the implications for your research. You have generated some exciting dialogue through the questions you posed to one another – keep up the good work! Serving as your critical friends, we have several thoughts and insights to share from the themes that emerged:

"People First" language:

We want to emphasize the importance of using "people first" language – for example, referring to "children with special needs," rather than saying "SPED kids" – and we strongly encourage the community to maintain this discipline as a way to uphold human dignity. This is especially important when we are referring to children who are still growing, changing, and becoming. It is even more important when we understand that "disability" is a social construction based on social norms of what qualifies as ability, achievement, success, etc. Check out this <u>resource</u> *for more information.*

[Note: we have since understood that there is controversy about this language usage, particularly in the Deaf and Autism communities].

The value of special education services:

Many of you did a good job of identifying and examining assumptions in the text and identifying and examining your own assumptions. The goal is not to confirm all of our assumptions, but to challenge them by embracing the opportunity to examine them carefully through multiple perspectives. Ultimately, through this process you will come to a deeper understanding and potentially to disconfirm your assumptions. We will never penalize you for proving yourself wrong!

Sometimes we feel discomfort or uncertainty about ideas when they challenge our assumptions, and some strategies to deal with this discomfort and uncertainty are to attempt to delegitimize the text by questioning the value of the research or by resisting the ideas with the argument that it is not your experience (e.g., you don't see any examples in your own settings of disproportionality in special education). We are in favor of and encourage you to speak back to any form of communication (i.e., questioning assumptions, perspectives, and conclusions of all the media you encounter, including articles, books, videos, etc.). However, part of taking a critical stance is being willing to move past defensiveness or lack of personal knowledge/naiveté to consider the research and evidence-based reality.

There is a tension between providing appropriate services and "tracking" – the "good" and "bad" of labeling. For example, Stacia's experience with ability grouping of first graders is that the intention was to offer children who were struggling readers more support by group, but then her school discovered that by fifth grade the same students never "graduated" to become proficient readers. Similarly, some of you were concerned about students who are English Language Learners being misidentified because their second language acquisition process is a "slower" learning process. Do you think it's possible that this hesitation to dually identify English Language Learners was part of the disparity between African American and Latinx students being identified?

We encourage you to use your critical stance to examine more closely the impact of structures, policies, and practices in your school. Some of you discussed incorrect referral practices while leaving unquestioned the need for referrals. It may be irrelevant that the structural bias is intentional; what matters more is the impact of the structural bias on children in schools.

Racial and class bias in special education is a complicated issue. Obviously, bias exists in schools (and in the world), and Children of Color and children from low-income families and children who are learning English may be unfairly placed (and "locked") into special education programs that underestimate their potential to achieve. Also, labeling could mean more funding for kids in need who would otherwise be overlooked or ignored by schools. There is a long history of critique and evidence of cultural bias in testing that you may want to explore using the reference list from this article: https://journals. sagepub.com/doi/abs/10.1177/8755123315576212

For those who are wanting to learn more about the origins of the special education system, Tom Skrtic's work in disability studies that critiques special education theory and practice would be a good source of information. Another side of special education is reflected in Rosa's comments about affluent white parents pursuing SPED diagnoses. Peter Demerath's book is a good source for understanding how different contexts impact the labeling culture. His book entitled "Producing success: The culture of personal advancement in an American high school" explores how labels (e.g., IEP's) are desirable in many affluent communities, since these are seen as helping students get ahead.

There were some comments that reflected an unquestioning acceptance of the status quo. The school system is a bureaucracy that leans toward standardization, rather than toward individualized whole-child practices. There are certain levels at which students need to perform. If they don't reach those levels, special education testing becomes the "obvious" path to take. However, we need to ask the questions: How are standardized proficiency levels decided and by whom, and where is there flexibility to take into account developmental differences among students? Where there are genuine disAbilities, how can we create a system that offers targeted support of the specific needs without stigmatizing the child or the family?

Impact of testing culture on labeling:

Some of you have more latitude and/or take more time to provide extra support to students, either because of the nature of your school setting or because you act defiantly within a more restrictive setting (smile). You do the best you can, even as you realize the ways in which standardized testing is creating a labeling culture. Testing drives the need for a strict pace that requires leaving kids behind and suggesting that something is wrong with them, rather providing children more time and exposure to content. You recognize that more and longer exposure to material is often what is needed, rather than labeling children as having an innate disAbility.

Research-related issues:

· There is a fundamental difference between qualitative research in general and teacher research that perhaps is not clear from the text. In teacher research, you MUST **analyze data in the process of collecting it, particularly because**

there is an action component in teacher research that is influenced by the data analysis. Please do not put off the analysis until you have collected all of the data!!

- You expressed lots of appreciation for the discussion on triangulation. Triangulation is more than a "good idea" –it is an essential part of research. Be sure to articulate how you are making sure to ground your findings in strong evidence.
- Asking each other for advice about the research process or for clarification about ideas and experiences is an excellent way to generate *dialogue*. The value of collaboration and sharing data is an important part of the research process and we encourage you to **use the peer space on [online discussion space] for doing that.**
- **Objectivity:** On the subject of objectivity, no one should be trying to **prove** anything. Your conclusions will never be neutral because your conclusions will likely lean in one direction or another, based on the strength of the evidence. But you are only making claims and supporting those claims with evidence, not offering the definitive answer to your research question. Remember that claims are the insights you gain from your research. They don't have to be positive outcomes!

CONCLUSION

Rather than engage in self-flagellation, we have continued to strive to dismantle racism in our curriculum and practice and in that of our teachers. Our teachers come into the master's program with a wide range of experiences and knowledge and also are at different levels of adult development, including racial identity development, as are we. Part of the challenge that all teachers face is to meet students where they are developmentally and to structure experiences that resonate with each individual in order to maximize their learning opportunities. The content we teach is not devoid of context and it is a constant negotiation of everyone's emerging understandings and struggles. Scholars and activists have been working for decades to tackle issues of racism and educational inequities; perhaps it has been too ambitious of us to expect dramatic transformation over the course of two years. Nevertheless, we have held ourselves to a high standard because we have to. As we write this book, we are exploring additional ways to more explicitly infuse antiracist teacher professional development into our work. We seek other teacher educators, policy makers, school administrators, teachers, and parents with whom to collaborate.

REFERENCES

Anyon, J. (1981). Social class and school knowledge. *Curriculum Inquiry*, *11*(1), 3–42. doi:10.1080/03626784.1981.11075236

Baird, A. A. (2012, March). *Sticky teaching*. Association for Psychological Science. https://www.psychologicalscience.org/observer/sticky-teaching

Baker, B. D., Farrie, D., & Sciarra, D. (2018). *Is school funding fair? A national report card* (7th ed.). Education Law Center.

Christensen, L. (2005, Winter). *Teacher Quality: Teachers teaching teachers*. Rethinking Schools Online. https://www.rethinkingschools.org/articles/teachers-teaching-teachers

Darden, E. C., & Cavendish, E. (2012). Achieving resource equity within a single school district: Erasing the opportunity gap by examining school board decisions. *Education and Urban Society*, *44*(1), 61–82. doi:10.1177/0013124510380912

Demerath, P. (2009). *Producing success: The culture of personal advancement in an American high school*. University of Chicago Press. doi:10.7208/chicago/9780226142425.001.0001

Flinders, D. J., Noddings, N., & Thornton, S. J. (1986). The null curriculum: Its theoretical basis and practical implications. *Curriculum Inquiry*, *16*(1), 33–42. doi:10.1080/03626784.1986.11075989

Friere, P. (2000). Pedagogy of the oppressed. *Continuum*.

Galtung, J. (1969). Violence, peace, and peace research. *Journal of Peace Research*, *6*(3), 167–191. doi:10.1177/002234336900600301

Galtung, J. (1990). Cultural violence. *Journal of Peace Research*, *27*(3), 291–305. doi:10.1177/0022343390027003005

Gannon, M. (2016, February 5). *Race is a social construct, scientists argue*. Scientific American. https://www.scientificamerican.com/article/race-is-a-social-construct-scientists-argue/

Garces, L. M., Ishimaru, A. M., & Takahashi, S. (2017). Introduction to *Beyond Interest Convergence*: Envisioning transformation for racial equity in education. *Peabody Journal of Education*, *92*(3), 291–293. doi:10.1080/0161956X.2017.1324654

Ginwright, S. (2018, May 31). *The future of healing: Shifting from trauma informed care to healing centered engagement*. Medium. https://medium.com/@ginwright/the-future-of-healing-shifting-from-trauma-informed-care-to-healing-centered-engagement-634f557ce69c

Gladwell, M. (2000/2002). *The tipping point: How little things can make a big difference*. Little Brown and Company.

Gulamhussein, A. (2013). *Teaching the teachers: Effective professional development in an era of high-stakes accountability*. The Center for Public Education.

Harry, B., & Klingner, J. K. (2014). *Why are so many minority students in special education?: Understanding race & disability in schools*. Teachers College Press.

Horsford, S. D., Alemán, E. A. Jr, & Smith, P. A. (2019). Our separate struggles are really one: Building political race coalitions for educational justice. *Leadership and Policy in Schools*, *18*(2), 226–236. doi:10.1080/15700763.2019.1611868

Horsford, S. D., Scott, J. T., & Anderson, G. L. (2019). *The politics of education policy in an era of inequality: Possibilities for democratic schooling*. Routledge.

Horsford, S. D., Stovall, D., Hopson, R., & D'Amico, D. (2019). School leadership in the New Jim Crow: Reclaiming justice, resisting reform. *Leadership and Policy in Schools*, *18*(2), 177–179. doi:10.1080/15700763.2019.1611872

Inglis, H. (2014, December 4). *What is Sticky Learning?* Seminariumblog. http://seminariumblog.org/books/sticky-learning/

Kendi, I. X. (2019). *How to be an antiracist*. One World.

Lorde, A. (1982, February). *Learning from the 60s* [Speech delivered at Harvard University]. Blackpast. https://www.blackpast.org/african-american-history/1982-audre-lorde-learning-60s/

Luke, A. (2010). Documenting reproduction and inequality: Revisiting Jean Anyon's "Social class and school knowledge.". *Curriculum Inquiry*, *40*(1), 167–182. doi:10.1111/j.1467-873X.2009.00474.x

Merriam Webster. (n.d.). White supremacy. In *Merriam Webster Dictionary*. Retrieved 2019 from http://www.learnersdictionary.com/definition/white%20 supremacist

Park, J. (2007, December 6). School finance. *Education Week*. https://www. edweek.org/we/issues/school-finance/

Pitman, D. (n.d.). *Discriminology*. https://www.discriminology.org

Race Matters Institute. (2019). *What do we mean when we say racial equity*. https://viablefuturescenter.org/racemattersinstitute/2014/03/12/what-do-we-mean-when-we-say-racial-equity/

Rochmes, J., Penner, E. K., & Loeb, S. (2017). *Educators As "Equity Warriors"* [CEPA Working Paper No.17-11]. Stanford Center for Education Policy Analysis: https://cepa.stanford.edu/content/educators-equity-warriors

Samuels, C. A. (2019, October 24). *The challenging often isolating work of school district chief diversity officers*. EducationWeek. https://www.edweek. org/ew/articles/2019/10/23/the-challenging-often-isolating-work-of-school. html?print=1

Srivastava, S. (2007). 'Let's talk': The pedagogy and politics of antiracist change. In Utopian pedagogy: Radical experiments against neoliberal globalization. University of Toronto Press.

Stern, C. (2020, February 18). *Schools get graded on racial equity*. The Daily Dose. https://www.ozy.com/the-new-and-the-next/the-next-school-testing-metric-racial-equity-report-cards/267776/

Stoops, T. (2018, September 27). *Overcoming the soft bigotry of low expectations for black males*. Carolina Journal. https://www.carolinajournal. com/opinion-article/overcoming-the-soft-bigotry-of-low-expectations-for-black-males/

Stovall, D. (2016). Out of adolescence and into adulthood: Critical race theory, retrenchment, and the imperative of praxis. *Urban Education*, *51*(3), 274–286. doi:10.1177/0042085915618718

Strauss, V. (2018, February 9). *This is what inadequate funding at a public school looks and feels like- as told by an entire faculty.* Washington Post. https://www.washingtonpost.com/news/answer-sheet/wp/2018/02/09/this-is-what-inadequate-funding-at-a-public-school-looks-and-feels-like-as-told-by-an-entire-faculty/?utm_term=.55aa517fc19f

Ture, K., & Hamilton, C. V. (1967/1992). *Black power: The politics of liberation.* Vintage Books.

Conclusion

In the process of finalizing this book for publication, the world came to an abrupt halt. The spread of COVID-19 reached global pandemic proportions. Non-essential businesses and schools were closed, social distancing was implemented, and shelter-in-place orders were given in an effort to "flatten the curve" and lessen the burden on our healthcare system in order to save lives. While at first glance a global pandemic might seem far removed from antiracist teacher professional development, we immediately saw ways in which they are intricately connected. We would be remiss if we did not at least briefly address some of these emerging issues and reflect on the ways in which we see antiracist teacher professional development as an essential part of a post-pandemic life. Most of these issues revolve around the use of online learning for P-12 classrooms and the glaring equity and access issues that have been highlighted as a result of this shift in instruction.

Overnight, teachers found themselves in the position of having to design distance learning opportunities for their students. School systems scrambled to figure out the possibilities of moving online, quickly learning that a significant percentage of students do not have access to the internet and/or to the technological devices needed to access any of the content that might be placed online. In some cases, teachers photocopied packets of work to mail to students, but there was little opportunity to follow up with students in order to assist them with the work. Many of the teachers with whom we work struggled with ever-changing messages coming from district offices: prepare to use this online platform, do not contact any of your students or require them to engage in learning opportunities, forget the online platform as we are switching to a new one, do not plan anything as the district will handle the planning of content in order to provide consistency, feel free to add on to the district's instruction in ways that make sense for your class(es)... It was clear that we were in uncharted waters as schools worked to fulfill their obligations to students while wrestling with how to reach all students in safe and appropriate ways and at the same time sustaining meaningful relationships with them. Teachers remained on the front line and were expected to work miracles in a system that was already broken. Had school systems -- and teachers -- already been critically aware, responding to a pandemic might have looked less like chaos and more like continuity of learning.

Let's look first at issues of equity and access. Although there were some great learning opportunities happening (e.g. video-conferencing), who was being left out? Some teachers reported an increase in building rapport with students because of the constant feedback with individual students on each learning activity. However, we heard reports from teachers that there were a handful of students in each of their classes whom they had not been able to contact. Often these students were members of already- disenfranchised groups -- Students of Color, students living in poverty, English Language Learners, and so forth. While we might be quick to celebrate the connections teachers *were* making with students, we cannot ignore the connections teachers *were not* making.

Furthermore, so many of those connections, particularly with young students, relied on parents who were able to help them connect. What about parents who were essential workers or those who had to work from home and could not devote time or provide technological devices? The class divide became more evident in this crisis. Using video conferencing exposed peers to others' living conditions, which impinged on their privacy and put some students in the position of being ridiculed. Online learning also privileged families who were familiar with the American schooling system; those who had not experienced the system themselves might not have been able to anticipate the knowledge and skills to be covered or how to support their children to develop these skills. For that matter, there were many parents who were familiar with the schooling system but still struggled to support the learning of their children. The public finally realized that teaching *is* a specialized profession that requires training and not something that "just anyone" can do. Students who had an abundance of financial resources continued to be provided with additional learning opportunities because their parents who could afford to supplement learning with their time and attention or with resources such as home libraries, materials, outdoor learning opportunities, and so forth. Then there were those with fewer financial resources who continued to fall further behind their peers.

Questions of equity have also emerged regarding the online learning platform. For one, how do we make it appropriate for all ages? Is it appropriate for kindergarten students to be online for instruction? Is it even appropriate for high school students? How do we employ screen time that is meaningful and does not contribute to the increased expectation for instant gratification and the unintended by-product of real-life social disconnection? Clement and Miles (2018) argue that increased technology is doing more harm for our students than good. Technology is not necessarily designed to cultivate identity and cultural responsiveness; rather increased screen time has led to decreased "ability to have open, honest, face-to-face, socially appropriate dialogue…" (Clement & Miles, 2018, p. 153). Furthermore, what about the role of relationships in online learning? Even if there were a way to guarantee connectivity (the ability for all students to get online), this would not guarantee connectedness (the presence of interpersonal relationships with students). It is labor-intensive work to maintain relationships online, even for those teachers who already highly valued relationships with students. And for those teachers who might not have prioritized relationships, it can be challenging to start this work in an online environment. Over the years budget cuts led to increased class sizes, which made it more challenging for community building and discussions in person, never mind in an online environment. Our teachers shared stories about virtual class meetings with anywhere from 30 to 72 students present. Where in this environment is the space to address social-emotional and identity development?

While we have worked in an online format to create antiracist professional development for teachers focused on identity development, critical pedagogy, relationships, and leadership, there were several elements in place that made this platform successful: 1. A small group of adult learners who worked together over the course of two years, 2. Face-to-face instruction at the beginning of the learning journey and interspersed throughout, and 3. A curriculum that was purposefully grounded in relationship building. Moving to online instruction is not just about organizing and delivering content; it is about creating the conditions under which students can grow and develop into antiracist citizens and agents of change.

So, what does all of this mean for the future? When and if we go back to brick and mortar, how might it look different? Most of the initial conversation focused on changing the structure of schools in order to contain the spread of the virus. There was talk of dividing the student population so that half attend school on Mondays and Wednesdays, the other half attend on Tuesdays and Thursdays, and the "off" days and Fridays are reserved for online learning. Other solutions included having high schools convert to online instruction full-time and using those buildings to spread out elementary and middle school students to help with social distancing measures.

The impact of the pandemic will likely extend over more than a single academic year. At this critical moment in time, it is essential to center these conversations around how we might use this crisis to rethink how we "do school" not just for the sake of containing a virus but for the sake of providing meaningful, equitable, and appropriate education for all. Vasquez (2020) from the National Equity Project provides a powerful look at how we might use this "disturbance" to create a new socially just system for schooling our youth. He argues for the development of strategic equity leaders who draw on the experiences of students and families to create a space that focuses on student learning, rather than seat hours, using project-based learning to drive education. He argues that this pandemic brought to light the ways in which our current school system perpetuates inequities, and that we need to seize this moment to interrupt and to change these structures. We add that this new vision of schooling needs to make space for antiracist instruction where children can learn who they are, how they relate to others, and how to dismantle inequitable systems and structures. Schools need to be spaces where everyone is actively and intentionally dispelling the myth of a hierarchy of human value.

Furthermore, we need to be mindful of the multiple layers of trauma that all of us have experienced and create spaces that help students (and teachers) process this trauma and feel safe and secure in creating learning spaces where all can be actively engaged in learning. This is especially true following the uprisings against the 2020 police killings of unarmed Black people, occurring as this book was going to print. The resulting groundswell in the following days and weeks by people of all races, all across the US and around the world, may mark a turning point in the growth of a powerful movement to demand that we address not only the problem of police brutality but of racism and racist systems in all its many forms. It is not clear what is possible now that might not have been possible before, but the call to change schooling – curriculum, discipline, assessments, and professional development – has a broader constituency than ever before.

In order for this to be successful, we need teachers to have access to teacher professional development that helps them focus on connections and engage in naming, reflecting, and acting on the inequities they now see. Or as Vasquez (2020) suggests, "We as individuals first have to SEE what the system is producing, then we have to ENGAGE with others to design something different, and finally we have to ACT" (para. 8). This is our chance. "The first step in designing a new way is to decide *now* that you won't return to normal — a normal that was never neutral and wasn't working well for most students, teachers or families" (Vasquez, 2020, para. 18).

REFERENCES

Clement, J., & Miles, M. (2018). *Screen schooled: Two veteran teachers expose how Technology overuse is making our kids dumber.* Chicago Review Press.

Vasquez, H. (2020). *What if we...don't return to school as usual.* National Equity Project. https://medium.com/national-equity-project/what-if-we-dont-return-to-school-as-usual-4aceb5227df5

Related Readings

To continue IGI Global's long-standing tradition of advancing innovation through emerging research, please find below a compiled list of recommended IGI Global book chapters and journal articles in the areas of antiracism, diversity in the classroom, in-service teacher education, and professional development. These related readings will provide additional information and guidance to further enrich your knowledge and assist you with your own research.

Adera, B. (2017). Supporting Language and Literacy Development for English Language Learners. In J. Keengwe (Ed.), *Handbook of Research on Promoting Cross-Cultural Competence and Social Justice in Teacher Education* (pp. 339–354). IGI Global. doi:10.4018/978-1-5225-0897-7.ch018

Alisat, L., & Clarke, V. B. (2017). An Integral Analysis of Labeling, Inclusion, and the Impact of the K-12 School Experience on Gifted Boys. In J. Keengwe (Ed.), *Handbook of Research on Promoting Cross-Cultural Competence and Social Justice in Teacher Education* (pp. 355–381). IGI Global. doi:10.4018/978-1-5225-0897-7.ch019

Alsup, P. R. (2019). STEM Career Interest at the Intersection of Attitude, Gender, Religion, and Urban Education. In J. L. Wendt & D. L. Apugo (Eds.), *K-12 STEM Education in Urban Learning Environments* (pp. 25–67). IGI Global. doi:10.4018/978-1-5225-7814-7.ch002

Amos, M. L., & Plews, R. C. (2019). The Impact of Language Use and Academic Integration for International Students: A Comparative Exploration Among Three Universities in the United States and Western Switzerland. *International Journal of Technology-Enabled Student Support Services*, *9*(2), 1–13. doi:10.4018/IJTESSS.2019070101

Amos, Y. T., & Kukar, N. M. (2017). Teaching and Learning Simultaneously: Collaboration between Teacher Education and a University ESL Program. In C. Martin & D. Polly (Eds.), *Handbook of Research on Teacher Education and Professional Development* (pp. 48–67). IGI Global. doi:10.4018/978-1-5225-1067-3.ch003

Atay, D., Kurt, G., & Kaşlıoğlu, Ö. (2017). Collaborative Teacher Development on Teaching World Englishes. In K. Dikilitaş & I. H. Erten (Eds.), *Facilitating In-Service Teacher Training for Professional Development* (pp. 165–184). IGI Global. doi:10.4018/978-1-5225-1747-4.ch010

Baker, A. D. (2019). Open Educational Resources in Teacher Preparation Programs: Teacher Candidates' Perceptions of Open Textbooks. *International Journal of Teacher Education and Professional Development*, *2*(1), 52–65. doi:10.4018/IJTEPD.2019010104

Baker-Gardner, R. (2016). Induction of Teachers in the English Speaking Caribbean. In T. Petty, A. Good, & S. M. Putman (Eds.), *Handbook of Research on Professional Development for Quality Teaching and Learning* (pp. 517–545). IGI Global. doi:10.4018/978-1-5225-0204-3.ch025

Bates, R. (2019). The Importance of Black Male Collegians' Conceptualizing Student Success at Historically White Institutions. In J. T. Butcher, J. R. O'Connor Jr, & F. Titus (Eds.), *Overcoming Challenges and Creating Opportunity for African American Male Students* (pp. 172–189). IGI Global. doi:10.4018/978-1-5225-5990-0.ch010

Bibeau, A. M. (2020). Gender Equality and Inequality: From the Foundations of Feminism to the Modern #MeToo Movement. In S. T. Brand & L. E. Ciccomascolo (Eds.), *Social Justice and Putting Theory Into Practice in Schools and Communities* (pp. 164–185). IGI Global. doi:10.4018/978-1-5225-9434-5.ch011

Blankenship, R. J., Paquette, P. F., & Davis, C. H. (2019). Field-Based Learning for Minority Educators: Developing Situationally Relevant Self-Awareness Practices in the Field Experience. *International Journal of Teacher Education and Professional Development, 2*(2), 1–23. doi:10.4018/IJTEPD.2019070101

Bright, A., & Gambrell, J. (2017). Calling In, Not Calling Out: A Critical Race Framework for Nurturing Cross-Cultural Alliances in Teacher Candidates. In J. Keengwe (Ed.), *Handbook of Research on Promoting Cross-Cultural Competence and Social Justice in Teacher Education* (pp. 217–235). IGI Global. doi:10.4018/978-1-5225-0897-7.ch011

Buchheister, K., Jackson, C., & Taylor, C. E. (2017). Defining Effective Learning Tasks for All. In C. Martin & D. Polly (Eds.), *Handbook of Research on Teacher Education and Professional Development* (pp. 561–581). IGI Global. doi:10.4018/978-1-5225-1067-3.ch031

Burbach, J. H., Martin, S. B., Arnold-Fowlkes, J., Sakaith, J., Julius, C., & Hibbs, A. (2017). This Is How I Learn: Co-Creating Space for Students' Voices. In J. Keengwe (Ed.), *Handbook of Research on Promoting Cross-Cultural Competence and Social Justice in Teacher Education* (pp. 178–192). IGI Global. doi:10.4018/978-1-5225-0897-7.ch009

Burgess, C. M., & Evans, J. R. (2017). Culturally Responsive Relationships Focused Pedagogies: The Key to Quality Teaching and Creating Quality Learning Environments. In J. Keengwe (Ed.), *Handbook of Research on Promoting Cross-Cultural Competence and Social Justice in Teacher Education* (pp. 1–31). IGI Global. doi:10.4018/978-1-5225-0897-7.ch001

Burke, K. P., & Ciccomascolo, L. E. (2020). Mentoring, Sponsorship, and Gender. In S. T. Brand & L. E. Ciccomascolo (Eds.), *Social Justice and Putting Theory Into Practice in Schools and Communities* (pp. 198–207). IGI Global. doi:10.4018/978-1-5225-9434-5.ch013

Burtin, A. S., Hampton-Garland, P., & Mizelle-Johnson, N. (2017). "I Don't See Color, I Grade on Content": An Approach to Addressing Embodied Microaggressive Behaviors in Preservice Teacher Programs. In J. Keengwe (Ed.), *Handbook of Research on Promoting Cross-Cultural Competence and Social Justice in Teacher Education* (pp. 236–252). IGI Global. doi:10.4018/978-1-5225-0897-7.ch012

Bush, J. C. (2017). Moving Forward with an Eye on the Past: A Historical Perspective of Teacher Research. In K. Dikilitaş & I. H. Erten (Eds.), *Facilitating In-Service Teacher Training for Professional Development* (pp. 112–128). IGI Global. doi:10.4018/978-1-5225-1747-4.ch007

Campanha, A. M., & Carvalho, A. C. (2017). The Rewards and Challenges of an Ongoing In-Service Teacher Training Programme. In K. Dikilitaş & I. H. Erten (Eds.), *Facilitating In-Service Teacher Training for Professional Development* (pp. 41–59). IGI Global. doi:10.4018/978-1-5225-1747-4.ch003

Carr-Winston, M. A. (2019). Consequences of Inequality and Exclusion on the Culture of Higher Education Institutions. In S. Wisdom, L. Leavitt, & C. Bice (Eds.), *Handbook of Research on Social Inequality and Education* (pp. 91–110). IGI Global. doi:10.4018/978-1-5225-9108-5.ch005

Castillo, D., & Vega-Muñoz, A. (2020). Sociological Perspectives on Migrant Children's Education: The Public Chilean Schools Case. In B. Arslan-Cansever & P. Önder-Erol (Eds.), *Sociological Perspectives on Educating Children in Contemporary Society* (pp. 107–137). IGI Global. doi:10.4018/978-1-7998-1847-2.ch005

Çelik, S. (2017). Setting New Standards for In-service Teacher Training: A Model for Responsive Professional Development in the Context of English Language Teaching. In K. Dikilitaş & I. H. Erten (Eds.), *Facilitating In-Service Teacher Training for Professional Development* (pp. 300–310). IGI Global. doi:10.4018/978-1-5225-1747-4.ch017

Cernik, J. A. (2019). Education and Rural America: Interconnected Problems. In S. Wisdom, L. Leavitt, & C. Bice (Eds.), *Handbook of Research on Social Inequality and Education* (pp. 149–166). IGI Global. doi:10.4018/978-1-5225-9108-5.ch008

Cetin, M., & Sahinkarakas, S. (2017). E-Mentoring as a Professional Teacher Development Tool. In K. Dikilitaş & I. H. Erten (Eds.), *Facilitating In-Service Teacher Training for Professional Development* (pp. 130–140). IGI Global. doi:10.4018/978-1-5225-1747-4.ch008

Chakraborty, M., & Chlup, D. T. (2016). The Relationship Between Social Justice Issues and Emotional Intelligence (EI): A Literature Review. In N. P. Ololube (Ed.), *Handbook of Research on Organizational Justice and Culture in Higher Education Institutions* (pp. 205–223). IGI Global. doi:10.4018/978-1-4666-9850-5.ch009

Chen, A. Y. (2017). Demographic Imperativeness: Critical Issues in Preparing Minority Teacher Candidates in Teacher Education. In J. Keengwe (Ed.), *Handbook of Research on Promoting Cross-Cultural Competence and Social Justice in Teacher Education* (pp. 101–119). IGI Global. doi:10.4018/978-1-5225-0897-7.ch005

Clausen, C. K. (2017). Exploring Technology Through Issues of Social Justice. In J. Keengwe (Ed.), *Handbook of Research on Promoting Cross-Cultural Competence and Social Justice in Teacher Education* (pp. 137–158). IGI Global. doi:10.4018/978-1-5225-0897-7.ch007

Correia, A. (2020). Flip the Script: English Learners Aren't Underperforming – We Are Underserving: A Move From Deficit Thinking to Democratic Education. In S. T. Brand & L. E. Ciccomascolo (Eds.), *Social Justice and Putting Theory Into Practice in Schools and Communities* (pp. 81–93). IGI Global. doi:10.4018/978-1-5225-9434-5.ch006

Coupet, S. Q., & Nicolas, G. (2017). We Drank the Cola in Collaboration: Voices of Haitian Teachers in Haiti. In J. Keengwe (Ed.), *Handbook of Research on Promoting Cross-Cultural Competence and Social Justice in Teacher Education* (pp. 159–177). IGI Global. doi:10.4018/978-1-5225-0897-7.ch008

Covington, A. C., Allen, A., & Lewis, C. W. (2016). Culturally Sustaining Pedagogy and Hip-Hop Based Education: A Professional Development Framework in Rap Cypher and Battle to Promote Student Engagement and Academic Achievement. In T. Petty, A. Good, & S. M. Putman (Eds.), *Handbook of Research on Professional Development for Quality Teaching and Learning* (pp. 486–495). IGI Global. doi:10.4018/978-1-5225-0204-3.ch023

Dahle-Huff, K. (2020). *Making Room for Race in Your Classroom Discourse: A Journey of Identity and Homecoming*. doi:10.4018/978-1-7998-2971-3.ch014

Davis-Maye, D., Yarber-Allen, A., & Jones, T. B. (2017). Feeling Silly and White: The Impact of Participant Characteristics on Study Abroad Experiences. In H. An (Ed.), *Handbook of Research on Efficacy and Implementation of Study Abroad Programs for P-12 Teachers* (pp. 400–414). IGI Global. doi:10.4018/978-1-5225-1057-4.ch022

Dewsbury, B. (2020). A Worthy Burden: Reflections on the Journey of a STEM Professor of Color in Higher Education. In S. T. Brand & L. E. Ciccomascolo (Eds.), *Social Justice and Putting Theory Into Practice in Schools and Communities* (pp. 29–43). IGI Global. doi:10.4018/978-1-5225-9434-5.ch003

Eakins, S. L. (2019). A School Model for Developing Access to Higher Education for African American: Social Capital and School Choice. In S. Wisdom, L. Leavitt, & C. Bice (Eds.), *Handbook of Research on Social Inequality and Education* (pp. 167–189). IGI Global. doi:10.4018/978-1-5225-9108-5.ch009

Elçi, A., Yaratan, H., & Abubakar, A. M. (2020). Multidimensional Faculty Professional Development in Teaching and Learning: Utilizing Technology for Supporting Students. *International Journal of Technology-Enabled Student Support Services*, *10*(1), 21–39. doi:10.4018/IJTESSS.2020010102

Ellis, M. K. (2020). Leading With Life: Using Personal Stories to Promote Social Justice in Pedagogy. In S. T. Brand & L. E. Ciccomascolo (Eds.), *Social Justice and Putting Theory Into Practice in Schools and Communities* (pp. 245–265). IGI Global. doi:10.4018/978-1-5225-9434-5.ch016

Estes, J. S. (2017). Preparing Teacher Candidates for Diverse Classrooms: The Role of Teacher Preparation Programs. In J. Keengwe (Ed.), *Handbook of Research on Promoting Cross-Cultural Competence and Social Justice in Teacher Education* (pp. 52–75). IGI Global. doi:10.4018/978-1-5225-0897-7.ch003

Estes, J. S., & McConnell-Farmer, J. L. (2020). Inspiring Teacher Candidates to Embrace Cultural Diversity. In J. Keengwe (Ed.), *Handbook of Research on Innovative Pedagogies and Best Practices in Teacher Education* (pp. 120–139). IGI Global. doi:10.4018/978-1-5225-9232-7.ch008

Flippin, M., Moore, A., & Clapham, E. D. (2020). Including All Abilities: Pedagogies, Programs, and Projects for Inclusion. In S. T. Brand & L. E. Ciccomascolo (Eds.), *Social Justice and Putting Theory Into Practice in Schools and Communities* (pp. 294–308). IGI Global. doi:10.4018/978-1-5225-9434-5.ch019

Flores-Mejorado, D., & Reed, D. (2019). The Influence of Self-Determination Theory on African American Males' Motivation. In J. T. Butcher, J. R. O'Connor Jr, & F. Titus (Eds.), *Overcoming Challenges and Creating Opportunity for African American Male Students* (pp. 72–98). IGI Global. doi:10.4018/978-1-5225-5990-0.ch004

Fondrie, S., Penick-Parks, M., & Delano-Oriaran, O. (2017). Developing Equity Literacy through Diverse Literature for Children and Young Adults. In J. Keengwe (Ed.), *Handbook of Research on Promoting Cross-Cultural Competence and Social Justice in Teacher Education* (pp. 193–216). IGI Global. doi:10.4018/978-1-5225-0897-7.ch010

Gedik, P. K., & Ortactepe, D. (2017). Teacher Identity (Re)Construction within Professional Learning Communities: The Role of Emotions and Tensions. In K. Dikilitaş & I. H. Erten (Eds.), *Facilitating In-Service Teacher Training for Professional Development* (pp. 86–97). IGI Global. doi:10.4018/978-1-5225-1747-4.ch005

Greene, H. C., & Manner, J. C. (2016). A National Crisis and a Call to Action: Preparing Teachers to Teach Children from Poverty. In T. Petty, A. Good, & S. M. Putman (Eds.), *Handbook of Research on Professional Development for Quality Teaching and Learning* (pp. 387–408). IGI Global. doi:10.4018/978-1-5225-0204-3.ch019

Hadjistassou, S., Avgousti, M. I., & Allen, C. (2020). Pre-Service Teachers' and Instructors' Reflections on Virtually Afforded Feedback During a Distant Teaching Practicum Experience. *International Journal of Teacher Education and Professional Development, 3*(1), 42–59. doi:10.4018/IJTEPD.2020010103

Harvell, K. D. (2019). The Art of Sankofa and Re-Establishing Kujichagulia: Interrogating the Educational Past of Black Folks. In J. T. Butcher, J. R. O'Connor Jr, & F. Titus (Eds.), *Overcoming Challenges and Creating Opportunity for African American Male Students* (pp. 41–71). IGI Global. doi:10.4018/978-1-5225-5990-0.ch003

Helfaya, A., & O'Neill, J. (2018). Using Computer-Based Assessment and Feedback: Meeting the Needs of Digital Natives in the Digital Age. *International Journal of Teacher Education and Professional Development, 1*(2), 46–71. doi:10.4018/IJTEPD.2018070104

Herridge, A. S., & Hobley, M. D. Jr. (2019). Impact of Mentoring and Support Programs on Academic Performance of African American Males: Analysis Through a Critical Race Theory Lens. In J. T. Butcher, J. R. O'Connor Jr, & F. Titus (Eds.), *Overcoming Challenges and Creating Opportunity for African American Male Students* (pp. 108–119). IGI Global. doi:10.4018/978-1-5225-5990-0.ch006

Hill, V. (2020). *Digital Citizenship: The Future of Learning*. IGI Global. doi:10.4018/978-1-7998-3534-9.ch009

Hitchens, C. W., & ... . (2017). Studying Abroad to Inform Teaching in a Diverse Society: A Description of International Elementary Education Teaching Experiences at Ball State University. In I. G. I. Heejung An (Ed.), *Handbook of Research on Efficacy and Implementation of Study Abroad Programs for P-12 Teachers* (pp. 52–70). Global. doi:10.4018/978-1-5225-1057-4.ch004

Hos, R., Cinarbas, H. I., & Yagci, H. (2019). A Head-Start to Teaching: Exploring the Early Field Experiences in Pre-service EFL Education in Turkey. *International Journal of Teacher Education and Professional Development*, 2(2), 68–84. doi:10.4018/IJTEPD.2019070105

Husbye, N. E., Alovar, Y., & Song, K. (2017). Patterns of Practice and Teacher Identity: Insights from the QTEL Professional Development Program. In C. Martin & D. Polly (Eds.), *Handbook of Research on Teacher Education and Professional Development* (pp. 527–537). IGI Global. doi:10.4018/978-1-5225-1067-3.ch029

Johnson, R., Kim, J. Y., & Lee, J. Y. (2016). Asians and the Myth of the Model Minority in Higher Education: A Psychocultural Reality in the 21st Century. In N. P. Ololube (Ed.), *Handbook of Research on Organizational Justice and Culture in Higher Education Institutions* (pp. 447–468). IGI Global. doi:10.4018/978-1-4666-9850-5.ch018

Jones, P. W., & Hope, W. C. (2019). African American Students, Racism, and Academic Injustice: Igniting a FUSE. In S. Wisdom, L. Leavitt, & C. Bice (Eds.), *Handbook of Research on Social Inequality and Education* (pp. 1–23). IGI Global. doi:10.4018/978-1-5225-9108-5.ch001

Juárez, L. M., Santillán, L., & Swoyer, J. G. (2020). Teacher Residency 2.0: Case Studies of an Innovative and Evolving Preparation Program Implementing Culturally Efficacious Instruction. In J. Keengwe (Ed.), *Handbook of Research on Innovative Pedagogies and Best Practices in Teacher Education* (pp. 206–223). IGI Global. doi:10.4018/978-1-5225-9232-7.ch012

Karataş, K., & Ardıç, T. (2019). The Role of Culturally Responsive Teacher to Ensure Social Justice in Education. In S. Wisdom, L. Leavitt, & C. Bice (Eds.), *Handbook of Research on Social Inequality and Education* (pp. 311–332). IGI Global. doi:10.4018/978-1-5225-9108-5.ch017

Kasemsap, K. (2017). Teacher Education and Teacher Professional Development: Current Issues and Approaches. In C. Martin & D. Polly (Eds.), *Handbook of Research on Teacher Education and Professional Development* (pp. 112–137). IGI Global. doi:10.4018/978-1-5225-1067-3.ch007

Katz, A. (2020). Building Connections Between Teacher Education Candidates and Urban Middle School Students Through Social Action: A Community Literacy Partnership. In J. Keengwe (Ed.), *Handbook of Research on Innovative Pedagogies and Best Practices in Teacher Education* (pp. 240–257). IGI Global. doi:10.4018/978-1-5225-9232-7.ch014

Keller, T. M. (2017). "The World is So Much Bigger": Preservice Teachers' Experiences of Religion in Israel and the Influences on Identity and Teaching. In H. An (Ed.), *Handbook of Research on Efficacy and Implementation of Study Abroad Programs for P-12 Teachers* (pp. 275–294). IGI Global. doi:10.4018/978-1-5225-1057-4.ch016

Kennedy, A. S., & Heineke, A. J. (2016). Preparing Urban Educators to Address Diversity and Equity through Field-Based Teacher Education: Implications for Program Design and Implementation. In T. Petty, A. Good, & S. M. Putman (Eds.), *Handbook of Research on Professional Development for Quality Teaching and Learning* (pp. 437–461). IGI Global. doi:10.4018/978-1-5225-0204-3.ch021

Kim, S. J. (2018). Creating Spaces for Critical Literacy for Bilingual Learners: Korean Kindergartners' Discussions About Race and Gender. In G. Onchwari & J. Keengwe (Eds.), *Handbook of Research on Pedagogies and Cultural Considerations for Young English Language Learners* (pp. 28–46). IGI Global. doi:10.4018/978-1-5225-3955-1.ch002

King, B. C. (2020). Becoming Ellis: The Story of a TransMale as Relayed by His Therapist. In S. T. Brand & L. E. Ciccomascolo (Eds.), *Social Justice and Putting Theory Into Practice in Schools and Communities* (pp. 125–135). IGI Global. doi:10.4018/978-1-5225-9434-5.ch009

Kowalsky, M. (2019). Envisioning Change and Extending Library Reach for Impact in Underserved School Communities. In S. Wisdom, L. Leavitt, & C. Bice (Eds.), *Handbook of Research on Social Inequality and Education* (pp. 202–219). IGI Global. doi:10.4018/978-1-5225-9108-5.ch011

Lawrence, J. E. (2019). Teaching Large Classes: Engaging Students Through Active Learning Practice and Interactive Lecture. *International Journal of Teacher Education and Professional Development*, 2(1), 66–80. doi:10.4018/IJTEPD.2019010105

Lee, M. (2020). Disability and Dominant Leadership Models Over Time. In S. T. Brand & L. E. Ciccomascolo (Eds.), *Social Justice and Putting Theory Into Practice in Schools and Communities* (pp. 274–293). IGI Global. doi:10.4018/978-1-5225-9434-5.ch018

Leon, R. (2019). An Empowering Experience: Black Males Developing Competencies Abroad. In J. T. Butcher, J. R. O'Connor Jr, & F. Titus (Eds.), *Overcoming Challenges and Creating Opportunity for African American Male Students* (pp. 205–229). IGI Global. doi:10.4018/978-1-5225-5990-0.ch012

Linton, J. N. & Journell, W. (2019). Meeting the Demand for Online Education: A Study of a State-Run Program Designed to Train Virtual K-12 Teachers. In Pre-Service and In-Service Teacher Education: Concepts, Methodologies, Tools, and Applications (pp. 511-533). IGI Global. http://doi:10.4018/978-1-5225-7305-0.ch025

Liu, Y., Liu, H., Xu, Y., & Lu, H. (2019). Online English Reading Instruction in the ESL Classroom Based on Constructivism. *International Journal of Technology-Enabled Student Support Services*, 9(2), 39–49. doi:10.4018/IJTESSS.2019070104

Lyu, K., Lyu, C., Li, J., & Shughri, G. (2019). Parental Involvement Contributes to Family Cultural Capital in J District in Shanghai: Based on Taoyuan Private Primary Migrant School. In S. Wisdom, L. Leavitt, & C. Bice (Eds.), *Handbook of Research on Social Inequality and Education* (pp. 448–469). IGI Global. doi:10.4018/978-1-5225-9108-5.ch025

Matsunobu, K. (2019). Intercultural Understanding of Music for Kyosei Living: A Case Study on Multicultural Music Education in an American Primary School. In R. K. Gordon & T. Akutsu (Eds.), *Cases on Kyosei Practice in Music Education* (pp. 49–64). IGI Global. doi:10.4018/978-1-5225-8042-3.ch004

McCarthy, J. (2018). Blended Learning Strategies for Engaging Diverse Student Cohorts in Higher Education. *International Journal of Teacher Education and Professional Development*, *1*(2), 29–45. doi:10.4018/IJTEPD.2018070103

McCormack, V. (2017). Project-Based Learning Integration with Teachers Immersed in a Professional Development Initiative. In C. Martin & D. Polly (Eds.), *Handbook of Research on Teacher Education and Professional Development* (pp. 442–452). IGI Global. doi:10.4018/978-1-5225-1067-3.ch025

McHaelen, R. Fleurette (Flo) King, Goldsmith, D. J. & Pomerantz, H. (2020). Opening the Doors for All LGBTQ+ Students. In Brand, S. T. & Ciccomascolo, L. E. (Ed.), Social Justice and Putting Theory Into Practice in Schools and Communities (pp. 136-161). IGI Global. http://doi:10.4018/978-1-5225-9434-5.ch010

Mede, E., & Dollar, Y. K. (2017). Evaluation and Facilitation of an In-Service Teacher Training Program: Impact on English Primary Teachers' Classroom Practices. In K. Dikilitaş & I. H. Erten (Eds.), *Facilitating In-Service Teacher Training for Professional Development* (pp. 230–245). IGI Global. doi:10.4018/978-1-5225-1747-4.ch013

Miller, I. K., & Maria Isabel, A. C. (2017). Exploratory Practice in Continuing Professional Development: Critical and Ethical Issues. In K. Dikilitaş & I. H. Erten (Eds.), *Facilitating In-Service Teacher Training for Professional Development* (pp. 61–85). IGI Global. doi:10.4018/978-1-5225-1747-4.ch004

Moch, P. L. (2020). Faith, Hope, and Strength: Achieving the Impossible. In S. T. Brand & L. E. Ciccomascolo (Eds.), *Social Justice and Putting Theory Into Practice in Schools and Communities* (pp. 44–57). IGI Global. doi:10.4018/978-1-5225-9434-5.ch004

Moore, A. (2020). Disability as a Social Justice Imperative: Historical, Theoretical, and Practical Implications. In S. T. Brand & L. E. Ciccomascolo (Eds.), *Social Justice and Putting Theory Into Practice in Schools and Communities* (pp. 210–226). IGI Global. doi:10.4018/978-1-5225-9434-5.ch014

Morgan, B. M. (2017). Bridging the L1-L2 Divide: Learner-Centered Instruction in the Heritage/L2 Spanish Classroom. In J. Keengwe (Ed.), *Handbook of Research on Promoting Cross-Cultural Competence and Social Justice in Teacher Education* (pp. 270–286). IGI Global. doi:10.4018/978-1-5225-0897-7.ch014

Mukminin, A., & Habibi, A. (2019). Promoting Access and Success for Disadvantaged Students in Indonesian Basic Education: Social Justice in Education. In S. Wisdom, L. Leavitt, & C. Bice (Eds.), *Handbook of Research on Social Inequality and Education* (pp. 403–413). IGI Global. doi:10.4018/978-1-5225-9108-5.ch022

Mumford, J. M., Fiala, L., & Daulton, M. (2017). An Agile K-12 Approach: Teacher PD for New Learning Ecosystems. In C. Martin & D. Polly (Eds.), *Handbook of Research on Teacher Education and Professional Development* (pp. 367–384). IGI Global. doi:10.4018/978-1-5225-1067-3.ch020

Mysore, A. R. (2017). Teacher Education and Digital Equity: Research in the Millennium. In J. Keengwe (Ed.), *Handbook of Research on Promoting Cross-Cultural Competence and Social Justice in Teacher Education* (pp. 120–136). IGI Global. doi:10.4018/978-1-5225-0897-7.ch006

Nkabinde, Z. P. (2017). Multiculturalism in Special Education: Perspectives of Minority Children in Urban Schools. In J. Keengwe (Ed.), *Handbook of Research on Promoting Cross-Cultural Competence and Social Justice in Teacher Education* (pp. 382–397). IGI Global. doi:10.4018/978-1-5225-0897-7.ch020

Ntombela, S., & Setlhodi, I. I. (2019). Transformation and Social Justice in South African Higher Education: An Unequal Turf. In S. Wisdom, L. Leavitt, & C. Bice (Eds.), *Handbook of Research on Social Inequality and Education* (pp. 238–252). IGI Global. doi:10.4018/978-1-5225-9108-5.ch013

O'Connor, J. R. Jr, Butcher, J. T., & Titus, F. (2019). The Importance of Understanding the Challenges of African American Male Students: Setting the Foundation for Future Educational Success. In J. T. Butcher, J. R. O'Connor Jr, & F. Titus (Eds.), *Overcoming Challenges and Creating Opportunity for African American Male Students* (pp. 1–17). IGI Global. doi:10.4018/978-1-5225-5990-0.ch001

Oakley, M. (2020). Abilities Before Disabilities: The Educational Challenges and Triumphs of a Blind Individual. In S. T. Brand & L. E. Ciccomascolo (Eds.), *Social Justice and Putting Theory Into Practice in Schools and Communities* (pp. 266–273). IGI Global. doi:10.4018/978-1-5225-9434-5.ch017

Olajide, S. O., & Aladejana, F. O. (2019). Effect of Computer Assisted Instructional Package on Students' Learning Outcomes in Basic Science. *International Journal of Technology-Enabled Student Support Services*, 9(1), 1–15. doi:10.4018/IJTESSS.2019010101

Owens, D., Lockhart, S., Matthews, D. Y., & Middleton, T. J. (2019). Racial Battle Fatigue and Mental Health in Black Men. In J. T. Butcher, J. R. O'Connor Jr, & F. Titus (Eds.), *Overcoming Challenges and Creating Opportunity for African American Male Students* (pp. 99–107). IGI Global. doi:10.4018/978-1-5225-5990-0.ch005

Padía, L. B. (2020). Teaching Safety, Compliance, and Critical Thinking in Special Education Classrooms. In S. T. Brand & L. E. Ciccomascolo (Eds.), *Social Justice and Putting Theory Into Practice in Schools and Communities* (pp. 227–244). IGI Global. doi:10.4018/978-1-5225-9434-5.ch015

Penland, J. J. & Laviers, K. (2020). Reimagined Higher Ed Classrooms: Meaningful Learning Through Culturally Unbiased Virtual and Augmented Reality. In Handbook of Research on Innovative Pedagogies and Best Practices in Teacher Education (pp. 85-101). IGI Global. http://doi:10.4018/978-1-5225-9232-7.ch006

Penland, J. L. (2017). Developing Resilience through Experiences: El Camino Al Exito. In J. Keengwe (Ed.), *Handbook of Research on Promoting Cross-Cultural Competence and Social Justice in Teacher Education* (pp. 287–303). IGI Global. doi:10.4018/978-1-5225-0897-7.ch015

Pinter, H. H., Bloom, L. A., Rush, C. B., & Sastre, C. (2020). Best Practices in Teacher Preparation for Inclusive Education. In J. Keengwe (Ed.), *Handbook of Research on Innovative Pedagogies and Best Practices in Teacher Education* (pp. 52–68). IGI Global. doi:10.4018/978-1-5225-9232-7.ch004

Pitre, N. J., & Clarke, V. B. (2017). Cultural Self-Study as a Tool for Critical Reflection and Learning: Integral Analysis and Implications for Pre-Service Teacher Education Programs. In J. Keengwe (Ed.), *Handbook of Research on Promoting Cross-Cultural Competence and Social Justice in Teacher Education* (pp. 76–100). IGI Global. doi:10.4018/978-1-5225-0897-7.ch004

Popejoy, K. Good, A. J. Rock, T. & Vintinner, J. P. (2019). Integrated Methods Block: Transforming Elementary Teacher Preparation Through the Integration of Content Methods and Early Clinical Experiences. In Pre-Service and In-Service Teacher Education: Concepts, Methodologies, Tools, and Applications (pp. 414-432). IGI Global. http://doi:10.4018/978-1-5225-7305-0.ch02

Queener, J. E., & Ford, B. A. (2019). Culturally Responsive Mentoring Programs: Impacting Retention/Graduation Rates of African American Males Attending Predominately White Institutions. In J. T. Butcher, J. R. O'Connor Jr, & F. Titus (Eds.), *Overcoming Challenges and Creating Opportunity for African American Male Students* (pp. 120–132). IGI Global. doi:10.4018/978-1-5225-5990-0.ch007

Rockinson-Szapkiw, A. J., & Caldwell, L. R. (2019). Improving STEM Career Aspirations in Underrepresented Populations: Strategies for Urban Elementary School Professionals. In J. L. Wendt & D. L. Apugo (Eds.), *K-12 STEM Education in Urban Learning Environments* (pp. 208–237). IGI Global. doi:10.4018/978-1-5225-7814-7.ch008

Rockinson-Szapkiw, A. J., & Wade-Jaimes, K. (2019). Gendered and Racial Microaggressions in STEM: Definitions, Consequences, and Strategies Urban Elementary School Professionals Can Use to Combat Them. In J. L. Wendt & D. L. Apugo (Eds.), *K-12 STEM Education in Urban Learning Environments* (pp. 162–182). IGI Global. doi:10.4018/978-1-5225-7814-7.ch006

Rossi, P. G., Magnoler, P., Mangione, G. R., Pettenati, M. C., & Rosa, A. (2017). Initial Teacher Education, Induction, and In-Service Training: Experiences in a Perspective of a Meaningful Continuum for Teachers' Professional Development. In K. Dikilitaş & I. H. Erten (Eds.), *Facilitating In-Service Teacher Training for Professional Development* (pp. 15–40). IGI Global. doi:10.4018/978-1-5225-1747-4.ch002

Roth, K. R. & Ritter, Z. S. (2020). Channeling Race: Media Representations and International Student Perceptions. In *Accessibility and Diversity in Education: Breakthroughs in Research and Practice* (pp. 712-737). IGI Global. http://doi:10.4018/978-1-7998-1213-5.ch036

Roumimper, K. R., & Falk, A. F. (2019). Peer Support of Graduate Students of Color Through a Formal Graduate Student Association. In S. Wisdom, L. Leavitt, & C. Bice (Eds.), *Handbook of Research on Social Inequality and Education* (pp. 111–129). IGI Global. doi:10.4018/978-1-5225-9108-5.ch006

Şan, S., & Gedikler, H. G. (2020). Social Perspective on Child Education: Society, Democracy, and Political Literacy in Child Education. In B. Arslan-Cansever & P. Önder-Erol (Eds.), *Sociological Perspectives on Educating Children in Contemporary Society* (pp. 185–205). IGI Global. doi:10.4018/978-1-7998-1847-2.ch008

Seals, C., Horton, A., Berzina-Pitcher, I., & Mishra, P. (2017). A New Understanding of our Confusion: Insights from a Year-Long STEM Fellowship Program. In C. Martin & D. Polly (Eds.), *Handbook of Research on Teacher Education and Professional Development* (pp. 582–604). IGI Global. doi:10.4018/978-1-5225-1067-3.ch032

Semingson, P., & Amaro-Jiménez, C. (2017). Using Multimodal Literacies to Support Language Development for English Language Learners. In J. Keengwe (Ed.), *Handbook of Research on Promoting Cross-Cultural Competence and Social Justice in Teacher Education* (pp. 320–338). IGI Global. doi:10.4018/978-1-5225-0897-7.ch017

Simpson, A. L. Jr, & Jones, K. (2019). The Mentoring and Connectivism of African American Male Students Who Participate in Recreational Sports Programs. In J. T. Butcher, J. R. O'Connor Jr, & F. Titus (Eds.), *Overcoming Challenges and Creating Opportunity for African American Male Students* (pp. 133–150). IGI Global. doi:10.4018/978-1-5225-5990-0.ch008

Spencer, D. Jr, & Guthrie, K. L. (2019). A Blueprint for Developing Black Male Leader Identity, Capacity, and Efficacy Through Leadership Learning. In J. T. Butcher, J. R. O'Connor Jr, & F. Titus (Eds.), *Overcoming Challenges and Creating Opportunity for African American Male Students* (pp. 18–40). IGI Global. doi:10.4018/978-1-5225-5990-0.ch002

Strause, S. S., & Tan, S. (2017). Empowering "Digital Immigrants": Challenges and Solutions. In K. Dikilitaş & I. H. Erten (Eds.), *Facilitating In-Service Teacher Training for Professional Development* (pp. 246–259). IGI Global. doi:10.4018/978-1-5225-1747-4.ch014

Subramaniam, K. (2020). Educational Attainment of Children and Socio-Economical Differences in Contemporary Society. In B. Arslan-Cansever & P. Önder-Erol (Eds.), *Sociological Perspectives on Educating Children in Contemporary Society* (pp. 63–78). IGI Global. doi:10.4018/978-1-7998-1847-2.ch003

Tawiah, S., & Setlhodi, I. I. (2020). Introducing Information and Communication Technology Training for Rural Women in South Africa: Innovative Strategies for the Advancement of Livelihoods. *International Journal of Adult Education and Technology*, *11*(1), 45–59. doi:10.4018/IJAET.2020010103

Thomas, U. (2017). Disposition and Early Childhood Education Preservice Teachers: A Social Justice Stance. In J. Keengwe (Ed.), *Handbook of Research on Promoting Cross-Cultural Competence and Social Justice in Teacher Education* (pp. 253–269). IGI Global. doi:10.4018/978-1-5225-0897-7.ch013

Thornton, N. A. (2017). Culturally Relevant Literacy Instruction: Promoting Shifts in Teachers' Beliefs and Practices. In C. Martin & D. Polly (Eds.), *Handbook of Research on Teacher Education and Professional Development* (pp. 308–336). IGI Global. doi:10.4018/978-1-5225-1067-3.ch017

Travers, C. S. (2019). Mapping Mindset and Academic Success Among Black Men at a Predominantly White Institution. In J. T. Butcher, J. R. O'Connor Jr, & F. Titus (Eds.), *Overcoming Challenges and Creating Opportunity for African American Male Students* (pp. 151–171). IGI Global. doi:10.4018/978-1-5225-5990-0.ch009

Trella, D. L. (2020). Addressing Poverty-Related Trauma in School Children. In S. T. Brand & L. E. Ciccomascolo (Eds.), *Social Justice and Putting Theory Into Practice in Schools and Communities* (pp. 1–16). IGI Global. doi:10.4018/978-1-5225-9434-5.ch001

Vighnarajah, S., & Jolene, L. S. (2018). Assessment of Diversity Through Student Isolation: Qualitative Investigation of Academic, Social, and Emotional Isolation. *International Journal of Teacher Education and Professional Development*, *1*(2), 1–13. doi:10.4018/IJTEPD.2018070101

Voroshilov, V. (2017). Professional Designing as One of Key Competencies of Modern Teacher: An Ability Which Every Teacher Needs to Have. In K. Dikilitaş & I. H. Erten (Eds.), *Facilitating In-Service Teacher Training for Professional Development* (pp. 276–299). IGI Global. doi:10.4018/978-1-5225-1747-4.ch016

Wagle, T. (2019). What Are We Missing? In S. Wisdom, L. Leavitt, & C. Bice (Eds.), *Handbook of Research on Social Inequality and Education* (pp. 190–201). IGI Global. doi:10.4018/978-1-5225-9108-5.ch010

Waite, B., & Colvin, J. (2018). Creating and Assessing Faculty Training on Global, Intercultural, and Inclusive Practices. *International Journal of Teacher Education and Professional Development, 1*(2), 72–86. doi:10.4018/IJTEPD.2018070105

Wallace, J. L., & Robertson, V. (2019). The Men of L.E.G.A.C.I. Student Success Program: Building Strategic Platforms for Collegiate Success. In J. T. Butcher, J. R. O'Connor Jr, & F. Titus (Eds.), *Overcoming Challenges and Creating Opportunity for African American Male Students* (pp. 190–204). IGI Global. doi:10.4018/978-1-5225-5990-0.ch011

Wang, Y., & Shuttlesworth, D. (2020). Close the Achievement Gap With Professional Development. *International Journal of Teacher Education and Professional Development, 3*(1), 88–101. doi:10.4018/IJTEPD.2020010106

Webster, N., Coffey, H., & Ash, A. (2016). UrbanLivesMatter: Empowering Learners through Transformative Teaching. In T. Petty, A. Good, & S. M. Putman (Eds.), *Handbook of Research on Professional Development for Quality Teaching and Learning* (pp. 462–485). IGI Global. doi:10.4018/978-1-5225-0204-3.ch022

Whitaker, R. W. II, Campbell, A. N., Gates, Z. Y., & Ellison-Metcalfe, L. (2020). Culturally Relevant and Meeting Academic Standards at the Same Time: Teaching Math to African American Students as a Matter of Social Justice. In S. T. Brand & L. E. Ciccomascolo (Eds.), *Social Justice and Putting Theory Into Practice in Schools and Communities* (pp. 17–28). IGI Global. doi:10.4018/978-1-5225-9434-5.ch002

Wisdom, S. L. (2019). State-Wide Teacher Walkouts Highlight Equality Gaps. In S. Wisdom, L. Leavitt, & C. Bice (Eds.), *Handbook of Research on Social Inequality and Education* (pp. 46–63). IGI Global. doi:10.4018/978-1-5225-9108-5.ch003

Wolfe, Z. M. (2019). Challenges to Implementing STEM Professional Development From an Ecological Systems Perspective. In J. L. Wendt & D. L. Apugo (Eds.), *K-12 STEM Education in Urban Learning Environments* (pp. 69–94). IGI Global. doi:10.4018/978-1-5225-7814-7.ch003

Yeh, E., Jaiswal-Oliver, M., & Posejpal, G. (2017). Global Education Professional Development: A Model for Cross-Cultural Competence. In J. Keengwe (Ed.), *Handbook of Research on Promoting Cross-Cultural Competence and Social Justice in Teacher Education* (pp. 32–51). IGI Global. doi:10.4018/978-1-5225-0897-7.ch002

Young, N., Conderman, G. J., & Jung, M. (2019). Preparing Pre-service Early Childhood Candidates for Diverse Classrooms: The Open Doors Program. *International Journal of Teacher Education and Professional Development*, 2(2), 37–52. doi:10.4018/IJTEPD.2019070103

Zhou, M. Y. (2019). Diversity and Teacher Education: Cultural and Linguistic Competency for Teachers. In Pre-Service and In-Service Teacher Education: Concepts, Methodologies, Tools, and Applications (pp. 272-295). IGI Global. http://doi:10.4018/978-1-5225-7305-0.ch014

About the Authors

Jenice L. View is an Associate Professor Emerita at George Mason University. Her work has included the critical teaching and learning of history, critical teacher professional development, and uses of arts integration. Her 15-year academic career followed nearly 20 years in the non-governmental sector at the local and national levels, and a stint as a middle school humanities teacher. One ongoing action research project "Learning Historic Places with Diverse Populations," explores how place-based learning and history education can help Students of Color reclaim their connection with historic sites. Her curriculum design and teacher professional development work in Mississippi to teach the civil rights movement has impacted teachers and students statewide and in 14 school districts in particular. Another ongoing research project includes *Examining the Trajectories of Black Mathematics Teachers: Learning From the Past, Drawing on the Present, and Defining Goals for the Future,* a three- year study funded by the National Science Foundation, that includes collecting oral histories of retired Black mathematics teachers. Another exploration examines the impact of oral history collection on high schoolers' understanding of historical content, and teachers' experiences of teaching Black history. She has published widely in peer-reviewed journals, scholarly books, and popular outlets. She is a co-editor of the book *Why public schools? Voices from the United States and Canada* (2013), and co-editor of the award-winning book *Putting the movement back into civil rights teaching: A resource guide for classrooms and communities* (2004/2020). The co-authored book, *Teaching the New Deal, 1932 to 1941* (2020), offers classroom teachers a multicultural examination of this period with lessons and other resources. In addition, she is the author of *We Who Defy Hate: An Interfaith Preparation for Social Justice Action* curriculum, written in conjunction with the 2018 Ken Burns film, "Defying the Nazis: The Sharps' War." As creator and host of "Urban Education: Issues and Solutions," an award-winning 30-minute GMU-TV cable television program, she produced

29 shows on a variety of education topics. She has served as a board member and consultant on civil rights and social justice education for a variety of community-based, non-profit, educational, and national organizations. Her work with Meadville Lombard Theological School includes serving as a retreat leader for the Beloved Conversations Meditations on Race and Ethnicity workshops. Dr. View holds degrees from Syracuse University, Princeton University, and the Union Institute and University.

Elizabeth K. DeMulder is a Professor of Education and Academic Program Coordinator of the Transformative Teaching program, a teacher professional development master's degree program housed in George Mason University's College of Education and Human Development. She earned a Ph.D. in Developmental Psychology from St. John's College, Cambridge University, studying children's attachment relationships with parents and influences on their social and emotional development. Dr. DeMulder was a Staff Fellow at the National Institute of Mental Health, conducting research on attachment relationships, family dynamics, and parental psychopathology and the influences of these factors on children's development. She joined George Mason University under the auspices of the National Science Foundation's Visiting Professorships for Women Grant Program. Dr. DeMulder's research has a strong interdisciplinary, applied, and collaborative orientation and concerns the complex influences of systems, interpersonal relationships, and learning environments that support and/or create barriers to children's and teachers' development. In her research on young children's development, she focuses on challenging structural barriers (e.g. related to navigating poverty, racism, second language learning, access to child care) to understand and advocate for anti-oppressive and justice-oriented systems that support families and children's healthy development. She has been involved in community-based action research in Alexandria and in South Arlington, Virginia, where she developed a family-centered preschool program for low-income families as a university/community partnership. In her study of teacher professional development and in her teacher educator role, she uses critical theory, critical pedagogy and inquiry, and action research frameworks to understand and support the development of teachers' complex meaning-making, critical consciousness, and anti-oppressive and justice-oriented teaching. Dr. DeMulder co-edited a book entitled Transforming Teacher Education: Lessons in Professional Development and has published her research in a variety of professional journals, including the *Journal of Curriculum and Instruction, Teaching Education, Democracy and Education, Reflective Practice, Child*

Development, and Developmental Psychology. She serves as the Vice President of the Mason Advocacy Chapter of the American Association of University Professors and as a member of Mason's Faculty Senate.

Stacia M. Stribling is an Assistant Professor in the George Mason University Graduate School of Education's Transformative Teaching Master's Program. She received her Bachelor's Degree from Mary Washington College and her Master's Degree from the IET Program at George Mason University. In 2010 Stacia completed her PhD in Early Childhood Education with a minor in Literacy at George Mason University. Her dissertation explored the use of critical literacy practices with kindergarten and second-grade students. Her current research interests include early childhood education, critical literacy, teacher professional development, culturally responsive pedagogy, and multiculturalism. Prior to moving to the world of academia, Stacia spent eight years as a first- and second-grade teacher in Fauquier County, three years as a member of the Language Arts Council for Fauquier County Public Schools, and three years as the lead mentor teacher for Grace Miller Elementary School. One of her passions is advocating for teacher research as an essential component of teacher professional development; she is a Consulting Editor for *Voices of Practitioners,* a teacher research journal published by the National Association for the Education of Young Children (NAEYC), and is the past Secretary/Treasurer of the Teacher as Researcher Special Interest Group of the American Educational Research Association (AERA). Stacia has been involved with numerous grants, most recently a project that explores the use of equity audits and culturally responsive teaching using a core group of teachers from the same school setting in order to help facilitate socially just change. She has presented her research at national and international conferences and has published numerous journal articles and book chapters. In addition to her education background, Stacia holds a degree in music performance. In her spare time, she and her husband own and operate a "pick-ur-own" orchard in the foothills of the Blue Ridge Mountains and raise two beautiful children adopted through foster care.

Laura L. Dallman is doctoral candidate at George Mason University's College of Education and Human Development. She is researching the influence of teacher emotional and cultural intelligence in establishing positive relationships with students whose cultural background differs from that of the teacher. Laura was an elementary school teacher for many years. She started and directed a preschool in Tbilisi, Georgia; taught in a local school in Portau-Prince, Haiti, and taught in international schools in Brussels, Belgium and Moscow, Russia. She also taught second and third grade and served as a resource teacher for Fairfax County Public Schools in Virginia. Before becoming a teacher, Laura worked in college admissions and as a paralegal for a Wall Street Law firm. She served as a legislative aide in the U.S. Congress and then directed the federal relations program for a professional organization of marriage and family therapists. In that role, Laura raised money for the organization's political action committee and organized the association's grassroots program, *Powerlines*, in addition to representing therapists on Capitol Hill. While in Tbilisi, Georgia, Laura also founded an international women's organization which raised funds for local disability orphanages in cooperation with Georgian women leaders. Laura presently serves as an assistant editor and reviewer of the *School-University Partnership Journal* and as an advisor to the Tuasil Aijtimaeiun Foundation for Educational Reform in Jordan. Laura graduated Phi Beta Kappa with a Bachelor of Arts degree from Augustana College, IL, and earned a Master of Divinity Degree from Yale University.

Index

Recommended Reference Books

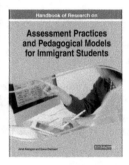

Handbook of Research on
Assessment Practices and Pedagogical Models for Immigrant Students

ISBN: 978-1-5225-9348-5
© 2019; 454 pp.
List Price: $255

Premier Reference Source
Preparing the Higher Education Space for Gen Z

ISBN: 978-1-5225-7763-8
© 2019; 253 pp.
List Price: $175

Premier Reference Source
Prevention and Detection of Academic Misconduct in Higher Education

ISBN: 978-1-5225-7531-3
© 2019; 324 pp.
List Price: $185

Premier Reference Source
Care and Culturally Responsive Pedagogy in Online Settings

ISBN: 978-1-5225-7802-4
© 2019; 423 pp.
List Price: $195

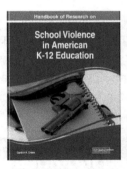

Handbook of Research on
School Violence in American K-12 Education

ISBN: 978-1-5225-6246-7
© 2019; 610 pp.
List Price: $275

Premier Reference Source
Critical Assessment and Strategies for Increased Student Retention

ISBN: 978-1-5225-2998-9
© 2018; 352 pp.
List Price: $195

Looking for free content, product updates, news, and special offers?
Join IGI Global's mailing list today and start enjoying exclusive perks sent only to IGI Global members.
Add your name to the list at **www.igi-global.com/newsletters.**

Publisher of Peer-Reviewed, Timely, and Innovative Academic Research

IGI Global
DISSEMINATOR OF KNOWLEDGE

www.igi-global.com ✉ Sign up at www.igi-global.com/newsletters f facebook.com/igiglobal t twitter.com/igiglobal

Ensure Quality Research is Introduced to the Academic Community

Become an IGI Global Reviewer for Authored Book Projects

Premier Reference Source

Emerging GIS Applications for Emergency and Disaster Management

Premier Reference Source

Managerial Strategies and Green Solutions for Project Sustainability

Premier Reference Source

Comparative Approaches to Using R and Python for Statistical Data Analysis

Premier Reference Source

Solutions for High-Touch Communications in a High-Tech World

The overall success of an authored book project is dependent on quality and timely reviews.

In this competitive age of scholarly publishing, constructive and timely feedback significantly expedites the turnaround time of manuscripts from submission to acceptance, allowing the publication and discovery of forward-thinking research at a much more expeditious rate. Several IGI Global authored book projects are currently seeking highly-qualified experts in the field to fill vacancies on their respective editorial review boards:

Applications and Inquiries may be sent to:
development@igi-global.com

Applicants must have a doctorate (or an equivalent degree) as well as publishing and reviewing experience. Reviewers are asked to complete the open-ended evaluation questions with as much detail as possible in a timely, collegial, and constructive manner. All reviewers' tenures run for one-year terms on the editorial review boards and are expected to complete at least three reviews per term. Upon successful completion of this term, reviewers can be considered for an additional term.

If you have a colleague that may be interested in this opportunity, we encourage you to share this information with them.

CPSIA information can be obtained
at www.ICGtesting.com
Printed in the USA
LVHW021911070421
683710LV00003B/42